T0358364

Opening up China's Markets of Crude Oil and Petroleum Products

Theoretical Research and Reform Solutions

Series on Chinese Economics Research

(ISSN: 2251-1644)

Series Editors: Yang Mu *(Lee Kuan Yew School of Public Policies, NUS)*
Fan Gang *(Peking University, China)*

Series on Chinese Economics Research – Vol. 9

Opening up China's Markets of Crude Oil and Petroleum Products

Theoretical Research and Reform Solutions

SHENG Hong

Unirule Institute of Economics, China

QIAN Pu

Unirule Institute of Economics, China &
The Institute of Economics in CASS, China

社会科学文献出版社
SOCIAL SCIENCES ACADEMIC PRESS (CHINA)

Published by

World Scientific Publishing Co. Pte. Ltd.
5 Toh Tuck Link, Singapore 596224
USA office: 27 Warren Street, Suite 401-402, Hackensack, NJ 07601
UK office: 57 Shelton Street, Covent Garden, London WC2H 9HE

Library of Congress Control Number: 2014953378

British Library Cataloguing-in-Publication Data
A catalogue record for this book is available from the British Library.

Series on Chinese Economics Research — Vol. 9
OPENING UP CHINA'S MARKETS OF CRUDE OIL AND
PETROLEUM PRODUCTS
Theoretical Research and Reform Solutions

ISBN 978-981-4603-96-6

In-house Editors: Sutha Surenddar/Sandhya Venkatesh

Typeset by Stallion Press
Email: enquiries@stallionpress.com

Printed in Singapore

Basic Conclusion

The reform to open the markets of crude oil and petroleum products is an underpinning point and a lever of the whole petroleum industry reform, which does not involve many aspects, and is less rigid comparing with reform measures that threaten the vested interest of the upstream industries of the oil monopoly enterprises, such as oil extraction and petroleum refining. Therefore, opening the markets of crude oil and petroleum products would get twice the result with half the effort. On the one hand, the reform benefits the society quickly and massively from the breakup of monopoly as it eliminates the losses of consumers caused by monopolistic high prices, and eliminates the net loss of social welfare caused by the limitation on enterprise entry. According to estimates of the welfare loss caused by the monopoly in 2011, this reform would obtain 79% or four-fifths of static effects of the petroleum industry reform (as shown in the figure below), in addition, it also would increase the total sales of more than RMB300 billion per year, thanks to the utilization of local oil refining enterprises.

On the other hand, the market-oriented reform in trading will have significant effects on the upstream production and will further promote the final overall reform of the oil system in China.

Therefore, it is a reform to achieve multiple ends with low costs.

Basic Conclusion

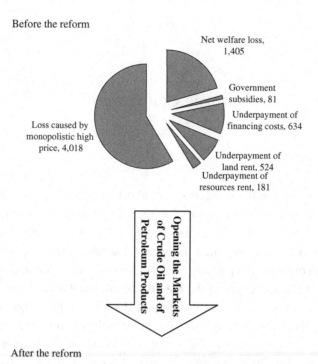

Before the reform

Net welfare loss, 1,405

Government subsidies, 81

Underpayment of financing costs, 634

Loss caused by monopolistic high price, 4,018

Underpayment of land rent, 524

Underpayment of resources rent, 181

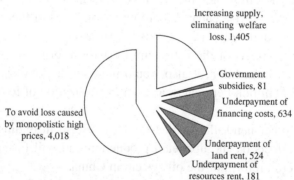

Opening the Markets of Crude Oil and of Petroleum Products

After the reform

Increasing supply, eliminating welfare loss, 1,405

Government subsidies, 81

Underpayment of financing costs, 634

To avoid loss caused by monopolistic high prices, 4,018

Underpayment of land rent, 524

Underpayment of resources rent, 181

Diagram on Static Effects of the Reform on Opening the Markets of Crude Oil and Petroleum Products (RMB100 million)

Abstract

- The economic traits of the oil and natural gas industry determine that the system of the oil and natural gas industry should be built upon market institutions, supplemented by proper government interventions, e.g., levying fuel oil taxes, adopting short-term intervention for serious price fluctuation, commandeering oil resources and products in time of warfare, and establishing resource reservation in times of peace.

- The current petroleum industry system of China demonstrates three features: dominance of state-owned enterprises, price regulation, and entrance restriction. Thus, the petroleum industry of China is highly monopolized, e.g., two to three monopoly enterprises have integrated monopoly in exploration, mining, refining, wholesale, retail, even import and exports.

- The monopoly in the oil and gas industry is an administrative monopoly, which is established by administrative departments through issuing administrative documents. These administrative documents are not issued through due legal procedure, but they determine and influence the affairs of vital interests to Chinese people, therefore, legally they stand on shaky ground.

- The current oil monopoly system and corresponding monopolistic behaviors of oil monopoly enterprises violate the constitutional principle of the socialist market economy and the *Anti-Monopoly Law* (《反垄断法》). Besides, the motivations and basis to establish oil monopolies are irrational economically.

- Diagram of welfare loss and distribution distortion of administrative monopoly

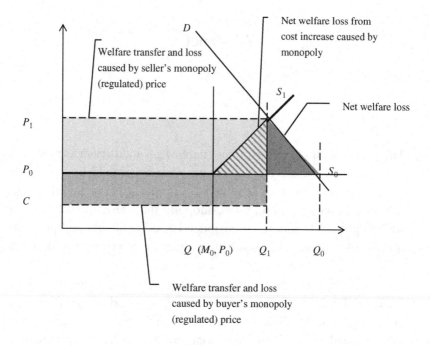

- The oil monopoly system has brought about great efficiency loss to the whole society. It is estimated the welfare loss in the oil industry reached as high as RMB3,477 billion from 2001 to 2011.
- The oil monopoly system also distorts income distribution and violates the principle of fairness. From 2000 to 2011, the three monopoly petroleum companies failed to surrender their profits of RMB1.4701 trillion. But when it comes to their income level, these companies enjoy far higher incomes above the social average level, e.g., the per capita salary of the China National Offshore Oil Corporation (CNOOC) in 2010 was about RMB340,000, 10 times the social average.
- The oil monopoly system stands against the market rules and makes oil monopoly enterprises unfair competitors. From 2001 to 2011, CNPC underpaid land rent of RMB395.8 billion, while petroleum enterprises underpaid resource rent of about RMB307.9 billion and financing cost of about RMB287.8 billion.

- The oil monopoly system makes an originally competitive market a monopoly market, and consequently it makes the market-based pricing system ineffective, so that the government regulation-based pricing mechanism stepped in. However, such a pricing mechanism is inefficient causing the set price to deviate from the price determined by the market and this mechanism will undoubtedly cause welfare loss. Meanwhile, it makes monopolists reduce their production and supply when the price is low but increase their production and supply when the price is high. The price is influenced by the quantities of production and stock in turn.

- The oil monopoly system also directly harms other competitors including private enterprises in the following aspects: (1) To prohibit market entry, or to drive those enterprises in the industry out of oil extraction and sales business; (2) to impose restrictions or discriminations on competitive enterprises that have already entered the oil industry; (3) to cooperate with local governments and reject competitors through administrative powers; (4) to directly violate the property rights of private enterprises, etc.

- The regulation on crude oil import has resulted in serious insufficiency of capacity utilization of other oil refining enterprises in addition to oil monopoly enterprises, causing a total loss of sales of about RMB300 billion every year.

- Because the quality standard of petroleum products of China is lower than other major countries, while the quality standard of petroleum products of Beijing is higher than the national standard, close to European standard (see the table below), we compared the adjusted price of petroleum products in Beijing and the average in other main countries.

	2006	2007	2008	2009	2010	2011	2012
European standard	European standard IV				European standard V		European standard V+
Beijing standard	European standard III			European standard IV			
National standard	National standard II				National standard III		

- To make the comparison fairer, we adopt the price before tax. The consumption tax and actual added-value tax is deducted from the price of petroleum products in Beijing. From 2006 to 2011, the comparison between the prices of petroleum products in China and weighted average prices in other main countries (RMB/L) is as follows:

	2006	2007	2008	2009	2010	2011
Gasoline						
Weighted average of foreign countries	2.30	2.57	3.06	2.18	2.64	3.38
China	2.07	2.26	2.80	2.72	3.22	3.92
Diesel						
Weighted average of foreign countries	2.33	2.54	3.50	2.13	2.64	3.52
China	2.15	2.44	3.03	2.95	3.51	4.25

- From 2006 to 2011, the losses of consumers caused by the high monopolistic (regulated) price were as high as RMB839.6 billion; from 2009 to 2011, the monopolistic (regulated) price of petroleum products in China (pre-tax) was about 31% higher than the average price of main countries, raising the loss to customers as high as RMB1.198 trillion.

- ## How Oil Monopolies Profit?

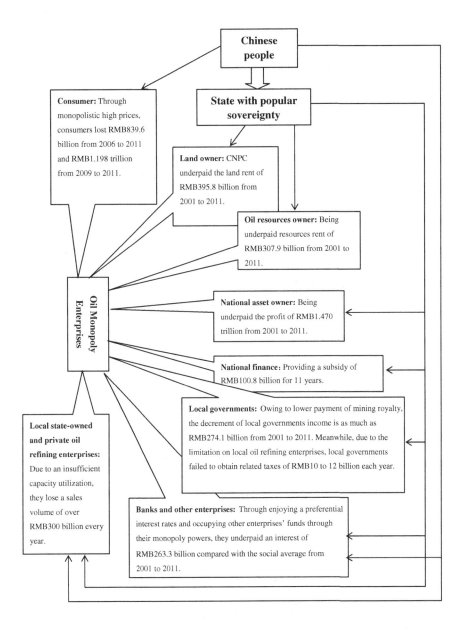

- The oil monopoly system also threatens national security and influences social stability. It provides the conditions and excuse for oil monopoly enterprises to create "gasoline shortages", causing tension and confrontation between the central government and local governments, and harms the interests of the central and western regions as well as minority areas. Meanwhile, the government is vulnerable to monopoly enterprises' blackmail on rainy days.
- Finally, the system itself is a violation of the framework of Chinese constitutionalism. Monopoly enterprises arrogate to use public powers and implement administrative power or quasi-administrative powers, while administrative departments arrogate to have legislative power and abuse legal enforcement power, in order to carry out the practice of monopoly and regulation contained in administrative documents.
- Therefore, it is a problematic system which should be reformed immediately at an extensive scale. The reform complies with principles of constitutionality, validity and economic rationality.
- Fundamental objectives of the oil system reform:

  (1) To establish a system based on the market institutions for the oil and gas industry;
  (2) To form a fair and effective competitive mechanism involving the upstream, midstream, and downstream sectors of oil and gas industry;
  (3) The government represents the state to grant the mining permit of oil and gas to economic agents in a competitive way;
  (4) The government should impose limited regulations only in special fields at specific times.

- Basic measures for the oil industry reform:

  (1) To cancel the monopoly powers and some of the administrative powers of the oil monopoly enterprises;
  (2) To establish an independent and neutral regulatory entity for the energy industry;
  (3) To fully open the market for the oil and gas industry;
  (4) To abolish the price regulation.

- Diagram on the static effects of the oil industry reform (RMB100 million)

Figure A: Before the reform

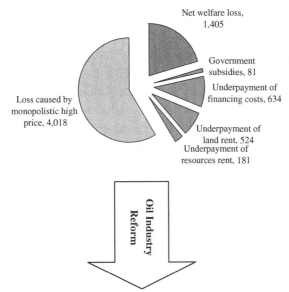

Net welfare loss, 1,405

Government subsidies, 81

Underpayment of financing costs, 634

Loss caused by monopolistic high price, 4,018

Underpayment of land rent, 524

Underpayment of resources rent, 181

Oil Industry Reform

Figure B: After the reform

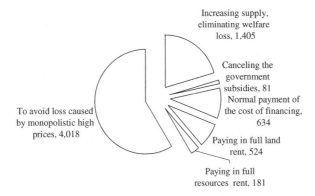

Increasing supply, eliminating welfare loss, 1,405

Canceling the government subsidies, 81

Normal payment of the cost of financing, 634

To avoid loss caused by monopolistic high prices, 4,018

Paying in full land rent, 524

Paying in full resources rent, 181

- The reform to open the markets of crude oil and petroleum products is an underpinning point and a lever of reform of the entire petroleum industry, which does not involve many aspects, and is less rigid compared to reform measures that threaten the vested interest of the upstream industries of the oil monopoly enterprises, such as oil extraction and petroleum refining. Therefore, opening the markets of crude oil and petroleum products would get twice the result with half the effort. On the one hand, the reform involving the breakup of monopoly benefits the society quickly and enormously, as it eliminates the losses to consumers caused by monopolistic high prices, and eliminates the net loss of social welfare caused by the limitation on enterprise entry into the crude oil and petroleum products market. The price of petroleum products will be lowered to the international level of the same quality, which will benefit consumers. According to the data from 2009 to 2011, the prices of both diesel and gasoline in China could be reduced by about 31%. So if the consumption leveled with 2011, the price paid by consumers could be decreased by RMB401.8 billion each year.

- Even according to the price of petroleum products in the trading center beyond the current monopoly system of China, the price will also fall with the opening of the markets for crude oil and petroleum products. The figure below demonstrates that the price of No. 93 oil in the trading center of the Yangtze River Delta is about 13% lower than the regulated price prescribed by the National Development and Reform Commission (NDRC).

- Comparison between the price of No. 93 oil generated in the Trading Center of Yangtze River Delta and that issued by National

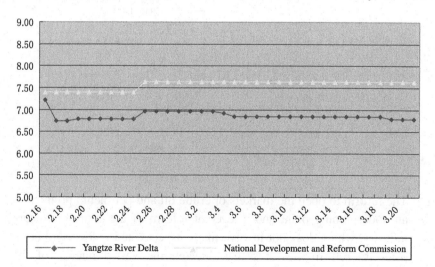

Development and Reform Commission (from February 16, 2013 to March 21, 2013 RMB/liter).

- In terms of welfare loss caused by the monopoly in 2011, the reform will obtain 79% or four-fifths of static effects of petroleum industry reform (as shown in the table below) and transform it into social welfare. Moreover, it will increase total sales of more than RMB300 billion every year due to the increase of the capacity utilization of local oil refining enterprises.

- Static effects of the reform on opening the markets of crude oil and petroleum products (RMB100 million)

Year	Net welfare loss	Government subsidy	Financing costs	Land rent	Resources rent	Loss caused by monopolistic high prices	Total	Percentage of reform effects
2011	1,405	81	634	524	181	4,018	6,843	79

- On the other hand, the market-oriented reform in trading will have significant effects on the upstream production and will further promote the final overall reform of the oil system in China.

- The analysis on the structure of reform motivations indicates that most people in China will support the oil industry reform. Since the monopoly is unpopular and the current oil monopoly system contradicts the principles of constitutionality and justice, the governing party and the central government are motivated to pursue reform measures. Meanwhile, consumers and private enterprises are also urging for a reform. Besides, other central state-owned enterprises, local state-owned enterprises, and local governments all support the reform. Only those administrative departments associated with the oil monopoly system and the executives and employees of oil monopoly enterprises may oppose the reform, with most of them supporting the reform.

- When we draw the blueprint for the reform on opening the markets of crude oil and petroleum products, we should choose one which incurs the lowest cost.

- The strategies for the reform on opening the markets of crude oil and petroleum products are as follows:

    (1) *Gradual opening*: As illustrated before, the markets should be opened in the following order: the crude oil import market, imports and exports markets of petroleum products, domestic market of petroleum products, and domestic market of crude oil;

    (2) *To reform outside of the system*: To maintain the current institutional arrangements for the monopoly enterprises in importing and exporting of crude oil and petroleum products while opening the markets of crude oil and petroleum products;

    (3) *Gradual entering*: In the process of opening the markets, it should be taken into account to grant permission to enterprises other than monopolistic ones, to enter the markets group by group;

    (4) *Subsidizing the reform*: For possible laid-off or unemployed workers from oil monopoly enterprises, if other petroleum enterprises cannot take in all of them, the government can establish an employment fund for the petroleum industry to digest the human resources;

    (5) *Trade of the planning rights*: For all oil monopoly enterprises, the government can abolish the price regulation on the selling of petroleum products in exchange for their agreement on opening the markets of crude oil and petroleum products.

- The reform in China has proven that when state-owned enterprises cannot absorb so many workers resulting in massive unemployment, non-state-owned enterprises become the main force in providing employment. For example, from 2008 to 2011, among all new jobs, non-state-owned enterprises provided for 96% of employment (according to the data from the State Statistics Bureau). Therefore, if the market-oriented reform should work out and be successful, it will facilitate the prosperity of non-state-owned enterprises and create numerous job opportunities, which will more than compensate the decrease in job opportunities in state-owned enterprises.

- Because the oil reserve-production ratio rises to 55, "Shale revolution" will lead to strategic supply growth of oil and natural gas, and natural gas will become the dominant energy in the new period; in addition, the growth rate of economies would slow down in China and India. The supply and demand relations will become relatively loose in the world oil markets, which is conducive to the reform of opening crude oil and refined oil markets.
- Roadmap of the reform.

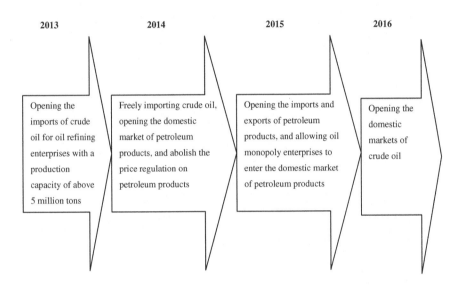

Contents

About the Author

Director of the Project: Sheng Hong

Administrator of the Project: Gao Yan

Members of the Project:
Sheng Hong, Gao Yan, Wang Jun, Qian Pu, He Shaoqi, Wang Jilin, Li Shuran, Zhao Nong, Li Renqing, Liu Xi

Members of Advisors:
Bai Rongchun, Deputy Director of State Energy Resources Commission, former Deputy Director General of Energy Bureau under the National Development and Reform Commission

Chen Yongjie, Deputy Secretary General of China Center for International Economic Exchanges

Feng Xingyuan, Deputy Director of Unirule Institute of Economics, Research Fellow of Chinese Academy of Social Sciences

Han Xiaoping, Chief Information Officer of China Energy Net

Liu Xiaoxuan, Research Fellow of Microeconomics Laboratory of Institute of Economics, Chinese Academy of Social Sciences

Ma Ke, Associate Editor of Caijing Magazine

Shi Xiaomin, Vice-Chairman of China Society of Economic Reform

Song Xiaowu, Chairman of China Society of Economic Reform

Wang Xiaoye, Research Fellow of Institute of Law, Chinese Academy of Social Sciences

Wu Jiandong, Vice-Chairman of China Wisdom Engineering Association, leader of smart energy research group of China Center for International Economic Exchanges

Zeng Xingqiu, former General Geologist of Sinochem Group

Zhang Kang, Member of Advisory Committee of China SINOPEC Group

Zhang Shuguang, Chairman of Academic Council of Unirule Institute of Economics

Zhang Xinzhu, Director of Research Center for Regulation and Competition, Chinese Academy of Social Sciences

Zhou Fangsheng, former Deputy Director General of Enterprise Reform Bureau of the State-owned Assets Supervision and Administration Commission under the State Council

Division of Responsibilities in the Project:

Sheng Hong, director of project group, author of Chapters 1, 4–6, author of part of Chapter 2 and part of Chapter 3; compiling editor of the full paper

Gao Yan, administrator of the project, member of discussion group;

Qian Pu, author of Chapter 2 and part of Chapter 3;

He Shaoqi, author of part of Chapter 2 and Sub-Report II;

Wang Jilin, author of part of Chapter 2, and of Sub-Report I;

Zhao Nong, member of discussion group;

Wang Jun, member of discussion group;

Li Renqing, member of discussion group;

Liu Xi, coordinator of the project.

Acknowledgments

This book is a new fruit of our research team. Having finished two previous research projects, *China's State-Owned Enterprises: Nature, Performance, and Reform, and China's Administrative Monopoly: Causes, Behaviors, and Termination*, we are better equipped with the knowledge and insights to further the research on a concrete industry: the oil industry.

What is more, the problems of the petroleum industry caught our attention 7–8 years ago when Unirule Institute of Economics was entrusted by a national agency to carry out a research project. However, Unirule was not able to fulfill it due to lack of funds. In recent years, we were gracefully supported by China Chamber of Commerce for Petroleum Industry so that this research could be carried out and completed.

The members of the research team, except those whose names appear on the cover of the book as the authors, are Yang Xiaojing, He Shaoqi, Wang Jilin, Li Shuran, and Liu Qian. Our special thanks go to Professor Gao Yan who plays a very important role. He, the Deputy Director of Unirule and Vice President of China Chamber of Commerce for Petroleum Industry, was the administrative leader of the research team, who contributes to the research by financing, organizing, arranging interviews with people concerned, and promoting the findings of the research.

As usual, we held workshops for the first and second drafts. Experts and scholars from the industry and the academia were invited to review and comment on the drafts. Experts from the petroleum industry were Zeng Xingqiu, Bai Rongchun, Zhang Kang, Han Xiaoping, Ma Ke, and Yang Lei. Economists who joined the workshops were Zhang Shuguang, Liu Xiaoxun, Zhang Xinzhu, Shi Xiaomin, Song Xiaowu, Chen Yongjie, and Feng Xingyuan. Other reviewers include Zhou Fangsheng, expert on state-owned enterprises (SOEs); Wu Jiandong, expert on energy issues; and Wang Xiaoye, jurist.

We would also like to thank China Chamber of Commerce for Petroleum Industry for arranging interviews with businessmen and executives in the petroleum industry. And our thanks go to the interviewees who shared with us real stories about the industry in China. They are Qi Fang, Li Jing, Wang Meng, Wang Xuhua, and Cao Hui.

The English draft of the report was polished by Mr. MA Junjie. And Sutha Surenddar, the editor of this book, also has our heartfelt gratitude.

As a collective work by so many people, this book is a successful product for readers who are interested in the subject. I, as the leader of the research team and one of the authors, am truly grateful to all who have helped us both mentioned above and unmentioned.

Sheng Hong
Director, Unirule Institute of Economics
May 21, 2014

List of Figures

Chapter 1

Chapter 2

Chapter 3

Chapter 6

List of Tables

Chapter 1

Chapter 2

Chapter 3

Chapter 1

Economic Nature and Significance
of Oil and Gas Industry

I. Private Goods and Production Competitiveness:
Basically Applicable to Market Economy

Oil and gas are apparently private goods which are exclusively possessed and consumed. For example, when a car owner buys 50 L gasoline to fill his/her oil tank, the gasoline would just serve his/her own car rather than others'. Similarly, the gas bought by a resident from the gas firm is only available for disposal, either to boil water or cook, by the resident himself/herself.

It is a long journey to convert crude oil and natural gas into petroleum products and usable gas. The process features exploration, drilling, mining, transportation, refining, and sales. The production activities of oil and gas are competitive from the very beginning, for a large number of enterprises have the same access to the market due to the broad distribution of oil and gas and the possibility of conducting exploration, well drilling, and mining in small scale (like drilling just one well). For example, the oil consumption worldwide in 2011 was about 4.59 billion tons (BP, 2012), while Arabian American Oil Company, the world's largest oil-producing company, produced about 650 million tons of crude oil (*Daqing Daily*, 2012) and Exxon Mobil Corporation, the world's largest oil-refining company has a refining capacity of 290 million tons (*Petroleum & Petrochemical Today*, 2012). Meanwhile, the world consumed about 2.45 trillion m^3 (BP, 2012) of natural gas of which only 670.5 billion m^3 was produced and supplied by Gazprom, the Russian gas giant (Liao Weijing, 2012). Moreover, these are "enterprise scale," much larger than "plant size" and "production scale." Therefore, oil and gas industry is a competitive industry.

The nature of private goods and production competitiveness of oil and gas industry determine that this industry can be basically operated by private enterprises through market-based pricing mechanism.

II. Scarce Natural Resources

Nevertheless, different from ordinary commodities, oil and gas are natural resources. If some natural resources are rich in reserve and can be obtained at a low cost, then people can consume resources, such as air, free of charge without worrying about exhaustion. On the contrary, some natural resources are not inexhaustible and the cost of obtaining them is high. This restricts people from obtaining them, and further makes them not-so-scarce (see Figure 1.1). As long as people are willing to pay the cost (to extract or mine), they have access to this resource which is not scarce, and they do not risk jeopardizing efficiency either. An example supporting this statement is obtaining water in the traditional society.

A third situation is that some resources become scarce as the cost of exploitation plummets with technical progress (see Figure 1.1). On this

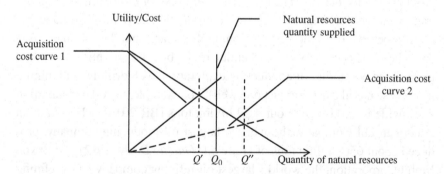

Figure 1.1. Schematic Diagram of Relation between Cost of Obtaining and Scarcity of Resources

Note: When the cost of obtaining is high (such as cost of obtaining curve 1), the consumed resources quantity Q', decided by its point of intersection with demand curve, is lower than natural resource supply quantity Q_0; when the cost of obtaining is reduced with technical progress (such as cost of obtaining curve 2), the water consumption quantity Q'' decided by its point of intersection with demand curve, is higher than natural resource supply quantity Q_0.

occasion, this natural resource can be called "scarce natural resource." If there is no exclusive property right of such a resource, and people are allowed to exploit and capture it freely, a "crowding phenomenon" will occur, which will lead to the "tragedy of the commons" or even extinction of natural species.

The problem can be solved by the following solutions in accordance with effectiveness and institutional cost: (1) spontaneous establishment of exclusive property rights recognized and protected by the government, such as land property right; (2) establishment of exclusive property rights by government in case of absence of spontaneous establishment, such as intellectual property right; (3) monopoly by some economic subject; (4) control over means and time of obtaining by the government to increase the cost of obtaining, such as restriction on standards of fishing tools or regulations on closed fishing season; (5) direct allocation of acquisition quota by government.

Given the characteristics of oil and gas, the best method is to establish the exclusive property right system. In many countries, there exists private land property rights. Therefore, the oil and gas mining companies have to get the consent of land property rights owner before mining on the land. In addition, the wide distribution of natural resources, such as oil and gas reserves, will cause competition among mineral owners, and then the market for transaction between mineral owners and the oil and gas mining companies will come into being. The land use fee or mining royalty at certain levels will be fixed after bargaining. This system which builds natural resource property rights, on land property rights, will fundamentally eliminate the "crowding phenomenon" and "tragedy of the commons." Even if land property rights and mineral property rights belong to the state, the state, as owner of land and natural resources, can also collect mining royalty through negotiation or tendering. The mining royalty, which includes factors of both absolute rent and differential rent (see Figure 1.2), can be back-counted by product price determined by the competitive market. Mining royalty varies with diverse differential rents of oil fields. In some cases, mining royalty can be collected in other forms, like the ratio of profit oil distribution.

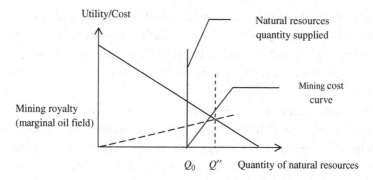

Figure 1.2.   Schematic Diagram of Scarce Resource, Resource Rent, and Property Right

III. Exhaustible Resources: Positive Discount Rate and Zero Discount Rate

In any period, the ceiling on the exploitation and capture of a natural resource is not the physical quantity of the resource. There is an optimal allocation of natural resources in the time bar. Natural resources can be divided into renewable resources and non-renewable ones. As for non-renewable resources, the optimal allocation in the time bar is that this natural resource can be most effectively used and be replaced by another resource at a similar cost, exactly on the time point of its depletion. As for renewable resources, the optimal allocation in the time bar is that the quantity of capture in a certain period shall be close to the difference between the actual quantity of biotic population and the threshold quantity, ensuring the normal reproduction of the biotic population.

Another difference between renewables and non-renewables is that the former, unlike the latter, is an asset with its value naturally increasing over time. For instance, forest resources may grow as time goes by and consequently increase in value. However, non-renewables usually neither grow nor increase in value over time. For instance, within the time span of an individual's natural life, the petroleum reserves of one oil field do not increase over time.

As for non-renewable resources, it is impossible to find the quota of best allocation in the time bar through competition among individuals. First of all, though the time dimension of resource allocation spans over generations, it is the contemporaries who determine the price in the market. For the contemporary generation, the current consumption is more relevant than the consumption in the future. Therefore, they value the former but underestimate the latter. In order to encourage people to postpone today's consumption to the future, it is essential to give them a kind of time compensation, i.e., interest. In contrast, the future consumption cannot be compared with today's consumption before it is discounted. There is no doubt that the discount rate of the contemporaries is positive. However, when estimated over generations, the discount rate shall be zero, because in the case that other factors remain unchanged, a person's consumption today has no difference with his future consumption, in value, 20 years later. But since the future generations are not born, it is the contemporaries who determine the market price of resources. Consumers prefer current consumption, while owners of resources prefer selling more natural resources, as the maximum benefit of the owners of resources is getting maximal incomes from selling resources, i.e., the maximal net present value of future benefits. Apparently, in the case that other factors are unchanged, compared with the discount rate of zero, the choice to make the discount rate positive is to exploit more resources at present. As a result, the natural resources actually exploited and sold exceed the quantity of best allocation on the time bar.

As for renewable resources, as long as there is an exclusive property right, it is possible (but not necessary) to find the quota which reflects the optimal allocation in the time dimension through market competition. Since renewable resources can grow or reproduce over time, as long as the owner of such resources anticipates that the asset value growth, brought by the growth and reproduction of the resource, can be obtained by himself or his future generations, and as long as the value growth rate is at least equal to the discount rate, the asset owner will allocate resources efficiently to maintain the quantity which can maximize the appreciation in assets, thus ensuring the best allocation of resource in the time dimension. However, when the growth and reproduction rate of the resource is too low and consequently the growth rate of its market value is lower than the individual discount rate, the owner can make excessive exploitation or capture.

As for how to make an effective allocation of exhaustible or non-renewable resources in terms of time, there is Hotelling's Law in economics research:

$$P't/Pt = \rho.$$

In this equation, $P't/Pt$ is the rate of change in net price (mining royalty) of resources; and ρ is the discount rate.

The formula shows that if the social value of non-renewable resources is to be maximized, the net price or property value of such resources Pt shall rise at the same ratio as the discount rate of social utility ρ. Actually, there is no net price of exhaustible resources rising according to the Hotelling's Law (Perman *et al.*, 2002, p. 237), indicating that the current non-renewable resources are not optimally allocated between generations. Apparently, if the cross-generation discount rate equals 0, the net price or property value of resources shall maintain at a constant level. But the contemporary individual discount rate is positive, it is impossible to achieve the best allocation of exhaustible resources in the time dimension (Research Group of Unirule Institute of Economics, 2009).

Therefore, for non-renewable resources, i.e., exhaustible resources, **the accurate information concerning the future depletion of oil and natural gas cannot be given from the price in the competitive market, which makes it impossible to realize the optimal allocation in the time dimension**. Even though the price will gradually rise with the gradual decrease of oil and natural gas reserves, and such anticipation on rise in price will make owners of oil and natural gas resources willing to save more for future exploitation, the discount rate will offset the effect of anticipation on rise in price (see Figure 1.3). For example, it is expected that the oil price will rise by 5% per year later, but if the discount rate is 5%, the effect of the price will be offset. Only when the expected rise in price is higher than the discount rate, can oil resources owners make the decision to postpone exploitation. The decision may not be correct as the price signal is still discounted.

In fact, at constant 2010 prices in US$, from 1880 to 2000, except for the two periods of oil crisis, the crude oil price always fluctuated around the level of over US$20 (see Figure 1.4), let alone the continuous ascending tendency. According to the Hotelling's Law, it can be reversely deduced

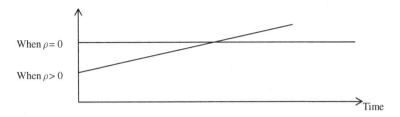

Figure 1.3.   Discount Rate and Net Price of Resources

Note: ρ shown in the figure is the discount rate. If the discount rate is equal to 0, the net price of resources shall be a horizontal line; if the discount rate is larger than 0, the net price of resources shall be a line leaning to the upper right. This figure reveals that when the discount rate is larger than 0, (1) resources will be depleted earlier than in the situation when the discount rate is equal to 0; (2) the contemporary generations consume more resources than the future generations.

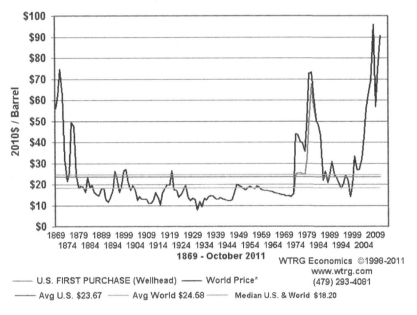

Figure 1.4.   History of Crude Oil Price (1869–2011, at 2010 price in US$)

Source: WTRG Economics (http://www.wtrg.com/prices.htm).

that there is a problem in the pace of oil exploitation, i.e., the exploitation is too fast.

Whats more, ever since 1980, the reserve and exploitation ratio of oil is above 30 all the time; and the reserve and exploitation ratio of natural gas is above 58. "Calculated on the basis that the 2007 oil and gas production remains unchanged, the current oil reserves can provide for the whole world for at least another 41.6 years, and the reserves of natural gas can provide for another 60.3 years." (Feng Lianyong, 2009, p. 62). Suppose the discount rate is 5%, the cash equivalent value of a certain oil resource in 41 years is about 13.5% of that today; the cash equivalent value of a certain natural gas resource in 60 years will be less than 5.4% of that today. That is not a concern of the contemporary generations, so it cannot be reflected in the market price today.

Although oil reserves and exploitation ratio declines in some regions, the ratio has been gradually rising at a global level since the 1980s, and reached approximately 55 by the end of 2011 (see Figure 1.5), which provides an even more blurry picture on the scarcity of oil in 55 years.

Therefore, **it is necessary to have a certain operation to arrange an appropriate quota to be exploited in each period to correct the failure of market in the allocation of natural resources in the time dimension**. But strictly speaking, it is very difficult to find or determine the appropriate quota, because the oil resource reserve and exploitation cost to determine the appropriate quota keep changing. The proven reserve of oil increases over time. Calculated by the estimated reserves and consumption growth rate at the time, the oil reserves in 1950 was able to provide for approximately 19.2 years, but in 1988 it was estimated that the reserves could provide for another 38.7 years (Judy Liess, 2002, p. 54); the remaining recoverable reserves of oil in the world were approximately 91.7 billion tons in 1980, but were 157.2 billion tons in 2003 (Yang Xueyan *et al.*, 2004, p. 12) and 176.8 billion tons in 2007 (Feng Lianyong, 2009, p. 62). Meanwhile, with technological development, the exploitation cost declines, which props up the increase of conditional reserves, i.e., the oil reserves worth exploiting at the current exploitation cost. For instance, the exploitation cost of offshore oil fields was approximately US$15 per barrel in the 1980s, but now it dropped to US$5 and again risen to US$8 (*France Le Figaro*, 2005). Besides, it is very difficult to tell what level of oil price can propel people to make researches on alternative energy sources that can replace oil exactly at its depletion.

In practice, there are two things correcting the fast exploitation of oil and natural gas resources caused by positive discount rate.

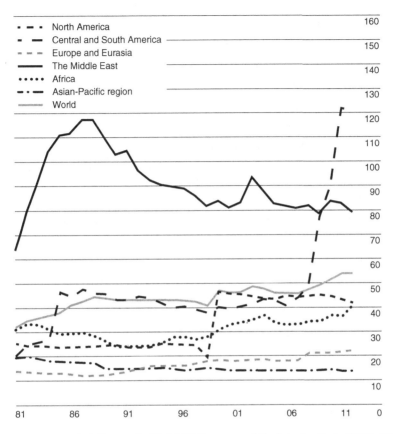

Figure 1.5. Trend of Changes in World Oil Reserve and Exploitation Ratio (1981–2011)
Source: BP, 2012, p. 7.

The first one is the gasoline tax levied by government. In the long run, the price elasticity of gasoline demand is large, so the higher price caused by gasoline tax can reduce the demand for oil products. **The other one is the Organization of the Petroleum Exporting Countries (OPEC).** OPEC raises the world oil market price higher than when there was no OPEC. This is achieved by allocating yield quota to member states or setting higher price, which further reduces the demand for oil. Member states of OPEC can also gain revenues called "OPEC tax" coined by western countries. The interaction between OPEC tax and gasoline tax corrects the excessive exploitation in the market caused by positive discount rate.

IV. Partial Effect of Peak Oil Theory and Alternative Energies

The crude oil price continued to rise after 2004, up to approximately US$100 per barrel in 2008, and remained above US$50 since then. During that period, OPEC made few achievements and failed to effectively bring down the price by increasing oil yields. A high price benefits petroleum exporting countries in the short-term, but in the long-term, it will bring about the emergence of alternative energy sources, which is finally unfavorable for petroleum exporting countries. The phenomenon seems to show that oil reserves have already approached the ultimate depletion stage, so the market price responds intensively.

It has been a common concern for the international oil industry and even for the whole world to determine when the oil reserves will be depleted. Therefore, the peak oil theory came into being. According to this theory, when the yield of a certain oil field or country exceeds the increment of proven reserves, it passes the peak oil stage. However, data show that after the 1990s, the world oil production has already exceeded the proven reserves (see Figure 1.6).

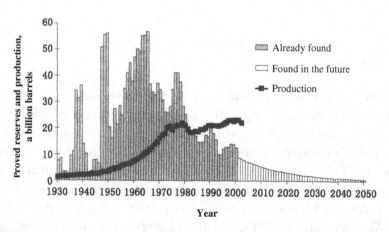

Figure 1.6. Gap between Newly-added Proved Reserves and Output of Oil (1930–2050, billion barrels)
Source: Quoted in Feng Lianyong, 2009, p. 78.

Therefore, many predict that the world peak oil will occur somewhere between 2008 and 2020; while some others hold that the peak may occur after 2030. No matter 2008 or 2030, both fall within the contemporaries, so the peak will influence the current market price. It shows the peak oil theory makes sense, at least partially, as the crude oil price rose significantly after 2004.

If the peak oil theory is correct, then it can be said that the current international oil market price approximately reflects the scarcity of oil as an exhaustible resource. It is also proven by the fact that the role of OPEC is weakening. Since the 1980s, the oil reserves and exploitation ratio in the Middle East has been declining (see Figure 1.5), while oil producing countries in that region are mainly members of OPEC. From 2003 to 2009, the spare oil production capacity of OPEC decreased from 600 million barrels per day to below 100 million barrels per day, which is not sufficient to adjust output so as to influence price (see Figure 1.7). It is true that OPEC's spare oil production capacity rose after 2009 and OPEC resumed its influence on the oil price, but the influences of OPEC weakened on the whole.

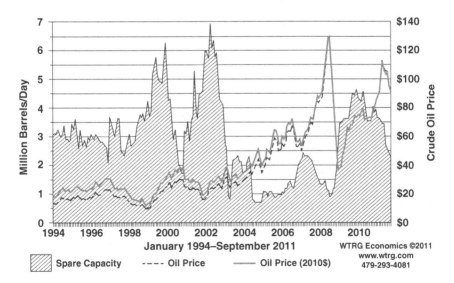

Figure 1.7. OPEC's Spare Capacity (1994–2010, million barrels/day)
Source: WTRG Economics (http://www.wtrg.com/prices.htm).

The rise in oil prices ushered in the development of alternative energy sources and accelerated the development of energy-saving technology. For instance, the development of both shale gas and shale oil has already produced strategic impacts. Thanks to the production of shale gas, over the past six or seven years, America's proportion of imported oils decreased from 60% to 40%, and the country did not import natural gas any more (News Center of China Shale Gas Network, 2013a). Shale gas was even over supplied due to low prices and was set on fire to consume the over-supply (News Center of China Shale Gas Network, 2013b).

Other alternative energy sources, such as solar energy, wind energy and electric vehicles, may embrace major breakthroughs in the near future. Dependence on oil will reduce and oil prices will be brought down. This also shows that after the contemporaries learned about the possibility of oil depletion, the market price approximately reflects the overall scarcity of oil and plays its proper role in setting the market price.

V. Demand Characteristics (1): Necessities of Public Life

Generally, oil products and natural gas products are used in transportation, residential uses, commerce, industries and electric generation sectors, etc. With development of vehicles and urban pipeline gas, oil products and natural gas products have already been widely consumed. Vehicles and pipeline gas supplies gradually become an important part of everyday life. In the United States, more than 60% of the petroleum products in demand are for transportation (2002, see Figure 1.8); and 24% of the natural gas in demand is for residential use (2004, see Table 1.1). In China, the proportion of petroleum products consumed by vehicles was around 40% in 2002 (Yang Xueyan *et al.*, 2004, p. 58); and the proportion of gas used by urban residents reached 24% in 2003 (Yang Xueyan *et al.*, 2004, p. 59). These figures are still rapidly increasing at present. It can be said that one of the major uses of oil and natural gas is as necessities of public life.

As necessities of public life, the first characteristics is "being necessary," which means that the price elasticity of demand for them is comparatively smaller; the other characteristics is "being public," which means that products made of such resources are of common concern and are widely influenced by public opinions. Price elasticity can also be

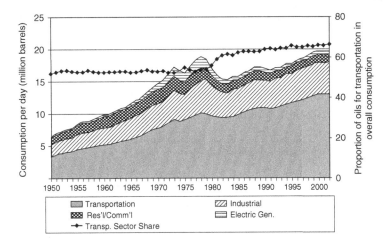

Figure 1.8. Consumption Structure of Petroleum Products in the US (1950–2002, million barrels, %)

divided into long-term elasticity and short-term elasticity. The short-term price elasticity refers to the influences of price changes on people's demand, under the situation that people's consumption modes of oil or natural gas products are fixed, such as in the situation that a car has been bought or a natural gas cooker has been installed. The long-term price elasticity means that the price changes may influence people's choice about energy consumption modes in the long-term and then influence the demand for such resources. For instance, if gasoline prices rise, people would rather take the bus than purchasing a car; if natural gas prices increase, people will choose other alternative energy sources to cook instead of using natural gas cookers. In both cases, the demand for petroleum and natural gas products will sharply fall.

Therefore, **the short-term price elasticity of both oil and natural gas is small, even equals zero sometimes; while their long-term price elasticity is large**.

This conclusion is supported by Tables 1.2 and 1.3. In Table 1.2, when crude oil price increases by 10%, the demand for gasoline decreases by 0.3%, that is to say, the price elasticity is −0.03. When the natural gas wellhead price increases by 10%, residents' demand for natural gas does not decrease, that is to say, the price elasticity is zero. In Table 1.3, no matter whether domestic or commercial institutions, in terms of natural

Table 1.1.   Consumption Structure of Natural Gas Products in the US in 2012 (Million cubic feet, %)

Use	Total	Residential	Commercial	Industrial	Transportation	Power generation
Quantity	23,351,180	4,177,138	2,904,807	7,099,549	32,940	9,136,746
Proportion (in %)	100	18	12	30	0.1	39

Source: US Energy Information Administration.

Table 1.2.   Price Sensitivity of Energy Demand in the US

Demand sector	+1% GDP	+10% Prices		+10% Weather	
		Crude oil	N. Gas Wellhead	Fall/ Winter	Spring/ Summer
Petroleum					
Total	0.6%	−0.3%	0.1%	1.1%	0.1%
Motor Gasoline	0.1%	−0.3%	0.0%	0.0%	0.0%
Distillate Fuel	0.8%	−0.2%	0.0%	2.7%	0.1%
Residual Fuel	1.6%	−3.4%	2.6%	2.0%	2.7%
Natural Gas					
Total	1.1%	0.3%	−0.4%	−4.4%	1.0%
Residential	0.1%	0.0%	0.0%	8.2%	0.0%
Commercial	0.9%	0.0%	0.0%	7.3%	0.0%
Industrial	1.7%	0.2%	−0.5%	1.3%	0.0%
Electric Utility	1.8%	1.6%	−1.5%	1.0%	4.0%
Coal					
Total	0.7%	0.0%	0.0%	1.7%	1.7%
Electric Utility	0.6%	0.0%	0.0%	1.9%	1.9%
Electricity					
Total	0.6%	0.0%	0.0%	1.5%	1.7%
Residential	0.1%	0.0%	0.0%	3.2%	3.6%
Commercial	0.9%	0.0%	0.0%	1.0%	1.4%
Industrial	0.8%	0.0%	0.0%	0.3%	0.2%

Table 1.3. Price Elasticity of Energy in Residential and Commercial Buildings in the US in 1993

Energy	Short-term elasticity	Long-term elasticity
Residential users		
Power	0.00 – –0.80	0.00 – –2.50
Natural gas	0.00 – –0.88	0.00 – –3.44
Fuel	0.00 – –0.70	0.00 – –3.50
Commercial users		
Power	–0.17 – –1.18	0.00 – –4.74
Natural gas	0.00 – –0.38	0.00 – –2.27
Fuel	–0.30 – –0.61	–0.55 – –3.50

Source: C. Dahl, *A Survey of Energy Demand Elasticities in Support of the Development of the NEMS*, Contract No. DE-AP01-93EI23499 (Washington, DC, October 1993).

gas in houses and gasoline, the highest short-term price elasticity (absolute value) is within 0–1, while the highest long-term price elasticity (absolute value) ranges from 2.27–3.5.

That characteristic of price elasticity of oil and natural gas will make the market price of both fluctuate greatly in the short-term. Since the short-term price elasticity is very small, when the supply reduces due to various reasons, a greater rise in price will be seen. But since the long-term price elasticity of oil and natural gas is large, after a period of time, the demand will fall, while the supply increases along with the rise in prices. This will bring down the price dramatically. A price fluctuation within a certain range is normal and can be flatted by establishing a futures market or transactions of hedging. But too many speculative factors in the futures market will also intensify price fluctuation. It is not always a good thing if the price fluctuation exceeds a certain range, because it will bring about welfare losses to enterprises and residents (Peter Lindert and Charles Kindleberger, 1985, pp. 554–558). **In severe circumstances, the dramatic rise in prices may become unaffordable for some enterprise and force them to close down, and some residents will suffer severe welfare losses as they cannot afford the high prices. On the other extreme, low prices may also jeopardize the oil and gas industry.**

Taking the "public characteristic" of oil and natural gas mentioned before into consideration, the prices of oil and natural gas are not only an economic issue, but also a political issue which has immediate influence on social stability.

Therefore, **in the light of such price characteristics of oil and natural gas, we do not exclude the possibility that the government should perform price controls in specific periods.** Even the United States, as a country more dedicated to economic freedom, once interfered when the oil price went too low in the 1930s and controlled gasoline prices during the oil crisis in the 1970s (Daniel Yergin, 1992, pp. 258–265, p. 615).

VI. Demand Characteristics (2): Requirement of Military Affairs

Another important demand characteristic of oil is military requirement. National defense is an important public good, which may cause severe losses to a country in the case of undersupply. In the earlier days of modern times, the losses may include cession of territory, compensation, and accepting unequal treaties undermining sovereignty and interest. After the Second World War, such losses are still featured, with territories being occupied and plundered of resources. In modern wars, oil is an important resource which ensures the maneuverability of armies, and undersupply of oil may result in failure of wars. To avert the losses caused by defeats in wars, the oil price cannot be too high. That is to say, under this circumstance, the oil price elasticity is zero.

The total demand of oil market is roughly composed of national defense demand, industrial and commercial demand, and residential demand. The former two demands have important influences on the characteristics of oil demand, i.e., the price elasticity of oil is low and close to zero.

If the oil supply sharply decreases (the supply curve S in the figure moves left to S') in the time of war, oil prices will dramatically rise and the industrial and commercial demand with larger price elasticity will sharply decrease, and the residential demand will decrease slightly in the short-term but sharply in the long run. However, the national defense demand will not decrease but increase. If the market is monopolistic, the monopoly

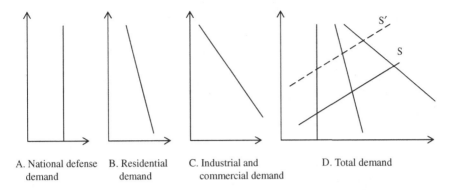

A. National defense   B. Residential   C. Industrial and   D. Total demand
   demand   demand   commercial demand

Figure 1.9.   Three Types of Demands for Oil
Note: The total demand is the accumulation of the former three demands.

enterprises may take advantage of the lack of elasticity in government oil purchases to force up oil prices to the level of monopoly price. Government may be unable to purchase sufficient oil due to lack of funds, which results in loss of wars. On the contrary, if a country has more oil reserves than its enemy, it will increase its oil supply by occupying oil producing areas and cut its enemy's oil supply by damaging oil fields and oil pipelines. Therefore, **since national defense is a prioritized public good, which means without national defense, the oil consumption of industry and commerce and that of residents' would become meaningless. As oil is the specific resource providing for the public goods of national defense, it shall be used for the purpose of national defense as a priority.**

To illustrate further, **since external threats to countries still exist in the time of peace, governments should maintain a certain quantity of oil reserves and control in case of accidents**. The quantity of the oil reserves may be determined according to the odds of war, consumption in unit time of war and the length of warfare emergency period.

Concerning how to use oil in national defense first, government should, on the basis of market system, take some specific measures. Such measures may include the following actions by the state: (1) monopolize the oil resources and establish state-owned petroleum enterprises to directly exploit, refine and sell oil; (2) control or hold shares in petroleum companies; (3) sign long-term order contracts with private petroleum companies; (4) establish an oil reserve system; and (5) directly expropriate oil of private petroleum companies in the time of war. **Among these measures, monopoly and state-owned enterprises lack efficiency and may control the domestic oil market, so they are unfit to implement these measures. What's more, when it comes to overseas oil exploitation, the government cannot monopolize the oil resources of other states, and foreign governments are very sensitive to the exploitation of oil as a strategic resource by foreign state-owned enterprises. Therefore, monopoly and state-owned enterprises are unfit to implement these measures. The latter several measures not only maintain the high efficiency of market and private enterprises, but also strengthen the control of government over oil resources, so they are more practical and fit.**

After the national defense demand is met as a priority, the remaining oil, if any, can be allocated in two methods to meet the residential demand, industrial, and commercial demand. One method is the market. It is noted that since the industrial and commercial demand are more elastic, the rise in price may lead to a significant drop in demand; what's more, the industrial and commercial users who can afford higher prices are more efficient. Though the residential demand lacks elasticity in the short-term, the use of automobiles is reduced in the long-term and consequently decreasing the demand for oil products. Therefore, under certain conditions, there is a competitive market and the oil supply is fairly sufficient, making this method practical. The other method is the ration system. Since the residential demand for oil lacks elasticity, and is a cause for public concern, a certain quota can be allocated to residents for the sake of social stability. Its disadvantage is that the establishment of ration system is costly and the efficiency is lower than that of the market.

In general, **government will carry out full control over oil resources in specific periods; or take direct control over part of oil resources under normal circumstances; these assumptions indicate that market system should be the leading system in the allocation of oil resources.**

VII. Rent Features of Oil and Gas Industry

Oil and natural gas resources are widely distributed. Some may be located in places with convenient transportation, while some may be in remote

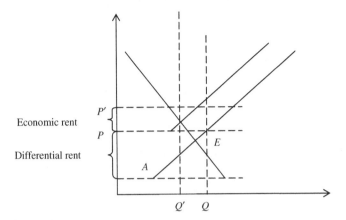

Figure 1.10. Schematic Diagram for Differential Rent and Economic Rent of Oil

Note: In the competitive market, the equilibrium price is *P*, and the equilibrium quantity is *Q*. At this time, the differential rent is the difference between the cost of the best oil field *A* and that of the worst oil field *E* at the market margin. When a price cartel (e.g., OPEC) arises, reducing the equilibrium quantity to *Q'* by controlling the quantity, the price will rise to *P'*. The gap between the value of *P'* and *P* reflects the value of scarcity and meets the definition of economic rent, i.e., the rent purely generated by scarcity. The economic rent is almost equal to absolute rent.

places; some may be buried shallowly, while some cannot be exploited without digging very deep; some are in places suitable for drilling, while some are not. Therefore, costs for oil and natural gas exploitation vary from place to place. In this respect, oil and gas fields are similar to farmlands. Like farmlands, oil and natural gas fields also have differential rent, i.e., the difference of costs for the same output from different oil and gas fields. In general, it is the cost difference between certain oil or gas field and the poorest oil or gas field in the market margin. In a competitive market, the differential rent usually belongs to land or resource owners.

In addition to differential rent, there is economic rent, which is similar to absolute rent. The definition of absolute rent is that when there still is demand for agricultural products when all lands are claimed over, even the worst land will have rent. This is caused by the macro scarcity of land as a whole with respect to all demands for land (land products). The characteristic that differentiates oil and natural gas from land is that oil and natural gas are exhaustible natural resources, while land can be repeatedly used. Macro scarcity means that the quantity of demand exceeds the best allocation amount in the time dimension at the market price in any period. As mentioned before, the monopoly of OPEC raises the market price of oil, but the price should not exceed that of alternative energy or potential new energy. So we can approximately take the gap between OPEC price and the price in a competitive market as economic rent.

Under the legal framework of China, the initial property of mineral resources belongs to the state. The person applying for mining rights shall pay for the mining right he gains. **That means the differential rent of both oil and gas fields, i.e., mining royalty, shall be collected by the state. However, only in a competitive market can differential rent be appraised, thus it is helpful for giving correct price signals to create a market structure where enterprises compete for the mining rights. Economic rent, on the other hand, is a rent purely produced by scarcity without people's contribution. So it should be attributable to the public and be collected by the state on behalf of the public. A specific form can be gasoline tax.**

VIII. Crisis Features of Oil and Gas Industry

Judging from the nature of oil and natural gas as exhaustible natural resources and the low price elasticity of their demand, it can be deduced that the market is relatively weak. When there is a sudden decrease in supply, prices will dramatically rise. If that causes a panic among people and convinces them there is at least a hint of a shortage of oil and natural gas in the long-term, or even a slight hint of depletion, people will store up more resources, which will further enhance the demand, causing bigger shortage in the market and finally pushing up the price. That will cause what is known as an "oil crisis."

During the first oil crisis in 1973, a 9% drop in oil supply caused a 600% rise in oil price (Daniel Yergin, 1992, pp. 641–642). During the second oil crisis in 1979, the oil supply actually failed to meet 4–5% of the demand, but it propelled countries into competition for oil purchases, causing an increase of 150% in oil price (Daniel Yergin, 1992, p. 713).

On the other extreme, under certain circumstances, oil price may be reduced below the cost, causing another kind of crisis, i.e., a crisis that threatens the very existence of the oil industry. For instance, during the great depression in the 1930s, since new oil fields were found, oil price slumped down to a minimum of 2 cents per barrel (Daniel Yergin, 1992, pp. 258–260).

The sudden sharp rise and drop in oil price are not only because there is a lack of elasticity in demand, but also due to people's panic. People worry that if they do not buy oil (or sell oil), others will. If such cases were true, people will find them on the unfavorable side of the situation since the price will only be higher whatsoever (or lower).

Therefore, a similarity can be found between an oil or energy crisis and a general economic or financial crisis, i.e., the microcosmic body therein is in a prisoner's dilemma: People obviously know that the price is far from the normal level, and such changes in price are unfavorable to all, purchasers or sellers, but they cannot take actions to change the tendency. For example, in financial crisis, people know that if everyone buys in, the slump of stock market will be stopped, but there is barely anyone who would like to buy in. Because once one person buys while all others undersell stocks, the buyer will suffer greater losses. At this time, only when a force greatly larger than general micro individuals buys in, can the price be influenced and be stopped from further decline, so as to save the whole market. In real life, there is no such strong force except the government. Therefore, **the nature of oil crisis determines that government shall directly influence markets at specific times. The government's major means is to conduct counter-cyclical buying and selling. The resources used for operation is oil itself. Put in other words, government must have some oil reserves**.

IX. Summary

1. Since oil and natural gas are private goods of competitive production, oil and gas industry can be competitively operated in the market by enterprises (including state-owned and private enterprises).

2. However, oil and natural gas are not common goods, but scarce natural resources. Only under the premise of establishing exclusive property system can the "tragedy of the commons," i.e., overcrowding exploitation and depletion of resources, which may occur in scarce natural resources, be avoided.

3. Unlike renewable natural resources, oil and natural gas, as non-renewable and exhaustible natural resources, need a mechanism of correction, because the contemporary generations make overexploitation and consumption due to the positive discount rate, i.e., underestimating the future tendency. In reality, the correction mechanism is the gasoline tax levied by the government and the "OPEC tax" of price raised by OPEC.

4. In recent years, the world oil reserves and exploitation ratio gradually rises, but peak oil arises in some regions, e.g., the Middle East. When the oil peak is just around the corner, if it does arrive within 30 years, the current market price is likely to be influenced and the importance of OPEC may decline. The market price may reflect the scarceness of oil more and more. It will exert appropriate influences on the production and consumption of oil, and the research, development, and production of alternative energy sources.

5. Since oil and natural gas have the characteristics of popular consumer goods and of military requirements, they have very low, even zero, price elasticity and wide social sensitivity. Thus, it needs government intervention in specific periods. For instance, in the case of large fluctuation in prices, government shall properly intervene; oil shall be completely or partially controlled in times of war, so as to meet the military requirements first, while it is essential to maintain certain oil reserves in times of peace.

6. As oil and natural gas are widely spread, differential rents exist; and as they are scarce on the whole, there is economic rent, i.e., the rent formed merely due to scarcity. Differential rent can be formed through market competition for resources, and shall be obtained by owners of resources, or by the state as in China's case. Since economic rent is absolute value of scarcity, it shall be collected by the government on behalf of the public and a specific form may be gasoline tax.

7. Since the demand for oil and natural gas lacks price elasticity and both resources are exhaustible resources, the oil and gas industry has some characteristic of crisis. Government shall adopt counter-cyclical means when a crisis occurs, which requires a large amount of reserves of oil and natural gas resources.

8. Since the formation of differential rent requires competition and competitive market structure can prevent monopoly enterprises from making use of wars or crisis to engross the market or drive up prices, from the perspective of national security and efficiency, it is essential to establish a competitive market in oil and gas industry.

9. The abovementioned characteristics of oil and gas industry determine that the system of oil and gas industry shall mainly be based on the market system, supplemented by proper government interventions, including levying gasoline tax, adopting short-term intervention for large price fluctuations, commandeering oil resources and products in the times of war, and establishing resource reserve in times of peace.

Chapter 2

Formation, Status Quo, and Nature of Petroleum Industry System in China

I. History of Evolution of Petroleum Industry System

1. Before 1978

The "Sino-Soviet Petroleum Corporation" established in March 1950 by China and Soviet Union in Xinjiang on the principle of equal rights and joint stock, was a prototype of the Chinese petroleum sector. In April 1950, **the Petroleum Administration was established under the Ministry of Fuel Industries** as an authority in charge of production and construction of the petroleum industry in China. In 1954, Soviet Union's shares in Sino-Soviet Petroleum Corporation were handed over to the People's Republic of China.

The State Council decided that from 1955, in addition to the oil exploration and development by the Petroleum Administration under the Ministry of Fuel Industries, the Ministry of Geology and Mineral Resources and the Chinese Academy of Sciences shall respectively undertake the geological survey and research activities related to oil resources. In July 1955, the second session of the first National People's Congress decided to cancel the Ministry of Fuel Industries and to establish the **Ministry of Petroleum Industry**, the Ministry of Coal Industry, and the Ministry of Power Industry. During the period 1955–1957, China organized the first large-scale general survey on oil and natural gas resources, when there were 9 oil and gas fields found in the Mainland, consisting of 6 oil fields and 3 gas fields. By the end of the 1950s, 4 oil and natural gas bases in Yumen, Xinjiang, Qinghai, and Sichuan were established in China. In 1959, the nationwide crude oil ouput reached 3.733 million tons, of which 2.763 million tons, or 73.9%, was from the 4 bases.

From the late 1950s to the 1970s, the emphasis of petroleum industry was to carry out exploration and exploitation. The petroleum sector concentrated human and material resources and organized large-scale exploration campaigns in Northeast China, North China, Sichuan, Hubei, and Shaanxi–Gansu–Ningxia (Shaan–Gan–Ning) Border Region, and successively discovered and developed oil fields including Karamay, Daqing, Shengli and Dagang; and oil–gas exploration moved from the land to the ocean with the discovery of the oil fields such as Bohai Oil field. Over a period of 13 years from 1966 to 1978, 125 oil and natural gas fields were discovered, including 91 oil fields and 34 gas fields. Oil reserves dramatically rose and 14 oil development bases, namely Daqing, Fuyu, Shengli, Huabei, Dagang, Liaohe, Jianghan, Henan, Jiangsu, Shan–Gan–Ning, Yumen, Qinghai, Xinjiang, and Yanchang, along with Sichuan natural gas development base, were formed. The oil production saw an annual average growth rate of 18.6%. In 1978, the oil production reached 104 million tons, making China the nineth largest oil producing country in the world. Part of the crude oil was exported, which became a main foreign exchange-earning channel. The nationwide annual processing capability of crude oil reached 92.91 million tons, and petroleum industry became an important pillar of China's national economy.

During that period, administrative departments in charge of oil were also adjusted several times. On June 22, 1970, the Ministry of Petroleum Industry, Ministry of Coal Industry and Ministry of Chemical Industry were merged into the **Ministry of Fuel and Chemical Industries**. On February 1, 1975, the Ministry of Fuel and Chemical Industries was cancelled to establish the **Ministry of Petroleum and Chemical Industries**, which was replaced by the **Ministry of Petroleum Industry** according to the decision of the first session of the fifth National People's Congress on March 8, 1978.

Before 1978, China's petroleum industry was a completely planned economy production system. The State Development Planning Commission and the State Economic and Trade Commission were responsible for the formulation of investment plans, tasks, and targets; the Ministry of Finance was responsible for allocating funds; the Ministry of Geology and Resources was responsible for exploration; the Ministry of Petroleum Industry was responsible for production and operation.

All enterprises were subordinate units of the Ministry of Petroleum and investment plan, product sales, personnel arrangement, cost accounting, pay grade and targets were determined by related departments. All oil and petroleum products were included in the national comprehensive balance plan and were uniformly allocated and managed by a grade system. Uniform oil buying and selling channels were formed domestically, and enterprises only needed to complete the set targets.

2. After 1978

After 1978, the low efficiency of China's petroleum industry was exposed. Oil production constantly declined and oil enterprises suffered serious losses. To address this situation, the state carried out several reforms in the petroleum industry.

(1) In 1981, with the approval of the State Council, the Ministry of Petroleum Industry implemented the lump sum production target of 100 million tons crude oil. After achieving the target of annual output of 100 million tons of crude oil, the Ministry can export the crude oil exceeding the target or saved from its own use and by reducing losses, and the money earned from the difference between the international price and the domestic price may be used as the fund for oil exploration and development. Since then, a dual-track system where plan and market coexist emerged in the oil circulation system.

(2) Offshore oil exploitation is characterized by high investment, high technology, and high risk. Under the circumstance of insufficient technology and funds, China urgently wanted to address difficulties in exploitation in the form of cooperation with overseas enterprises. Therefore, in March 1982, the China National Offshore Oil Corporation (CNOOC) was set up under the Ministry of Petroleum Industry. **QIN Wencai, Deputy Minister of Petroleum Industry, assumed the office of CNOOC's General Manager. Under the leadership of Vice-Premier Kang Shien and leaders of the Ministry of Petroleum Industry, the first session of leading group formulated the foreign cooperation mode and participated in the drafting of the *Regulations of the People's Republic of China on the Exploitation***

of Offshore Petroleum Resources in Cooperation with Foreign Enterprises (1982) (《中华人民共和国对外合作开采海洋石油资源条例》); China National Offshore Oil Corporation was granted the exclusive right in the exploitation in operation with foreign enterprises. The institutions for offshore and onshore oil development independently carried out cooperative or self-run oil exploration and development with 5 m depth of water as the boundary.

(3) In 1983, the government integrated oil refinery enterprises of every sector and organized China Petrochemical Corporation (SINOPEC); in September 1988, the government cancelled the Ministry of Petroleum Industry and restructured it as China National Petroleum Corporation (CNPC) in charge of management of onshore petroleum companies. From then on, China's oil industry formed a monopoly pattern with three enterprises. CNPC monopolized oil exploration and exploitation; SINOPEC monopolized oil refining; CNOOC monopolized offshore oil exploration and exploitation. In 1997, the government established Star Petroleum Co. Ltd.,[1] which has the right to conduct business of the whole petroleum industry.

Before 1998, petroleum was subject to separate operation. China National Petroleum Corporation was responsible for the exploration and production of onshore crude oil; CNOOC was responsible for the exploration and production of offshore crude oil; China Petrochemical Corporation was responsible for the refining of crude oil; and China National Chemicals Import and Export Corporation exclusively monopolized the import and export trade of oil. The downstream wholesale and retail links were mainly operated by non-state-owned enterprises.

In 1998, China's petroleum industry was reorganized, and separate operation was changed to mixed operation. The national oil business was divided among three group companies, namely, China Petrochemical Corporation (in 2000, Star Petroleum Co. Ltd., was incorporated into SINOPEC Group), China National Petroleum Corporation, and CNOOC

---

[1] It is based on the general exploration and scientific research team of Petroleum Geology and Marine Geology Bureau under the former Ministry of Geology and Mineral Resources and related affiliated petroleum system.

on geographic basis, i.e., the south, the north, and the offshore. Those three companies were all vertically integrated full-service companies. CNPC and SINOPEC respectively obtained the exploration and exploitation of oil and natural gas resources in 12 provinces in the north and 19 provinces in the south, and gained the midstream and downstream businesses of oil refining, wholesale and retail in their respective provinces and import–export operation right.

In 1994, the State Council approved and transmitted the *Suggestions on the Reform of Crude Oil and Petroleum Products Circulation Systems* (《关于改革原油、成品油流通体制的意见》) of the State Development Planning Commission and the State Economic and Trade Commission and strengthened the macro-management on the production and circulation of crude oil and petroleum products, which put oil circulation back on the planning track. In May 1999, the General Office of the State Council issued the *Suggestions on Clearing and Rectifying Small Refinery Plants and Regulating the Circulation Order of Crude Oil and Petroleum Products* (《关于清理整顿小炼油厂和规范原油成品油流通秩序的意见》) (G.B.F. [1999] No. 38, hereinafter referred to as "**Document No. 38**"), which established the administrative monopoly status of CNPC and SINOPEC in the wholesale market of petroleum products.

The competent authorities of petroleum industry also went through several changes. In 1980, the **National Energy Commission** was established, in charge of the ministries of petroleum industry, of coal industry and of power industry. In this stage, the National Energy Commission implemented integrated management over the petroleum industry. In 1982, the integrated management was cancelled and the management mode prior to 1980 was resumed, i.e., the Ministry of Petroleum Industry took full charge of petroleum industry. In 1988, the Ministry of Petroleum Industry was cancelled and the **Ministry of Energy** was established to carry out unified management over petroleum, coal, and power industries. In 1993, the Ministry of Energy was cancelled and the government formed the **Bureau of Petroleum and Chemical Industry** under the State Economic and Trade Commission, while CNPC and SINOPEC still exercised part of industry management functions. The government relieved the management over petroleum industry and adopted a guiding mode of management. From 1998 to 2001, Sheng Huaren assumed the office of director and secretary of CPC Committee of the State Economic and Trade Commission. He once held the post of general manager and secretary of Party Committee of China Petrochemical Corporation, as well as director of Planning Department under the Ministry of Chemical Industry. In 2001, the Bureau of Petroleum and Chemical Industry was cancelled, when petroleum industry had no competent authorities. In 2003, the government established the National Energy Administration, which carried out integrated administration on petroleum industry. In 2005, the State Council set up a leading work team for energy issues, which was a high-level deliberation and coordination organ. In 2008, the National Energy Administration was established under the National Development and Reform Commission.

From the process of institutional changes in the overall petroleum industry, it can be seen that the current situation of petroleum industry monopoly is not the result of market competition. From the complete monopoly of petroleum industry to the establishment of the three big companies, to the reorganization of these three big companies, all are top–down changes implemented by administrative departments by administrative means, and these reforms have a strong administrative tone all along the way (Research Group of Unirule Institute of Economics, 2012).

II. Formation of Monopoly Right of Petroleum Enterprises

In 1979, under the former State Economic and Trade Commission, the Ministry of Geology and Resources took the lead and formed the drafting office for the *Mineral Resources Law* (《矿产资源法》) jointly with the authorities of the industries including petroleum, chemical, metallurgy, coal, building materials and nuclear industry. In 1982, the Ministry of Geology and Resources was changed to the Ministry of Geology and Mineral Resources. The Ministry of Geology and Mineral Resources recommended that oil and natural gas shall be listed as "specified minerals" in the mineral law and related power of examination and approval shall be centralized in the competent department under the State Council. In 1986, China's first *Mineral Resources Law* was issued; although administrative departments of oil changed many times, the pattern of state-level licensing concerning oil and natural gas remained unchanged. Petroleum industry has maintained the highly centralized management mode.

At the time of establishment, CNOOC, SINOPEC, and CNPC were respectively granted monopoly management power and even administrative power of the industry within a certain scope.

The *Regulations of the People's Republic of China on the Exploitation of Offshore Petroleum Resources in Cooperation with Foreign Enterprises* (《中华人民共和国对外合作开采海洋石油资源条例》) (1998, revised in 2001) granted CNOOC with the exclusive right for exploitation in cooperation with foreign enterprises. Since the entry threshold of funds and technology is relatively higher, the risk is higher. For the purpose of diversifying risks, cooperation and joint operation are common forms employed for the development of offshore oil resources by major international petroleum companies. Therefore, the provisions of the *Regulations* are nearly equal to granting CNPC with the exclusive right in offshore development. Though CNPC and SINOPEC also obtained the management right of offshore oil and natural gas resources in 2009, the pattern of monopoly by the three enterprises in oil and natural gas resources was not yet wholly broken.

In 1983, in the *Report on Establishment of China Petrochemical Corporation* (《关于成立中国石油化工总公司的报告》) of the State Economic and Trade Commission, the State Development Planning Commission, the State Commission for Restructuring the Economic System and the Ministry of Finance, which was approved and forwarded by the CPC Central Committee and the State Council, it was decided that the established China Petrochemical Corporation is to be responsible for implementing centralized leadership, overall planning and unified management over important oil refining, petrochemical industry, and chemical fiber enterprises in China. In 1998, SINOPEC also obtained the exclusive right in exploration and development of onshore oil in cooperation with foreign enterprises.

Upon the establishment of CNPC, the *Circular on the General Office of the State Council on the Transmission of the Report of the Ministry of Energy Concerning Organization of China National Petroleum Corporation* (《国务院办公厅转发能源部关于组建中国石油天然气总公司报告的

通知》) (G.B.F. [1988] No. 44, hereinafter referred to as "**Document No. 44**") granted CNPC with the exploration and development and exclusive right of onshore oil (**including island, beach, and shallow sea with water depth of 05 m**) resources. The *Regulations of the People's Republic of China on the Exploitation of Onshore Petroleum Resources in Cooperation with Foreign Enterprises* (《中华人民共和国对外合作开采陆上石油资源条例》) (1993, Decree of the State Council No. 131) promulgated in 1993 also awarded CNPC with the exclusive right in exploitation of onshore oil in cooperation with foreign enterprises.

According to Document No. 44, CNPC also exercised part of government administration functions, authorized or entrusted by the Ministry of Energy and other governmental departments. Specifically, such functions include the following: **to manage and administer the exploration, development, production, and construction of onshore oil and natural gas; to be in charge of the transportation and sale of oil and natural gas throughout China**; to manage and sell the oil and natural gas and related products, by-products and diversified products beyond the amount of goods under unified central planning specified by the state; to cooperate with foreign companies in the exploration and development of oil and natural gas fields; **to assist the Ministry of Energy in handling the issue of oil and natural gas exploration license, rolling exploration and development license and mining license in the whole country and those within the foreign and contracted area approved by the state.**

Document No. 38 further intensified the control of CNPC and SINOPEC over crude oil and their monopoly in oil refining and the wholesale link of petroleum products. Private enterprises and other enterprises intending to enter the upstream industry of petroleum have to adopt the method of cooperating with CNPC, exploit the low-yield oilfield lots considered as valueless by CNPC and take all investment risks. What's more, 20% of the oil exploited by them must be freely delivered to CNPC and the rest must be completely sold to CNPC at the price fixed by CNPC. In the refining sector, SINOPEC and CNPC were authorized to integrate local refinery plants. In the wholesale of petroleum products, all petroleum products (gasoline, kerosene, diesel) produced by all refinery plants at home must be completely delivered to the wholesale enterprises of CNPC and SINOPEC. The release of that document made it virtually impossible for any independent petroleum products wholesale enterprise other than CNPC and SINOPEC to exist.

The release of Document No. 38 closely followed the *State Council's Institutional Restructuring Plan* (《国务院机构改革方案》) deliberated and approved at the first session of the Ninth National People's Congress in March 1998. In the Plan, it was decided to build CNPC and SINOPEC into two mega conglomerates, being eager to grant them with the monopoly management right in the industry prior to their establishment. One of the purposes is to support both groups to rapidly expand, so as to cope with the fierce competition with transnational petroleum enterprises after joining the WTO. China's petroleum and petrochemical industries have developed under the protection and support of national policies for a long time. For example, the state restricted the import volume of crude oil and petroleum products by means of a quota system, licensing system, high tariff barriers, and market access, and prohibited foreign enterprises from engaging in the wholesale and retail business of crude oil and petroleum products in China. The petroleum enterprises developing under such protective policies cannot be strong enough to compete with transnational corporations. Therefore, the related parties believed that "to grant both groups with monopoly management right prior to opening-up can rapidly enhance their strengths and also build a barrier defending foreign capitals" (Yang Zhongxu, 2012).

To establish two conglomerates and to grant them with monopoly management right were also in line with the policy environment to extricate state-owned enterprises from difficulties at that time. The result of the third national industry general survey in January 1997 showed that the whole group of state-owned enterprises was already in the situation of insolvency. In the international market at this time, since the international oil price continued to decline, CNPC and SINOPEC were also in the dilemma of poor profit performance. At the First Plenary Session of the 15th Central Committee of the Chinese Communist Party in 1997, it was put forward that approximately three years would be spent in helping most large and medium-size state-owned enterprises running under deficit, out of the red. In the subsequent national economic layout, government capitals were withdrawn from competitive industries, but in some industries and fields, including petroleum industry, the control of government capitals was further enhanced.

The *Suggestions on Further Rectifying and Regulating Market Order of Petroleum Products* (《关于进一步清理整顿和规范成品油市场秩序的意见》) (Document No. 72) promulgated in 2001, not only further enhanced the monopoly rights of CNPC and SINOPEC in the wholesale market, but also granted both of them the exclusive right in the retail sector. In Document No. 72, it was required that newly-built gasoline stations be uniformly constructed by CNPC and SINOPEC through investment or holding exclusively, and both groups had great decision-making power in the layout and planning of national wholesale market of petroleum products (see Figure 2.1).

What accompanied Document No. 38 and Document No. 72 were the *Implementation Suggestions on Clearing and Rectifying Circulation Enterprises of Petroleum Products and Regulating the Circulation Order of Petroleum Products* (《关于清理整顿成品油流通企业和规范成品油流通秩序的实施意见》) (Document No. 637, 1999) and the *Notification on Strict Control over Problems of Newly-built Gasoline Stations* (《关于严格控制新建加油站问题的通知》) (Document No. 543, 2001) issued by the former State Economic and Trade Commission. The Document No. 637 required that "any gasoline, kerosene and diesel produced by all national oil refinery plants shall be subject to the wholesale operation of wholesale enterprises of groups, other enterprises and units shall not run the wholesale operation." The Document No. 543 required that "the gasoline station newly approved to be established in any region shall be

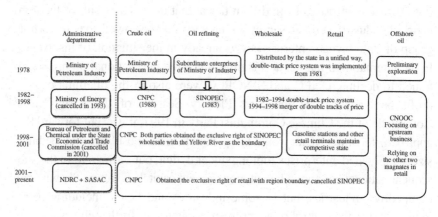

Figure 2.1.   Changes in Petroleum System (After 1978)

uniformly constructed by CNPC and SINOPEC and other enterprises, units or individuals shall not construct gasoline stations." Those documents further enhanced the monopoly rights of both petroleum groups in the wholesale and retail links of petroleum products.

III. Basic Framework and Features of Current System

1. Property Right System Structure

The *Interim Regulations on the People's Republic of China on Mining Industry* (《中华人民共和国矿业暂行条例》) promulgated in 1951 set forth the management system of the state on the property right of mineral resources and the national mining industry that "mineral deposits belong to the State." The first Constitution promulgated in 1954 also stipulated that "mineral reserves, rivers, as well as the forest, wasteland and other resources which belong to the state as stipulated in laws shall be owned by the whole people." The ***Mineral Resources Law of the People's Republic of China*** (《中华人民共和国矿产资源法》) **(1996)** implemented currently also stated this tenet that "mineral resources belong to the State. The state ownership of mineral resources is exercised by the State Council."

The *Mineral Resources Law* stipulates that "**the state-owned mining enterprises are the mainstay in mining mineral resources,**" but it does not exclude enterprises of other ownership from entering the field of mining exploitation. Article 19 of the Law stipulates that the people's governments at various levels shall "adopt measures to maintain the normal order in the mining areas of state-owned mining enterprises and other mining enterprises within their respective administrative areas." The *Circular on the General Office of the State Council on the Transmission of the Guidance of the State-owned Assets Supervision and Administration Commission Concerning Promoting the Adjustment of State-owned Capital and the Reorganization of State-owned Enterprises* (《国务院办公厅转发国资委关于推进国有资本调整和国有企业重组指导意见》) promulgated in 2006 enhanced the control of state-owned enterprises over "major infrastructures and significant mineral resources" and stated that state-owned capital shall maintain sole proprietorship or absolute majority shareholding in such infrastructures and resources.

Table 2.1.   2010 Proportion of State Holding Enterprises of Petroleum Industry in the Whole Nation (2010, %)

	Total assets (in %)	Total industrial output value (in %)	Main business income (in %)
Exploitation of oil and natural gas	96.61	94.70	95.42
Oil refining	59.58	70.92	71.41

Source: Calculated according to the *China Statistical Yearbook* (2011).

In fact, such a vertically integrated monopoly management in petroleum enterprises cannot ensure that the earnings of "state-owned minerals" are owned by the whole people. The whole people exercise their property right in mineral resources through the "state," than through entrustment and agency at various levels. In the multiple tiers, there is a serious information asymmetry between the consignor and the consignee, and the choice on the state-owned enterprise operator is not completely conducted through the market. As a result, the whole people, as the initial consignor, cannot really exercise their residual claim and residual control right.

On the one hand, on the acquisition of oil resources, state-owned enterprises obtained the development right of petroleum by a lower rent price instead of going through the competitive mechanism of bidding and the owner of factors — the state (the whole people) did not obtain sufficient rewards. If consulting the proportion of other states for collecting mining royalty, for the oil price below US$40, 10% of the price shall be paid as resource rent; for the oil price above US$40, resource rent shall be paid by the standard of China's special oil gain levy. During the period 2001–2010, the resource rent underpaid by petroleum enterprises was approximately RMB288.1 billion (Research Group of Unirule Institute of Economics, 2012).

On the other hand, due to the low price in resource factors, a part of resource rents become the profit of "state-owned" monopoly enterprises', which had not handed over any profits during a long term (1994–2006), and only handed over no more than 10% of profits after 2007. The rent that should have belonged to all citizens was dissipated and transferred.

2. Pricing Mechanism

The pricing system implemented currently in China is in accordance with the *Administrative Measures for Oil Prices (for Trial)* (《石油价格管理办法（试行）》) (NDRC-Price [2009] No. 1198) that crude oil price is set by enterprises base on the international market prices; since more than half of crude oil is imported, its price is actually the prevailing international market price. However, since the production and import of crude oil are mainly controlled by oil monopoly enterprises, there exists neither domestic crude oil market, nor domestic crude oil market price. The international crude oil prices play their role mainly through changing the inside price of oil monopoly enterprises.

The prices of petroleum products are subject to the government guidance price or government pricing. The National Development and Reform Commission (NDRC) set the gasoline and diesel benchmark retail price in every province (autonomous region, municipality directly under the Central Government) or central city. **The gasoline and diesel benchmark retail price is, on the basis of international market crude oil prices, determined by taking into account the domestic average processing cost, tax, reasonable circulation link expenses, and proper profits, but no specific formula is published**. When the moving average price change of international market crude oil has exceeded 4% in 22 consecutive working days, the prices of domestic petroleum products can be adjusted correspondingly. With respect to the referenced international crude oil prices, the NDRC mainly consults the prices of **Brent, Dubai, and Cinta**. Similar to the situation of crude oil, since the oil monopoly enterprises control the production and import of petroleum products, only some areas have petroleum products transaction centers composed of non-state-owned enterprises. Therefore, there exists neither any unified domestic market of petroleum products, nor any unified domestic market price of petroleum products.

3. Entry Control

(1) *Entry Control over Exploration and Exploitation.* According to the *Mineral Resources Law of the People's Republic of China* (《中华人民共和国矿产资源法》) promulgated in 1986 (revised in 1996), "oil belongs

to specified minerals, while the State Council may authorize other relevant competent departments to handle the registration of exploration of specified minerals; the competent departments authorized by the State Council may conduct examination of and grant approval to mining of such specified minerals as oil, natural gas, radioactive minerals, and issue mining licenses." It is stipulated in the *Measures for the Registration Administration of Mineral Resources Exploitation* (《矿产资源开采登记》) promulgated in 1998 that "whoever exploits oil and natural gas mineral resources shall, **upon the examination and consent of the organ designated by the State Council**, be registered by the competent department of geology and mineral resources under the State Council and issued a mining permit." In terms of access to oil and gas industry, the "examination and consent of the organ designated by the State Council" must be obtained first and a strict examination and approval system must be performed.

In the *Investment Project List Approved by Government* (《政府核准的投资项目目录》) (2004 version) issued by NDRC, the stipulations about oil and natural gas development projects are as follows: (1) Crude oil: The development projects of new oilfields with annual output of 1 million tons and above shall be approved by the competent department of investment under the State Council, other projects shall be determined by enterprises with oil exploitation right at their own discretion and shall be reported to the competent department of investment under the State Council for record. (2) Natural gas: The development projects of new natural gas fields with annual output of 2 billion cubic meters and above shall be approved by the competent department of investment under the State Council, other projects shall be determined by enterprises with natural gas exploitation right at their own discretion and shall be reported to the competent department of investment under the State Council for record.

With respect to the development of oil and natural gas projects, on the one hand, new entrants are subject to strict approval and verification mechanisms; and on the other hand, incumbent enterprises are granted with obvious preferential policies.

(2) *Entry Control over the Refining Sector.* In the refining link, Document No. 38 set forth that "China National Petroleum Corporation (hereinafter

referred to as "CNPC") and China Petrochemical Corporation (hereinafter referred to as "SINOPEC") may adopt such methods as transferring, joint operation, shareholding and acquisition for reorganizing small oil refineries which are qualified after clearing and rectification, except those of CNPC and SINOPEC." It endowed SINOPEC and CNPC with the power to integrate local refinery plants.

The *Specialized Planning for the Medium and Long Term Development of Petroleum Refining Industry* (《炼油工业中长期发展专项规划》) and the *Specialized Planning for the Medium and Long Term Development of Ethylene Industry* (《乙烯工业中长期发展专项规划》) promulgated by the State Council in 2006 set forth that the petroleum refining industry shall exercise access system. The two documents specified that the scale of newly-built oil refineries must be more than 8 million tons and that the geographical layout of the new refineries shall generally be in the places which lack oil. On the one hand, they raised entry threshold of the industry; and on the other hand, the space for private enterprises and other enterprises to enter the industry is compressed.

(3) *Control over Transportation Sector.* The administrative monopoly power also expands to the transporation sector and the field of other products. It is explicitly stipulated in the *T.Y.H. Decree No. 150* promulgated by the Ministry of Railways in 2003 that without the approval and seals of CNPC and SINOPEC, any railways bureau shall not accept transportation business of petroleum products. That compelled local and private oil refineries to adopt highway transportation at costs several times higher compared to railway transportation. In the Document No. 230 *Program for Expanding Pilots of Ethanol Gasoline for Vehicles* (《车用乙醇汽油扩大试点方案》) and the *Implementation Rules for Expanding Pilots of Ethanol Gasoline for Vehicles* (《车用乙醇汽油扩大试点工作实施细则》) (Document No. 230) issued by NDRC in 2004, it is stipulated that "the ethanol gasoline for vehicles shall be produced and supplied exclusively by CNPC and SINOPEC."

In terms of the construction and operation of long distance pipeline network, in accordance with the *Investment Project List Approved by Government* (《成品油市场管理办法》) (2004 version) issued by NDRC, as for oil pipeline network (excluding oilfield gathering and transportation pipeline network), trans-province (region, city) main pipeline network projects shall be approved by the competent department of investment under the State Council; as for gas pipeline network (excluding oil and gas field gathering and transportation pipeline network), trans-province (region, city) projects or projects with annual gas transportation capacity of 500 million cubic meters and above shall be approved by the competent department of investment under the State Council and other projects shall be approved by the competent department of investment under provincial governments. At present, pipeline networks are almost monopolized by both CNPC and SINOPEC. CNPC has the richest resources of natural gas pipeline network. Having made a huge investment, accumulatively RMB187.6 billion, in the construction of pipeline network in the 11th Five-Year Period, the company now owns 36.11 million meters of natural gas pipeline network and almost completely monopolizes the long distance natural gas transportation pipeline network in China (Research Group of Unirule Institute of Economics, 2012).

(4) *Entry Control over Wholesale and Retail.* The *Measures for Management of Petroleum Products Market* (《成品油市场管理办法》) effective as of 2007, lifted the ban under which private enterprises were prohibited from engaging in wholesale business, but at the same time raised the "threshold" for petroleum products wholesale and retail enterprises. For example, to apply for the qualification for wholesale of petroleum products, an enterprise shall satisfy the conditions as follows: It must have an oil refining enterprise which observes the industrial policies of the state, is capable of processing crude oil of at least 1 million tons at a time, and has a capacity of producing more than 500,000 tons of gasoline and diesel matching the quality standards of the state every year. At the same time, the applicant must be a qualified Chinese enterprise legal person with a registered capital of at least RMB30 million; where the applicant is a branch of a Chinese enterprise legal person, its legal person must have the qualification for engaging in the wholesale of petroleum products; it must have a petroleum products depot with a capacity of more than 10,000 cubic meters constructed in line with the local urban and rural planning

and oil depot layout planning; the related departments in charge of state land and resources, planning and construction, safety and supervision, public security and fire-fighting, environmental protection, meteorology and quality inspection, etc. shall have checked and accepted the depot; and the applicant must be equipped with such facilities to unload petroleum products as conduit pipes, railway special lines, highway transport vehicles or the ports for the shipping of petroleum products with a capacity of over 10,000 tons.

In terms of the qualification for retails, the first-time applicant must have secular and stable channels to supply petroleum products, and have signed with an enterprise qualified for wholesale business of petroleum products a petroleum products supply agreement for at least three years, which shall be in line with its business scale.

In addition to higher entry threshold, the existence of Document No. 38 and Document No. 72 further compressed the living space of private enterprises and other enterprise in the field of wholesale and retail of petroleum products.

(5) *Import and Export Control.* Import and export control includes the trade control over crude oil and petroleum products.

China exercises national trade management over the import of crude oil and petroleum products, government controls the total quantity and makes uniform arrangement on import volume. Non-state-owned trading enterprises are allowed to engage in import of small quantity.[2] To obtain the management right in import of crude oil and petroleum products, an enterprise shall apply to the Ministry of Commerce and obtain approval. The applicant must satisfy the application conditions on import of crude oil and petroleum products (fuel oil) for non-state trading enterprises, annually issued by the Ministry of Commerce, while the threshold for enterprises' application for qualification is very high.

---

[2]For specific stipulations, refer to the *Experimental Method for Operation and Management on State-run Trading and Importing of Crude Oils and Fertilizers* (《原油、成品油、化肥国营贸易进口经营管理试行办法》) (Decree of the Ministry of Foreign Trade and Economic Cooperation of the People's Republic of China, 2002, No. 27).

Table 2.2. Conditions for Enterprises Applying for Import of Crude Oil and Petroleum Products

Main conditions for a non-state-run trading enterprise applying for import of crude oil	Main conditions for a non-state-run trading enterprise applying for import of petroleum products
It should be a foreign trade operator with a registered capital not lower than RMB50 million and a bank line of credit of at least US$20 million;	Its registered capital shall not be lower than RMB50 million;
It shall have the use right of a water transport terminal whose capacity is at least 50,000 tons (or a railway terminal with an annual reloading of 2 million tons);[a]	It shall have the ownership or right of use of loading and unloading facilities such as petroleum products import terminal whose capacity is at least 10,000 tons or special railway lines (limited to frontier land transportation enterprises);
It shall have the use right of crude oil storage tank whose capacity is at least 200,000 cubic meters;	It shall have petroleum products storage tank with a capacity of at least 50,000 cubic meters;
It shall have a track record of crude oil import in the recent two years.	Its bank line of credit must be over US$20 million.

[a]Before 2009, it was required to own a crude oil import terminal of at least 50,000 tons and crude oil storage tank of at least 200,000 tons; in 2009, it was changed to the use right.

At present, only six state-owned trading companies have obtained the right of import and export operation of crude oil and petroleum products (excluding fuel oil). They are: China National Chemicals Import and Export Corporation, China International United Petroleum & Chemicals Co. Ltd., and China National United Oil Corporation, plus the CNOOC, Zhuhai Zhen Rong Company, and Zhenhua Oil with the right of import operation only.[3] There are 22 non-state-owned enterprises which obtain trading import crude oil qualification. Since 2003, crude oil import state trade has removed the quota restrictions and may organize import according to the market demand. On the contrary, non-state-run trading import

---

[3]A subsidiary of China North Industries Group Corporation (hereinafter refered to as "Norinco Group"), Zhenhua Oil imported crude oil mainly supplies Huajin Group held by Norinco Group and Huajin Group is a major shareholder of Liaotong Chemicals.

of crude oil is strictly restricted in quota, use and sales. For private enterprises, the non-state-run trading import quota of crude oil remains in name only for the following reasons:

First, by 2010, there were 22 enterprises qualified for crude oil non-state-run trading import, of which two-thirds were with state-run background (Jiang Lei, 2010), including the companies registered under CNPC and SINOPEC. The annual quota for non-state-run trading crude oil import issued by the Ministry of Commerce mostly went to local enterprises of state-owned petroleum companies, while private enterprises could only obtain a small fraction of the quota (Zhang Qi'an, 2011). For example, SCI International's research on local refineries in Shandong showed that there was only one enterprise qualified for crude oil non-state trading import, which received a quota of just about 100,000 tons.

Second, to obtain import quota, private enterprises shall satisfy not only the application conditions of the Ministry of Commerce, but some additional conditions. In April 2002, the former State Economic and Trade Commission announced that the crude oil non-state-run trading quota shall only be used for the processing of refinery plants of CNPC and SINOPEC. What's more, "at the time of import, it is essential to hold production scheduling certificate of both companies if they want to pass customs" (China Chamber of Commerce for Petroleum Industry, 2010). That means without the production scheduling certificate, oil will not pass the customs even if the non-state-run trading quota is obtained.

Third, the imported crude oil shall be resold to CNPC and SINOPEC for unified sales arrangement, and shall not be supplied to local refineries or circulated.

Except Zhenhua Oil, state-run trading enterprises qualified for petroleum products import are the same as those qualified for crude oil. In 2004, the quota on the state-run trade of petroleum products import was cancelled and an automatic import licensing management was adopted. However, non-state-run trading enterprises engaged in petroleum products import could only import fuel oil. Therefore, all petroleum products import businesses are in fact completed by state-owned enterprises.

(6) *Entry Control over Oil Reserves.* Since 2003, China has initiated the construction of national strategic oil reserve bases. The three

state-owned enterprises, CNPC, SINOPEC, and CNOOC, participated in the national project of strategic oil reserve from the beginning and carried out oil reserve construction with national investment. At present, the national oil reserve project is mainly constructed through the national investment, and it is expected that the national oil reserve capacity will be raised to approximately 85 million tons by 2020, the total scale of reserves will reach the net import quantity of 100 days around and reach the "threshold line" of 90 days for strategic oil reserve capacity specified by the International Energy Agency (IEA). In Japan, the *Petroleum Reserve Law* (《石油储备法》) stipulates that the oil reserved by the state and enterprises shall respectively supply the whole nation for at least 90 days and 60 days. At the end of 2010, Japan's oil reserves reached approximately 600 million barrels, the government and non-government reserves were both above the threshold line.

While the government is constructing reserve bases at huge costs, only several hundred thousand tons out of the total oil reserve capacity of 230 million tons[4] in China's private petroleum enterprises can be fully used, accounting for less than 1% of the total, with all the residual storage capacity idled (Wang Xiaozong and Wu Peng, 2011). Private enterprises accounting for half of the domestic oil retail have been kept off the gate of national strategic oil reserve at the excuse that "there are great difficulties in regulating them."

In 2010, the national oil reserve center began to hold open qualification bid for using social storage capacity to store the national oil reserve. Three out of the six bid-winning enterprises were completely private enterprises. That was the first time that the national oil reserve system opened to private enterprises, and was deemed as a significant breakthrough after the "New 36" released by the State Council in order to encourage and guide non-government investment. Now the rent contract expires, but no oil was ever allocated to the three enterprises (Zhai Ruimin, 2012).

---

[4]The data of All-China Federation of Industry and Commerce refer to the private enterprises' storage capacity of approximately 60 million tons.

4. Key Problems of the Current System: Highly Monopoly Guaranteed and Promoted by Administrative Departments

It is very clear that the problem of petroleum system is the problem of administrative monopoly, i.e., the monopoly established and maintained by administrative departments. Here, the word monopoly refers to not only the exclusive monopoly, duopoly, and oligopoly, but also all measures or acts hindering other enterprises from entering some industry in general.

As mentioned above, petroleum industry is one of the industries with the highest degree of monopoly in China, and every sector in the industry is subject to the control over entry set by the government. The exploration and exploitation are controlled by the Ministry of Land and Resources; prices are set by NDRC; and the import and export are determined by the Ministry of Commerce. On the surface, from exploration and exploitation, petroleum products refining to downstream wholesale and retail, import and export and product pricing, all are under the control of competent departments. In fact, the control subject is, to a great extent, the CNPC, SINOPEC as well as decisions of ministries and commissions under their indirect promotion (*Caijing*, 2012).

Therefore, the current petroleum industry system lacks control over administrative monopoly and is a highly monopoly made by related administrative departments by control means for establishing, guaranteeing, expanding, and promoting state-owned enterprises.

IV. Structure of Administrative Documents of Petroleum Industry System has No Legal Force

1. Structure of Administrative Documents of Petroleum Industry System

In conclusion, there are no laws adopted by legislative body among those comprehensively and spatially making up the monopoly system in China's petroleum industry, and all of them are administrative documents promulgated by administrative departments. Here, we list them as follows:

1988, the *Circular on Organization of China National Petroleum Corporation* (《关于组建中国石油天然气总公司报告的通知》) (G.B.F.

[1988] No. 44) of the Ministry of Energy which was transmitted by the General Office of the State Council;

1993, the *Regulations of the People's Republic of China on the Exploitation of Onshore Petroleum Resources in Cooperation with Foreign Enterprises* (《中华人民共和国对外合作开采陆上石油资源条例》) (1993, Decree of the State Council No. 131);

1998, the *Measures for the Registration Administration of Mineral Resources Exploitation* (《矿产资源开采登记管理办法》);

1998, the *Regulations of the People's Republic of China on the Exploitation of Offshore Petroleum Resources in Cooperation with Foreign Enterprises* (《中华人民共和国对外合作开采海洋石油资源条例》) (1998, revised in 2001);

1999, the *Suggestions on Clearing and Rectifying Small Refinery Plants and Regulating the Circulation Order of Crude Oil and Petroleum Products* (《关于清理争端小炼油厂和规范原油成品油流通秩序的意见》) (G.B.F. [1999] No. 38) of the former State Economic and Trade Commission and other departments which was transmitted by the General Office of the State Council;

1999, the *Implementation Suggestions on Clearing and Rectifying Circulation Enterprises of Petroleum Products and Regulating the Circulation Order of Petroleum Products* (《关于清理整顿成品油流通企业和规范成品油流通秩序的实施意见》) (Document No. 637, 1999) promulgated by the former State Economic and Trade Commission;

2001, the *Suggestions on Further Clearing, Rectifying and Regulating the Market Order of Petroleum Products* (《关于进一步清理整顿和规范成品油市场秩序的意见》) (G.B.F. [2001] Document No. 72) of the State Economic and Trade Commission and other departments which was transmitted by the General Office of the State Council;

2001, the *Circular on Strict Control over Problems of Newly-built Gasoline Stations* (《关于严格控制新建加油站问题的通知》) (Document No. 543, 2001) promulgated by the former State Economic and Trade Commission and other departments;

2002, the *Interim Methods for Operation and Management on State-run Trading and Importing of Crude Oils, Petroleum Products and Fertilizers* (《原油、成品油、化肥国营贸易进口经营管理试行办法》)

(Decree of the former Ministry of Foreign Trade of the People's Republic of China 2002, No. 27);

2003, the *Tie Yun Han No. 150 Decree* (铁运函150号令) promulgated by the Ministry of Railways;

2004, the *Investment Project List Approved by Government* (《政府核准的投资项目目录》) promulgated by NDRC;

2004, the *Program for Expanding Experiments of Ethanol Gasoline for Vehicles* (《车用乙醇汽油扩大试点方案》) and the *Implementation Rules for Expanding Experiments of Ethanol Gasoline for Vehicles* (《车用乙醇汽油扩大试点工作实施细则》) (Document No. 230) promulgated by NDRC;

2006, the *Specialized Planning for the Medium and Long Term Development of Petroleum Refining Industry* (《炼油工业中长期发展专项规划》) and the *Specialized Planning for the Medium and Long Term Development of Ethylene Industry* (《乙烯工业中长期发展专项规划》) promulgated by the State Council;

2006, the *Guidance on Promoting the Adjustment of State-owned Capital and the Reorganization of State-owned Enterprises* (《关于推进国有资本调整和国有企业重组指导意见》) of the State-owned Assets Supervision and Administration Commission which was transmitted by the General Office of the State Council;

2007, the *Measures for Management of Petroleum Products Market* (《成品油市场管理办法》) promulgated by the Ministry of Commerce;

2009, the *Management Measures for Petroleum Price* (*for Trial*) (《石油价格管理办法（试行）》) (NDRC-Price [2009] No. 1198) promulgated by NDRC.

Among them, Document No. 38, i.e., the *Suggestions on Clearing and Rectifying Small Refinery Plants and Regulating the Circulation Order of Crude Oil and Petroleum Products* (《关于清理整顿小炼油厂和规范原油成品油流通秩序的意见》) and Document No. 72, i.e., *Suggestions on Further Clearing, Rectifying and Regulating the Market Order of Petroleum Products* (《关于进一步清理整顿和规范成品油市场秩序的意见》), are fundamental and core documents for the entire framework of the administrative documents. Both of them systematically set the monopoly system of the whole petroleum industry, stress the restrictions over the free transaction of crude oil and petroleum products, and the entry control over oil refining field, as well as definitely establish the monopoly right of CNPC and SINOPEC.

2. Administrative Documents Concerning Petroleum Industry System Violate the *Constitution* and the *Legislative Law* (《立法法》) in Procedure

When seriously reviewing such administrative documents constituting the basis for the oil monopoly system, we will find a common characteristic, that is, all of them are not laws, but administrative documents promulgated by the State Council or its departments.

What's more, only two of these administrative documents, namely the *Interim Methods for Operation and Management on State-run Trading and Importing of Crude Oils, Petroleum Products and Fertilizers* (《原油、成品油、化肥国营贸易进口经营管理试行办法》) formulated by the former Ministry of Foreign Trade and the *Measures for Management of Petroleum Products Market* (《成品油市场管理办法》) formulated by the Ministry of Commerce, can be called administrative "rules." Other documents, especially Document No. 38 and Document No. 72 making up the basis of the whole oil monopoly system, are at the lowest level among the group of administrative documents. By their names, they are only administrative "suggestions," rather than "regulations" or "rules."

In accordance with the *Legislative Law* of China, only a document which is drafted and formulated under the presiding of the State Council, adopted according to procedures stipulated in the *Legislative Law* and signed by the Premier of the State Council can be called an "administrative regulation"; and only a document which is drafted and formulated under the presiding of a department of the State Council, adopted according to procedures stipulated in the *Legislative Law*, and signed by the person in-charge of the department can be called as administrative "rule."

However, both Document No. 38 and Document No. 72 were formulated under the leadership and direction of the former State Economic and

Trade Commission, not following the procedures stipulated by the *Legislative Law*. Such procedures include the following:

> "In the process of drafting an administrative regulation, the drafting body shall gather opinions widely from the relevant agencies, organizations and citizens. The gathering of opinions may be in various forms such as panel discussion, feasibility study meeting, hearing, etc." (Article 58).
>
> "Upon completion of a draft administrative regulation, the drafting body shall submit the following to the State Council's legislative affairs office for review: the draft administrative regulation and its commentaries, the different opinions of all parties concerned on major issues covered by the draft and other relevant materials." (Article 59).
>
> "An administrative rule of department shall be decided by ministerial affairs meeting or commission affairs meeting." (Article 75).
>
> And "Administrative rules shall be promulgated by way of a decree signed by the person in charge of the department." (Article 76).

One of the most important evidence is that the promulgation of both documents have no signature of the person in charge of the department, so they are obviously beyond the scope of generalized "regulations" recognized by the *Legislative Law* and they do not have the legal force which shall be due for administrative regulations and rules formulated according to due procedures on the basis of satisfying a higher level law specified by the *Legislative Law*.

In addition, neither Document No. 38 nor Document No. 72 is a policy. Because a policy is a short-term response made by administrative departments to economic cycle or economic trend with a short effective period, and it is implemented by changing economic parameters, inducing, encouraging, or restraining some type of economic behaviors of economic entities, rather than forcible measures. However, what Document No. 38 and Document No. 72 require is a long-term institutional framework and they imposed forcible measures, so they are not policies.

But it was such low-level administrative documents without legal force that determine the material affairs that shall be determined in the laws made by legislative body. Article 8 of the *Legislative Law* stipulates that "Only national law may be enacted in respect of matters relating to:"

...

(VIII) Fundamental economic system and basic fiscal, tax, customs, financial and foreign trade systems

...

To establish monopoly right in an industry involves a question about "basic economy system," that is, whether China practices planned economy system, monopoly system, or market economy system; in other words, whether to specially establish monopoly right by violating the basic principle of "socialist market economy" specified in the *Constitution* shall be determined by law. Therefore, it is apparently an arrogation of legislative power to establish monopoly right in oil industry by promulgating "suggestions" of department.

It's worth noting that, as previously mentioned, when the former State Economic and Trade Commission took the lead to formulate Document No. 38 and Document No. 72 in 1999 and 2001, and formulated related administrative documents including the *Implementation Suggestions on Clearing and Rectifying Circulation Enterprises of Petroleum Products and Regulating the Circulation Order of Petroleum Products* (《关于清理整顿成品油流通企业和规范成品油流通秩序的实施意见》) (Document No. 637, 1999) and the *Notification on Strict Control over Problems of Newly-built Gasoline Station* (《关于严格控制新建加油站问题的通知》) (Document No. 543, 2001), the Director and Secretary of the CPC Committee of the former State Economic and Trade Commission was Sheng Huaren, whose tenure lasted from 1998 to 2001. However, before that period, during the period from 1990 to 1998, his position was General Manager and Secretary of the CPC Committee of CNPC. After he left the office of an enterprise's principal and became a leader of an administrative department, he immediately organized the formulation of administrative documents which are obviously favorable to that enterprise without going through due procedures. Thus, he is suspected of having vested interests involved, and his motives are questionable.

Therefore, under the basic framework of the *Constitution* and the *Legislative Law*, Document No. 38 and Document No. 72 violate the legislative principle of China, so they are wrong in procedure. Therefore, they have no legal force as of the first date of their birth, or they are "illegal." For details, see "Sub-Report II."

3. Administrative Documents Concerning Petroleum Industry System Violate the *Constitution* and the *Anti-Monopoly Law* in Principle

Article 15 of the *Constitution* stipulates that "The state practices socialist market economy." The basic principle of "market economy" is that market entities are equal in rights, and they compete under the principle of fairness. Document No. 38 puts forward that "clearing and rectifying small oil refineries," "crude oil produced at home and imported crude oil shall be uniformly allocated by the state and shall not be sold without authority," and "petroleum products (gasoline, kerosene, diesel, similarly hereinafter) produced by all oil refineries at home shall be completely handed over to wholesale enterprises of CNPC and SINOPEC, while other enterprises and units shall not wholesale and every oil refinery shall not sell by themselves," and so on. These are all discrimination against different market entities. And the requirements that crude oil shall be allocated by means of planned economy and the wholesale operation of petroleum products shall be monopolized by specific enterprises obviously violate the principle of market economy, and thus also violate the principle of the *Constitution*.

It is stipulated in Chapter V of the *Anti-Monopoly Law* "Abuse of Administrative Authority to Eliminate or Restrict Competition" that:

> "Administrative authorities and other organizations authorized by laws or regulations to administrate public affairs shall not misuse their authority to force, openly or disguisedly, individuals or entities to sell, purchase, or use the products of operators designed by said authorities" (Article 32);
> "Administrative authorities and other organizations authorized by laws or regulations to administrate public affairs shall not misuse their authority to force operators to engage in monopolistic practices in violation of this Law"(Article 36); and
> "Administrative authorities shall not misuse their authority by drafting regulations containing provisions that eliminate or restrict competition." (Article 37).

The requirement in the Document No. 38 and Document No. 72 that petroleum products shall be handed over to CNPC and SINOPEC for wholesale and operation is obviously for the purpose of "limiting units or individuals" "to buy or use the goods supplied by designated operators."

Document No. 38 requires that crude oil produced at home "and imported crude oil shall be uniformly allocated by the state and shall not be sold without authority" and that "petroleum products are subject to centralized wholesale"; Document No. 72 requires that "the market access of petroleum products shall be strict" and that "petroleum products are subject to the centralized wholesale of CNPC and SINOPEC." These are obviously "regulations containing exclusion and restriction over competition."

With the requirement in Document No. 38 and Document No. 72 for the centralization of wholesale of crude oil and petroleum products, the market shares of both CNPC and SINOPEC have exceed the limit specified in the *Anti-Monopoly Law* that "two operators take two thirds of the shares in the related market." Therefore, the two documents obviously "force operators to engage in monopoly actions stipulated in this law."

Therefore, the basic content of both Document No. 38 and Document No. 72 also severely violate higher level laws such as the *Constitution* and the *Anti-Monopoly Law*.

4. Administrative Documents Concerning Petroleum Industry System have No Economic Rationality in Logic

Administrative documents represented by Document No. 38 and Document No. 72 raise three reasons for establishing monopoly in petroleum industry:

(1) "Small oil refineries are too many and are blindly developing without restraint. They not only intensify the contradiction between the over-capacity and the unreasonable layout in refinery industry, but also compete with large and medium-sized state-owned oil refining enterprises for crude oil and market, thus disturbing and breaking the normal order of the production and circulation of crude oil and petroleum products."

(2) "Since small oil refineries are small sized and most of them are lag behind in production technology, they have such problems of low

yield of light oil and low efficiency, the poor product quality and serious waste of resources; some small oil refineries even conduct smuggling in disguised form in the name of processing imported fuel oil; indigenous methods for oil refining are rampant and have serious hazard."

(3) There are a too many wholesale and retail enterprises of petroleum products and gasoline stations are redundantly constructed with disordered management, leading to pressing problem of disordered circulation channel and market order of petroleum products.

The first reason hypothesized that large and medium-sized state-owned oil refining enterprises are superior to small oil refineries; therefore the competition between the two sides in raw material market and product market was described as "small oil refineries compete with large and medium-sized state-owned refinery enterprises for crude oil and for market." Obviously, the logic is wrong here. Since all market entities are equal in the market, large and medium-sized state-owned oil refining enterprises also compete with small oil refineries "for crude oil and for market," but why the conclusion that "large and medium-sized state-owned oil refining enterprises interfere and break the normal production and circulation processes of crude oil and petroleum products" is not reached? In fact, through market-oriented reform, the competition between state-owned enterprises and private enterprises in market has already been a normal phenomenon in China's society. If that logic is established, most markets in China can take advantage of that excuse to prohibit the entry of private enterprises. And that is obviously impracticable and will damage China's market rules.

The second reason is that small oil refineries have small scale, poor quality and low efficiency, so they shall be kept off the market in a forcible way by administrative departments. In fact, in a dynamic way, large enterprises with efficiency actually develop from small enterprises. As long as there are fair competition rules, an enterprise with right strategies, effective management, and proper systems will develop and grow into a large enterprise; and some large enterprises may decline because they stand still and refuse to make progress, or make no attempt to make progress. If there have violation of market rules, restricted competition and ban on entry for the purpose of protecting the monopoly right of one or two enterprises, such enterprises may fall behind due to protection.

To say the least, if the purpose of policies is to promote the technical upgrading and efficiency of oil refineries, it is not proper to adopt discrimination policy against ownership, but to adopt the promoting policy that everyone is treated equally without discrimination.

The third reason is that there are too many wholesale and retail enterprises of petroleum products, resulting in redundant construction and showing an uncontrolled market order. That is a misunderstanding or even a distortion of market economy. Market economy allows enterprises to enter any industry. Therefore, especially in the initial stage of transition from planned economy to market economy, enterprises may pour in for there are few enterprises in the industry and more opportunities to make profits, so it seems that there is a large number of enterprises in the short term; but if there are too many enterprises and most enterprises find it difficult to survive as a result, some enterprises will go bankrupt or withdraw from the industry, and finally, it will tend to an equilibrium of enterprises in one industry. That was proved by the process of the reform and opening-up in China. For most industries, the influx of enterprises occurred in the initial stage of the opening-up, but through competition, a stable order has been formed in the industry.

Therefore, from the perspective of market economy mechanism, the "reasons" on which Document No. 38 and Document No. 72 were based upon, have no economic rationality.

V. Summary

1. The current petroleum industry system of China basically has the following three characteristics: The first one is that state-owned enterprises are in a dominant position; the second one is price control; and the last one is restrictions on entry.
2. The oil and gas industry in China is highly monopolized. It shows that two to three monopoly enterprises have overall monopoly in exploration, exploitation, refining, wholesale and retail, even import and export.
3. The monopoly in oil and gas industry is an administrative one, i.e., a kind of monopoly established by administrative departments through

issuing administrative documents. Such administrative documents are not promulgated through due legal procedures, but they determine the affairs influencing the vital interests of Chinese people, so they are illegal.

4. The current oil monopoly system and corresponding monopolistic behaviors of oil monopoly enterprises violate the constitutional principle of socialist market economy and the *Anti-Monopoly Law*.

5. The "reasons" on which the administrative documents establishing oil monopoly right are based, have no economic rationality.

Chapter 3

Performance of Oil Monopoly System

I. Causing Great Loss of Efficiency

1. Oil Monopoly Enterprises' Efficiency is Low and Keeps Declining

From 2006 to 2011, according to the annual report of CNPC, the nominal return on equity (ROE) decreased from 25.16% to 13.26%, while the ROE of industrial enterprises above the designated size nation-wide rose year by year, beginning to exceed that of CNPC in 2009 and reaching 16.33% in 2011, 3% higher than that of CNPC (Figure 3.1).

However, if we deduct the improper revenues that oil monopoly enterprise gained from monopoly high prices, the unpaid payable costs including rent, mining royalty, interest differential brought by preferential interest rate, as well as government subsidies, the actual profit obviously decreases. See Tables 3.1 and 3.2.

That situation becomes worse with the aggravation of monopoly and the intensifying of monopoly privilege. For instance, the real ROE of both CNPC and SINOPEC was negative even after 2009. Especially for SINOPEC, the problem is even more serious. See Figure 3.2.

In comparison with other enterprises abroad, the per capita benefit of oil monopoly enterprises in China is much lower. According to the annual reports of CNPC and SINOPEC, in 2011, the sales of CNPC was US\$310.3 billion and it has approximately 880,000 employees;[1] the sales of SINOPEC was US\$387.9 billion and it had approximately 1.06 million

---

[1] It includes 552,810 employees which belong to the Group and 323,605 various market-oriented temporary and seasonal workers.

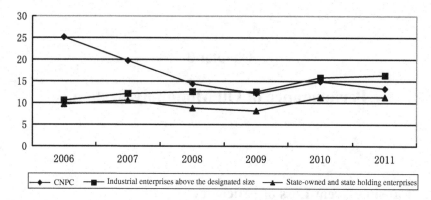

Figure 3.1. Comparison between CNPC and Other Enterprises in Nominal ROE (2006–2011, %)

Source: Calculated according to the data in the annual reports of CNPC (2006–2011) and *China Statistical Yearbook*.

employees. The data of World's Top 500 released in the *Fortune* in July 2011 revealed that the sales of Royal Dutch Shell was US$378.2 billion and it had about 90,000 employees around the world.

Reversely, to create the same operation revenue, the empoyees that SINOPEC and CNPC need are approximately 11 and 12 times of that of Royal Dutch Shell, respectively. That is, taking Shell as the standard, SINOPEC and CNPC have redundant employees, 10 and 11 times respectively, of the number of employees of Shell (Figure 3.3).

In terms of the control over period expense,[2] in comparison with Mobil, CNPC also shows a higher proportion. Given that the gross profit rates of the two do not vary too much, it can be further deduced that the excess returns brought by monopoly are enjoyed by the upper administrative management (see Table 3.3).

2. Bringing about Huge Social Welfare Losses

The current petroleum industry system of monopoly and control not only causes low enterprise efficiency, but also brings about huge social welfare

---

[2] The period expense includes sales expense, general, and administration expenses.

Table 3.1. Real ROE of CNPC (2001–2011, Unit: **RMB100 million, %**)

Item	2001	2002	2003	2004	2005	2006	2007	2008	2009	2010	2011
Total nominal profit	681	692	983	1,512	1,938	1,898	2,042	1,613	1,398	1,899	1,843
Less: Short-calculated costs and extra incomes											
Government subsidies	—	—	—	—	4	6	12	169	11	16	67
Short-paid financial expense	44	44	69	76	102	103	102	140	202	242	293
Short-paid industrial land rent	136	140	149	152	155	160	189	187	192	207	219
Short-paid gasoline station land rent	—	—	56	60	62	65	72	73	78	87	95
Short-paid resource rent	121	112	140	180	294	192	182	148	136	92	92
Income from high prices	—	—	—	—	—	−343	−295	−756	1,571	1,957	1,903
Total actual profit	380	396	569	1,045	1,321	1,715	1,780	1,652	−792	−702	−826
Actual net profit	274	289	409	743	940	1,309	1,359	1,200	−742	−670	−826
Total equity	2,906	3,167	3,566	4,430	5,437	5,676	7,834	8,484	9,081	10,101	10,825
Actual rate of return on common stockholder's equity (ROE) (in %)	**9.4**	**9.1**	**11.5**	**16.8**	**17.3**	**23.1**	**17.3**	**14.1**	**−8.2**	**−6.6**	**−7.6**

Source: Annual reports of CNPC over years and other sources.

Table 3.2. Real ROE of SINOPEC (2001–2011, Unit: RMB100 million, %)

Item	2001	2002	2003	2004	2005	2006	2007	2008	2009	2010	2011
Total nominal profit	209	220	300	535	615	754	834	220	861	1,022	1,026
Less: Short-calculated costs and extra incomes	0	0	0	0	0	0	0	0	0	0	0
Government subsidies	0	0	0	0	94	52	49	503	0	11	14
Short-paid financial expense	52	49	53	70	76	94	138	110	154	186	233
Short-paid industrial land rent	0	0	0	0	0	0	0	0	0	0	0
Short-paid gasoline station land rent	0	0	122	131	137	143	158	160	170	190	209
Short-paid resource rent	39	36	47	61	94	70	67	57	64	60	30
Income from high prices	0	0	0	0	0	−578	−518	−1,093	2,036	2,399	2,115
Total actual profit	118	135	78	273	214	973	940	483	−1,563	−1,824	−1,575
Actual net profit	79	87	50	165	137	684	662	546	−1,563	−1,826	−1,575
Total equity	1,390	1,465	1,629	1,864	2,156	2,818	3,335	3,502	4,065	4,527	5,095
Actual rate of return on common stockholder's equity (ROE) (in %)	5.7	5.9	3.0	8.9	6.4	24.3	19.8	15.6	−38.4	−40.3	−30.9

Source: Annual reports of SINOPEC (2001–2011) and other sources.

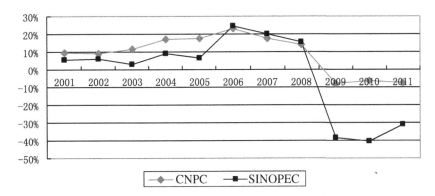

Figure 3.2. Real ROE of CNPC and SINOPEC (2001–2011, %)

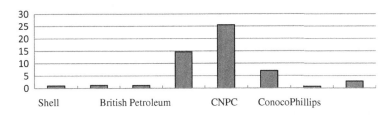

Figure 3.3. Comparison of the Number of Employees Needed for the Same Operation Revenue (2011)

Table 3.3. **Sales, General, and Administration Expenses (2006–2010, Unit: RMB million, %)**

	CNPC		Mobil	
	Expenses (RMB million)	Proportion in total income (in %)	Expenses (RMB million)	Proportion in total income (in %)
2006	79,479	11.54	92,775	3.91
2007	90,669	10.86	96,785	3.81
2008	99,400	9.28	103,175	3.45
2009	105,423	10.34	95,778	4.89
2010	121,072	8.26	95,440	3.97

Source: Wang Hong, Cheng Hao, Analysis on the Economic Performance of Administrative Monopoly Enterprises, *Chinese and Foreign Entrepreneur*, 2011 (07 second).

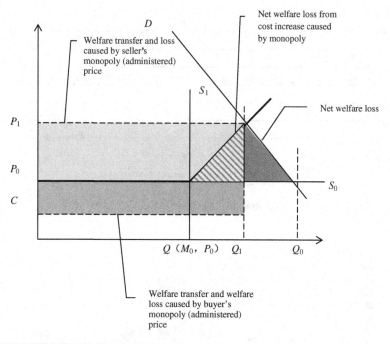

Figure 3.4. Schematic Diagram of Welfare Loss and Distribution Distortion Caused by Administrative Monopoly

Note: S_0 is the long-term average cost curve of the industry and it is formed by connecting the lowest average cost points on the long-term average cost (LAC) curve of several enterprises; S_1 is the marginal cost curve of the industry when the number of enterprises is M_0. P_0 is a competitive market price; P_1 is an administrative monopoly price; Q (M_0, P_0) is the maximum output when the number of enterprises entered is M_0 and the selling price is P_0; Q_0 is the equilibrium output in the competitive market; Q_1 is the equilibrium output in the event of administrative monopoly (Research Group of Unirule Institute of Economics, 2012). For details, see Sub-Report I.

losses. According to the analysis that we made in the *Reasons, Conduct and Abolition of Administrative Monopoly in China* (《中国行政性垄断的原因、行为与破除》), the welfare losses caused by the administrative monopoly in petroleum industry include: (1) net welfare losses caused by monopoly (dark grey part Figure 3.4); (2) underestimated cost, i.e., welfare transfer and welfare losses caused by the buyer's monopoly (administered) price (grey part in the Figure 3.4); (3) welfare transfer and welfare losses caused by the seller's monopoly (administered) price (light grey part in Figure 3.4, including bar part, Research Group of Unirule Institute of Economics, 2012); and (4) net welfare losses of cost increase caused by monopoly (bar part in Figure 3.4). The monopoly profit is the difference between the welfare transfer caused by the seller's monopoly price and the net welfare losses from cost increase caused by monopoly (light grey part in Figure 3.4).

With respect to the underestimated cost and monopoly profits, from the perspective of their approach to expenditure, their upper limit is that they all finally become non-productive dissipation; and from the perspective of opportunity cost, they are also welfare losses. The calculated welfare losses are shown in Table 3.4.

According to the calculation above, during the period 2001–2011, welfare losses and transfer of total RMB3.477 trillion was caused in petroleum industry.

Moreover, the welfare loss caused by petroleum monopoly kept increasing over time, especially in the years following 2010 and even reached RMB600 billion to RMB700 billion annually (Figure 3.5).

II. Distorting Distribution of Income, Violating Principle of Fairness[3]

Although the real performance of oil monopoly enterprises was not very good and even caused huge social welfare losses, there were nominal profits (actually short-paid rent and mining royalty), but the enterprises did not pay or underpay profits over a long term. But at the same time, the incomes of both management and employees of oil monopoly enterprises were significantly higher than the social average level.

1. Unpaid or Short-paid Profits

During the period from 2000 to 2011, the book net profits of the three petroleum companies were RMB1.539 trillion and the profits paid to the

---

[3] This section is mainly cited from the *Reasons, Conduct and Abolition of Administrative Monopoly in China* (2012) of Unirule Institute of Economics.

Table 3.4.   Summary of Welfare Losses of Oil Monopoly Enterprises over the Years (2001–2011, Unit: RMB100 million)

Year	2001	2002	2003	2004	2005	2006	2007	2008	2009	2010	2011	Subtotal
Net welfare loss	1,405	1,405	1,405	1,405	1,405	1,405	1,405	1,405	1,405	1,405	1,405	15,452
Government subsidies	—	—	—	—	98	58	61	672	11	27	81	1,008
Short-paid financing costs	96	96	130	160	197	200	241	268	383	474	634	2,878
Short-paid land rent	136	140	327	343	355	369	419	421	440	484	524	3,958
Short-paid resources rent	194	190	238	285	473	308	309	290	311	301	181	3,079
Loss caused by monopoly high prices	—	—	—	—	—	−922	−813	−1,850	3,607	4,356	4,018	8,396
Total	1,830	1,830	2,100	2,192	2,528	1,418	1,621	1,206	6,156	7,046	6,843	34,770

Note: For details, see Sub-Report I.

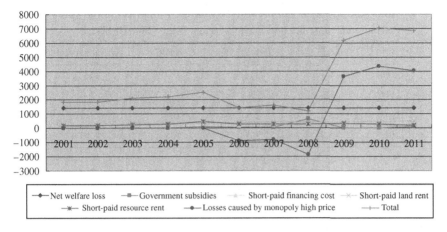

Figure 3.5. Social Welfare Losses Caused by Oil Monopoly Enterprises (2001–2011, Unit: RMB100 million)

state by them were approximately RMB68.9 billion, accounting for about 4.48% of the net profits. That is, **the short-paid profits of the three monopoly petroleum companies are up to RMB1.4701 trillion.**

2. Income of the Salaried Class

The employment form in petroleum enterprises is divided into employment by contract and market-oriented employment. And employees belong to the former with official establishment. In the three enterprises, there exists a quite high proportion of market-oriented employment. For instance, it was shown in the annual report of CNPC for the year ending 2011, that there were 323,605 temporary and seasonal employees, accounting for around 34% of its total employees. There is a large difference between the above-mentioned forms in wage and welfare. According to the data in the annual reports of the three petroleum companies, the incomes of employees of the former firm were considerably higher than the social average level. In 2010, the annual remuneration of employees of CNOOC was around RMB340,000, approximately 10 times of the social average level. See Table 3.5 and Figure 3.6.

Table 3.5.   Comparsion between Incomes of Employees of the Three Petroleum Companies and Social Average Wage (2008–2011)

	CNPC	SINOPEC	CNOOC	Social average
2008	4.1	2.2	9.7	1.0
2009	3.5	2.4	8.8	1.0
2010	3.7	2.5	10.6	1.0
2011	3.7	2.6	6.8	1.0

Source: Employee's compensation of the three petroleum companies is calculated according to their annual reports; social average data come from the *China Statistical Yearbook*; employees' compensation includes wage and salary, employee's welfare, retirement plan fund, as well as social security fund.

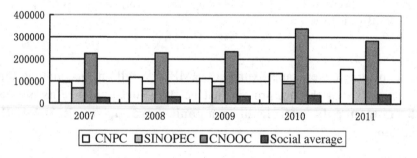

Figure 3.6. Comparison between Remuneration in Petroleum Industry and Social Average Remuneration in China (2007–2011, Unit: RMB)
Source: Company annual reports and the *China Statistical Yearbook* (2007–2011).

3. Executive Compensation and Company-Paid Consumption

The data provided by the annual reports of the company show that the per capita remunerations of executives in CNPC in the year from 2007 to 2011 were respectively RMB962,900; RMB892,300; RMB861,800; RMB1.1022 and RMB863,000 million, while the real operating profit ratios of the enterprise were 8.90%, 7.46%, −7.38%, 2.50% and 4.03%. In view of the company's real performance, it seemed that there was no relationship between the remunerations to the executives and the performance of the enterprise. See Figure 3.7.

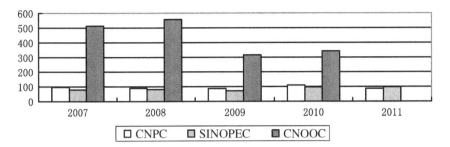

Figure 3.7. Remuneration to Executives in Petroleum Industry (2007–2011, Unit: RMB10,000)

Note: Average value calculated from the top three digits of the highest remuneration. CNOOC did not calculate the stock option income.

Source: Annual reports of all listed companies (2007–2011).

Table 3.6. Company-Paid Consumption and Hidden Remuneration of CNPC (2007–2010, Unit: RMB100 million, RMB10,000)

Year	Company-paid consumption (Unit: RMB100 million)	Per capita hidden remuneration (Unit: RMB10,000)
2007	567.97	14.56
2008	535.14	14.46
2009	647.56	14.51
2010	749.5	16.55

Source: Gao Minghua, *Report on Executive Remuneration Index of China Listing Companies* (2011), Economic Science Press.

According to the research in the *Report on Executive Remuneration Index of China Listing Companies* (《中国上市公司高管薪酬指数报告》) (2011), apart from explicit remuneration, the executives and common employees of CNPC also had company-paid consumption and hidden remuneration and such data were not directly disclosed in annual reports. However, the company-paid consumption and hidden remuneration (see Table 3.6) can be roughly deduced from the cash flow generated from non-business operations disclosed from annual reports. And the hidden remuneration of executives is much higher than the average data revealed.

4. Others

In addition to high pay and company-paid consumption, reports about the high welfare and squander of huge sums by the three petroleum enterprises were very common. For instance, Chen Tonghai, former General Manager and former President of SINOPEC, squandered over RMB40,000 every day (*Guangzhou Daily*, 2009); SINOPEC spent RMB1.56 million on luxury ceiling lamps (An Pei, 2009); CNPC spent RMB2 billion on "group house-purchase" (Long Shu, 2012); and CNPC invested RMB4.1 billion in Guangzhou for new office buildings (www.dayoo.com, 2009), etc.

III. Unfair Competitors: Obtaining Production Factors Freely or at Low Price

The market rules mean fair competition. Even though rules in a certain market are fair, competitors enjoy privileges in factor market and thus become unfair competitors, which violate market rules. Certainly, oil monopoly enterprises have already been in the position of monopoly in domestic market, so they are far from competitors; however, seen from the national macro economy and international market, they still are unfair competitors.

1. Absence of Rent

(1) *Absence of Industrial Land Rent of CNPC.* CNPC Company Limited and CNPC signed a lease contract of land use right on March 10, 2000 to lease a land of approximately 1.145 billion square meters from CNPC for a term of 50 years, with an annual rent expense of RMB2 billion and the total rent for the land above shall be adjusted through the agreement between the company and CNPC every decade. According to the lease agreement, the unit land rent is RMB1.75/m^2 per year.

In accordance with the fixed-base index number for industrial land stipulated by the Ministry of Land and Resources,[4] the annual rental price

---

[4] The fixed-base index number for industrial land takes the average price for the industrial land in the nationwide key cities in 2000 as the base, and the index number is the ratio between annual actual average price for industrial land and the average price for industrial land in 2000.

Table 3.7. Short-paid Land Rent of Listed Companies of CNPC by Market Price (2001–2011, Unit: RMB100 million)

	2001	2002	2003	2004	2005	2006	2007	2008	2009	2010	2011
Short-paid land rent	136	140	149	152	155	160	189	187	192	207	219

Source: Calculated according to the data on the website of Ministry of Land and Resources. For details, see Sub-Report I.

for industrial land is calculated at 3% of the industrial land price. After calculation, during the period from 2001 to 2011, the short-paid industrial land rent of CNPC is RMB188.8 billion (see Table 3.9). But that value may be underestimated, because the land leased by CNPC is commercial land in part, rather than pure industrial land.

(2) *Absence of rent for land used for gasolines of CNPC and SINOPEC*. The domestic state-owned land use system roughly experienced the land assignment system before 1990, the system combining land assignment with agreement grant from 1990 to 2002, as well as the land leasing system with bid, auction, and listing as core after 2003. In terms of national laws and regulations, the *Interim Regulations on the People's Republic of China Concerning the Assignment and Transfer of the Right to the Use of the State-owned Land in the Urban Areas* (《中华人民共和国城镇国有土地使用权出让和转让暂行条例》) promulgated in 1990, determines the transition from free allocation system of land to negotiating transfer system; the *Regulations for Bid, Auction and Listing Transfer of the Right to the Use of the State-Owned Land* (《招标拍卖挂牌出让国有土地使用权规定》) promulgated in 2002, determined the bid, auction and listing system for the state-owned land and in the same year, as a supplementary to the *Circular on the General Office of the State Council on the Transmission of the Suggestions of the State Economic and Trade Commission and Other Departments Concerning Further Rectifying and Regulating Market Order of Petroleum Products* (《国务院办公厅转发国家经贸委等部门关于进一步整顿和规范成品油市场秩序一件的通知》) (i.e., Document No. 72), the Ministry of Land and Resources promulgated the *Circular on Effectively Strengthening the Management on the Land for Gasoline Stations* (《关于切实加强加油站

Table 3.8.   Estimation on Absence of Rent of Land for Gasoline Stations of CNPC and SINOPEC (2003–2011, Unit: RMB100 million)

Year	2003	2004	2005	2006	2007	2008	2009	2010	2011
Short-paid land rent	178	190	199	209	231	234	248	277	305

Source: For details, see Sub-Report I.

用地管理的通知》), which stipulated that the land for gasoline stations shall be included in the project with restricted land supply, and that the land for gasoline stations shall be uniformly subject to the paid use system, and invitation to bid and auction shall be conducted according to regulations.

We suppose that the price formed in land bid, auction, and listing is the market price and the bid, auction, and listing system was practised on the land for gasoline stations at home from 2003. But from 1990 to 2002, land assignment system coexisted with agreement grant system and the land rent is underestimated since the land negotiated price is significantly lower than the market price. We have estimated the short-paid rent for land used for gasoline stations of CNPC and SINOPEC from 2003 to 2011 (Table 3.8).

2. Absence of Resource Rent

In China, those which reflect mineral resource rent are mainly resource tax and resource compensation. Before 2011, the oil resource tax rate was on a quantitative basis. The resource tax rate was RMB8–24/ton before 2004 and was raised to RMB14–30/ton after that year with serval upward adjustments. Though the resource tax was raised in absolute value, with the raise of oil price, the upper limits of rates of resource tax and oil price decreased from around 1.75% in 2001 to 1.11% in 2009. One of the purposes for the collection of the mineral resource compensation is to maintain the property rights and interests on mineral resource of the state, which also reflects the nature of resource rent. The rate of oil resource compensation collected in China is 1% of sales revenue. Put together, the sum of resource tax and resource compensation collected for oil is 2% of the price of oil. In 2011, China carried out a reform on the collection of crude oil resource tax to change it into a tax based on price rather than on quantity. After that the tax rate was 5% to 10% of the sales of crude oil.

In 2006, China began to collect special oil gain levy on the price of oil resource over US$40 per barrel and since that collection aims at the excessive income, the special oil gain levy can be regarded as differential mineral rent. But there is an essential difference between special oil gain levy and resource rent. First, in theory, that oil enterprises replaced the payable resource rent with the special oil gain levy means that they confused the concepts of rent and tax. The special oil gain levy imposed on enterprises is a tax levied on enterprises' excessive profit, generally called "windfall profit tax"; but currently, the main problems existing in state-owned enterprises are the use of resources at a low price or for free, and the absence of rent — cost for use of resources. Rent should be added into cost as a reflection of the price for resource factors, no matter how much profits enterprises make. At present, due to the use of resource factors by enterprises at a low price, and the inadequate remuneration gained by factor owners, the rent becomes the profit of monopoly departments.

In addition, special oil gain levy cannot fully realize the owner's equity of resources. Special oil gain levy can be interpreted as mining royalty levied on a price above US$40 per barrel, and it reflects the nature of differential resource rent. But for a price below US$40, the rate of resource rent is very low and cannot completely realize the owner's equity of resources.

The collection, in the form of special oil gain levy, makes space for competition between enterprises and government, while the tax rate is difficult to be adjusted once it is determined. After the release and implementation of new resource tax program, executives of CNPC and SINOPEC constantly appealed to adjust the tax exemption threshold of special oil gain levy. And as early as the State Council carried out preliminary research for the purpose of promoting resource tax reform, CNPC had united with SINOPEC, etc. to submit to related departments, the plan for adjustment of special oil gain levy

(Zhan Ling, 2011). On December 29, 2011, three months after the issue of resource tax reform plan, the Ministry of Finance released the *Circular on Enhancing the Special Oil Gain Levy Threshold* (《关于提高石油特别收益金起征点的通知》) (C.Q. [2011] No. 480), and raised the threshold for the special oil gain levy as of November 1, 2011 from US$40 to US$55. It is estimated that with the implementation of the new policy, calculated by the output of 2011, the two companies will directly reduce payment for special oil gain levy of RMB39.2 billion. And CNPC will reduce levy payment by nearly RMB30 billion. According the previous statements of CNPC, after the resource tax reform was promoted in an all-round way, the resource tax cost of CNPC was increased by around RMB29 billion. That means that the raise on threshold for special oil gain levy almost offsets the cost increase caused by resource tax.

In the *Interim Provisions on the Mining Royalty for the Exploitation of Onshore Petroleum Resources in Cooperation with Foreign Enterprises of China* (《中外合作开采陆上石油资源交纳矿区使用费暂行规定》), the highest proportion of mining royalty shall be 12.5%. The mining royalty in China is generally above 10%. Therefore, in the calculation of payable resource rent in this report, the resource rent of the oil with its price below US$40 is calculated by 10% of the price, while that of the oil with its price exceeding US$40 is calculated by the standard of the special oil gain levy in China. After deducting the paid resource rent, the short-paid rent of oil enterprises during 2001–2010 was approximately RMB307.9 billion.

Table 3.9. Annual Short-paid Oil Rent of State-Owned Petroleum Enterprises (2001–2011, Unit: RMB100 million)

Item	2001	2002	2003	2004	2005	2006	2007	2008	2009	2010	2011
Short-paid oil rent	194	190	238	285	473	308	309	290	311	301	181

Note: The price of crude oil realized in the full year; during the period of 2001–2005, the benchmark is the price of SINOPEC; during the period of 2006–2010, the benchmark is the weighted average price of CNPC and SINOPEC.

3. Financing Cost Lower than the Market Price

The banking industry-oriented financial system at home and the monopoly characteristic of domestic banking industry, determine the scarcity of financial resource as a production factor, while the scarcity results in the planning of domestic financial resources allocation and the allocation favoring state-owned enterprises, which gives rise to the inefficiency and distortion of financial resource allocation. At the level of economic operation, as state-owned enterprises are not better than non-state-owned enterprises in terms of overall benefit, the scale and cost of bank credit funds that they obtained are obviously lower than those of non-state-owned enterprises. For instance, in 2007, the total sales and the total employment from non-state-owned enterprises accounted for over 90% in the manufacturing sector, while some 80% of bank credit funds flowed to state-owned enterprises over the previous 10 years (Liu Xiaoxuan and Zhou Xiaoyan, 2011).

Domestic oil monopoly enterpries, as mega central state-owned enterprises, have been "favored" by the financial resource plan allocation and gained a large amount of financial resources at a cost significantly lower than the market rate, which led to misallocation of financial resources. Fundamentally, it is to subsidize oil monopoly enterprises by use of national savings. What's more, since oil monopoly enterprises have very strong monopoly forces compared to firms in the upstream and downstream of the industry, they usually freely occupy capitals of other enterprises in order to further reduce the financing cost. We present the financing costs of CNPC, SINOPEC, and CNOOC over the years, the market interest rate of bank capital, and the under-paid financial expenses of the three oil monopolies (see Table 3.10). As for the market interest rate of capital, by calculating the weighted average of the actual interest rate of every manufacturing enterprise with reference to the data of manufacturing enterprises (excluding state-owned enterprises) from 2000 to

Table 3.10. Annual Short-Paid Financing Costs of CNPC, SINOPEC, and CNOOC (2001–2011, Unit: RMB100 million)

Year	2001	2002	2003	2004	2005	2006	2007	2008	2009	2010	2011
Short-paid financial expense	96	96	130	160	197	200	241	268	383	474	634

2007, we get the market interest rate of 4.68% (Research Group of Unirule Institute of Economics, 2011).

4. Government Subsidies

CNPC and SINOPEC are "the most profitable companies" in China, but they often require various fiscal subsidies from the state. For instance, in 2008, CNPC and SINOPEC obtained national subsidies of RMB50.3 billion and RMB16.914 billion respectively, quoting that "such government subsidies are to make up the inversion between the domestic petroleum products price and crude oil price, and losses caused in the corresponding year by the group in taking measures to meet the supply of domestic petroleum products market" (Annual report of SINOPEC for the year of 2008, 2009). But in that year, CNPC and SINOPEC generally made profits, and the net profits attributable to the parent company were respectively RMB113.798 billion and RMB29.689 billion. According to the statistics, CNPC and SINOPEC both obtained national fiscal subsidies of RMB100.795 billion during the period 2001–2011 (Table 3.11).

Table 3.11. National Fiscal Subsidies Gained by SINOPEC and CNPC over the Years (2001–2011, Unit: RMB100 million)

Year	SINOPEC	CNPC
2001	—	—
2002	—	—
2003	—	—
2004	—	—
2005	94	4
2006	52	6
2007	49	12
2008	503	169
2009	—	11
2010	11	16
2011	14	67
Total	722	286

Source: Corporate annual reports of CNPC and SINOPEC (2001–2011).

IV. Deserting Pricing Mechanism of Market

Since the market of oil products is intrinsically a competitive market, the price of oil products can be set through market competition. The market price can give a real-time reflection of the change in supply and demand of oil products, and can influence the decision of enterprises and consumers in return to guide the effective allocation of resources.

However, administrative departments establish monopoly right to restrict the entry of competitors by arrogating laws, which changes the competitive market into a monopoly market, making it impossible to set price through competition. The price set by monopolists will be a monopolistic high price deviating from the equilibrium price. Therefore, the price is controlled by the government only. See the aforesaid oil pricing mechanism.

It is much less efficient to set price via government than via the market mechanism, because the domestic price is a "spontaneous price" determined by the supply and demand of the country, while the price pegged to and harmonized by the international price is not relevant, as it reflects the supply and demand of the international market. Moreover, since the price remains unchanged for at least 22 days, it cannot influence the supply and demand and adjust resource allocation, which leads to efficiency loss. Economics shows that whether the controlled price is higher or lower than the market price, it will bring about efficiency losses (Figures 3.8 and 3.9) and it is very rare to have the controlled price equal to the market price.

Apparently, China's controlled petroleum products price deviates from the market price. Since the prices of petroleum products in European countries and the US are set by the market, the difference between the petroleum products price of China and that of the European countries and the US is seen from the comparison between them. Figure 3.10 shows that the price control of petroleum products in China is basically inefficient.

In this pricing mechanism, two monopoly enterprises CNPC and SINOPEC will, for the purpose of maximizing their own interests, reduce production and supply when the price is falling and increase production and supply when the price is rising. As a result, when the price falls, there will be supply shortage and private gasoline stations cannot obtain any petroleum products at a retail price lower than the controlled retail price,

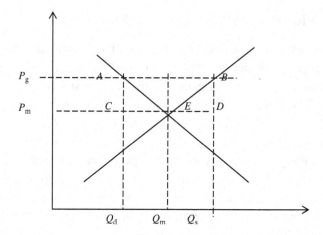

Figure 3.8.   Situation When the Controlled Price is Higher than the Market Equilibrium Price

Note: When the controlled price (P_g) is higher than the market price (P_m), the quantity supplied will exceed the quantity demanded in market equilibrium (Q_m) and reach Q_s, while the quantity demanded will be lower than the quantity demanded in market equilibrium and deline to Q_d. At this time, a surplus amounting to ($Q_s - C_d$) will arise. And its value amounts to the area of CDQ_sQ_d. As long as that part of value is idled, the subsequent loss will equal to the amount of that value multiply time. In addition, the value amounting to the area of EBQ_sQ_m is the net social welfare loss. The reason is that when the price is set by market, there is fundamentally no need to produce that part of oil products.

and thus, consumers are deprived of the benefit of a reduced price, and they have to take more time to queue up for oil. When the price rises, these companies increase production, regardless of demand, and transfer the risks of inventory pressure to the downstream or export firms.

In addition, China's controlled price mechanism is still flawed with other technical problems.

First, the change in the crude oil price in the international market mentioned in the *Measures* is only the crude oil price in Brent, Dubai, and Cinta, and it does not consult the crude oil price of New York Stock Exchange which can best reflect the change in international oil price. Meanwhile, the criterion that "the average price change exceeds 4% in 22 working days" is likely to leave little room for the domestic oil price to respond and adapt to the change in the international oil price (Pan Hongqi, 2011).

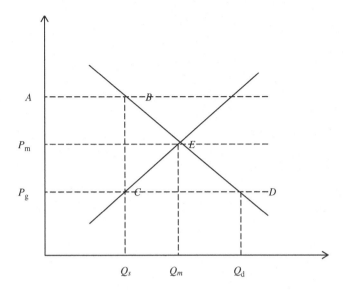

Figure 3.9. Situation When the Controlled Price is Lower than the Market Equilibrium Price

Note: When the controlled price (P_g) is lower than the market price (P_m), the quantity supplied will reduce from the quantity demanded in market equilibrium (Q_m) to Q_s, while the quantity demanded will increase from the quantity demanded in market equilibrium to Q_d. At this time, it will cause a shortage of ($Q_s - C_d$). And such a phenomenon will bring about a net social welfare loss amounting to the area of *BEC*, wealth transfer amounting to *ABCP_g*, even welfare losses. And shortage will result in invalid behavior such as queuing.

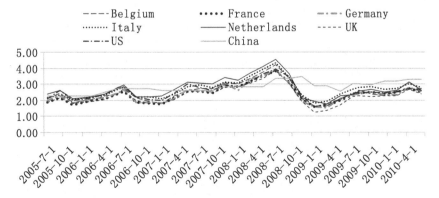

Figure 3.10. Deviation between the Controlled Price of Petroleum Products in China and the Market Price in Other Countries (2005–2010)

Source: Data in the website of US Energy Information Administration (EIA), and data released by the NDRC.

Second, the rise and fall of the oil price are not balanced. That the average price change exceeds the criterion of 4% is likely to give rise to "rapid rise and slow drop," because the same value of rise or fall is easier to reach. +4% as the base value is low when the price is rising and more difficult to reach. −4% as the base value is high when the price is falling.

Third, the international crude oil price consulted by the NDRC is inconsistent with the standard consulted by the two petroleum groups. According to the *Administrative Measures for Oil Prices*, the crude oil price is set on prevailing international market prices by enterprises. That is to say, the choice of the benchmark price in domestic crude oil transaction is independently determined by the "two barrels of oil" (referring to CNPC and SINOPEC). According to the information released by CNPC, in 2011, the price system for self-produced crude oil consulted by CNPC was Cinta, Duri, and Minas.[5] In comparison with the spot price in globally main oil-producing regions since May 2011, the crude oil prices in Cinta, Duri, and Minas are higher prices. CNPC's selling of domestic crude oil to refineries, at the crude oil prices of these three places in the international market, caused nominal losses to oil refining sector. In 2012, both CNPC and SINOPEC made an adjustment on their benchmark price that SINOPEC changed its benchmark oil from Duri to Dubai and CNPC changed its benchmark oil price from Cinta to Dubai. Since the benchmark oil price was lowered, the special oil gain levy to be paid by both petroleum companies was lowered by RMB30 billion.

Fourth, the most fundamental issue is that petroleum products price mechanism pegged to the international oil prices is not the price under the co-ordination of supply and demand. The price of goods in the market should be determined by the relationship between supply and demand. But in a market with administrative monopoly, since the market pricing mechanism fails, the government does not control crude oil prices while the administered price of petroleum products is higher than that in the international market. As a result, China exports petroleum

---

[5]Approximately 78% of self-produced crude oil is linked to the crude oil price of Cinta; 19% is linked to the crude oil price of Duri; 3% is linked to the crude oil price of Minas.

products at a low price in large amounts while showing a high reliance on crude oil.

The existence of monopoly jeopardized the market pricing mechanism in the oil industry and led to a series of problems. China loses the pricing power in the international market because there is no internal mechanism to set the price for crude and petroleum oil products.

V. Directly Damaging Private Enterprises and Other Enterprises

1. Barring or Forcing Out Incomers from the Field of Oil Exploitation and Sale

In the 1990s, there once was a period when private enterprises and other enterprises were encouraged to enter the oil exploitation industry. But after the revision of the *Mineral Resource Law* in 2000, articles stipulating that oil fields may be outsourced were cancelled and the golden age of private enterprises in oil exploitation was ended.

It is stipulated in the *Suggestions on Clearing and Rectifying Small Refinery Plants and Regulating the Circulation Order of Crude Oil and Petroleum products* (《关于清理整顿小炼油厂和规范原油成品油流通秩序的意见》) (G.B.F. [1999] No. 38) promulgated in 1999, that all petroleum products in China shall be handed over to the wholesale businesses of CNPC and SINOPEC for operation and other enterprises shall not engage in wholesale business. Oil refineries are prohibited from sales through their own channels.

Document No. 38 also stipulates that "wholesale enterprises of petroleum products shall be cleared and rectified within the year of 1999 and the wholesale enterprises ineligible for operation shall be cancelled. The qualified wholesale enterprises of petroleum products after clearing and rectification, except those of CNPC and SINOPEC, may be reorganized by CNPC and SINOPEC by legally adopting such methods as transferring, joint operation, shareholding and acquisition." That is equal to driving out those competitive enterprises that were already in the wholesale business of petroleum products.

To control the monopoly in the wholesale market of petroleum products is to control the retail market as well. This is a serious infringement of the free market rights of private enterprises and other enterprises. Besides, the *Suggestions on Further Rectifying and Regulating Market Order of Petroleum Products* (《关于进一步清理整顿和规范成品油市场秩序的意见》) (Document No. 72) promulgated in 2001, stipulates that "all newly-built gasoline stations in every region shall be uniformly constructed by CNPC and SINOPEC as their wholly-owned or holding subsidiaries," which restricted private enterprises and other enterprises from entering the retail field of petroleum products.

2. Imposing Restrictions or Discriminations on Competitive Enterprises that have Already Entered the Petroleum Industry

In the 1990s, a large number of private enterprises entered the oil refining business. After the implementation of Document No. 38 and Document No. 72, the crude oil supply of such enterprises was limited. A large number of local oil refineries and private oil refineries have to leave their production capacity idled for lack of crude oil. It was reported in *Caijing* that "by the end of 2011, the annual comprehensive refining capacity of 21 large local refinery enterprises in Shandong Province is 65 million tons and the completed output in 2011 is 31. Fifty million tons, with nearly half of the capacity idled, among which the crude processing volume is merely around seven million tons" (Shi Zhiliang *et al.*, 2012).

Since CNPC and SINOPEC control the retail link of petroleum products, once both groups stop oil supply to private gasoline stations, private gasoline stations will have no oil to supply and have no choice but to close down or be acquired by the two groups.

According to the information from Oil Circulation Commission under the China General Chamber of Commerce, by the end of 2006, there were 663 private petroleum wholesale enterprises and 45,064 private gasoline stations in China; but by 2008, two-thirds of private petroleum wholesale enterprises and one-thirds of private gasoline stations closed down (Zhao Xinshe, 2008).

3. Excluding Competitors through Local Government by Monopoly Power

For example, it was reported in *Caijing* that Anhui Provincial Government signed a strategic cooperation agreement with SINOPEC to give all gasoline stations in the downtown area to SINOPEC. The *Interim Administrative Provisions for Promoting Ethanol Gasoline for Vehicles in Anhui Province* (《安徽省推广使用车用乙醇汽油管理暂行办法》) issued by Anhui Province in March 2005 stipulated that ethanol gasoline shall be sold in the whole Anhui Province and shall be exclusively allocated and supplied by Anhui Branch of SINOPEC (Shi Zhiliang *et al.*, 2012).

On December 5, 2009, Hubei Provincial Government signed the *Strategic Cooperation Agreement on Accelerating the Construction of Wuhan 800,000 ton/year Ethylene Project* (《关于加快推进武汉80万吨/年乙烯项目建设战略合作协议》) with SINOPEC. That agreement proposed "to support the new construction, joint venture and acquisition of SINOPEC, and strive to build 500 stations." The 500 gasoline stations are located in transportation junctions such as expressway, airport, railway station, and important regions such as new districts and new roads in Hubei Province.

On November 24, 2010, the Department of Commerce of Hubei Province released an announcement on the first batch of proposed new gasoline stations in 2010. The announcement shows that this batch covers 290 gasoline stations and the builders are Hubei Petroleum Company under SINOPEC and Jingzhou Jiangjin Oil Station Operation Co. Ltd., among which the latter is a holding company of SINOPEC. That means that the 290 proposed gasoline stations are actually incorporated into SINOPEC (Research Group of Unirule Institute of Economics, 2012).

4. Directly Violating the Property Rights of Private Enterprises

In this respect, a typical event is Northern Shaanxi Oilfield Incident. In the oil industry, the *Circular on Suggestions Concerning Clearing and Rectifying Small Refinery Plants and Regulating the Circulation Order of Crude Oil and Petroleum Products* (《关于清理整顿小炼油厂和规范原油成品油流通秩序意见的通知》) (i.e., Document No. 38) promulgated by the former State Economic and Trade Commission and other departments in May 1999, had profound influence on the industry. Document No. 38 defined the monopoly right of the three major petroleum companies in the whole industry chain from exploitation, refining, wholesale to retail, which established the major basis for monopoly groups to monopolize the oil industry. The issue of Document No. 38 also directly influenced the situation of non-state-owned enterprises' exploitation in Northern Shaanxi oilfield; in October of the same year, the former State Economic and Trade Commission and other departments carried out an investigation on the situation of oil resource development in Northern Shaanxi with the provincial government of Shaanxi Province and issued the *Investigation Report on the Oil Exploration Order in Northern Shaanxi Region* (《关于陕北地区石油开采秩序情况调查的报告》) (i.e., "Document No. 1239"). The release of the report opened the prelude for the renationalization of the oil resources exploited by non-state-owned oil exploitation companies.

Document No. 1239 directly denied the method of exploiting oil fields through attracting investment, which' was adopted by the county-level governments in Northern Shaanxi Region. It required integrating and banning of the latter two classes among the three classes of entities exploiting oil fields in Northern Shaanxi. Drilling and production companies established by county-level governments were be integrated into Shaanxi Yanchang Petroleum Industrial Group by transferring, acquisition, merger and asset shares; as for the third class, "illegal" investors are required to immediately withdraw and freely transfer the oil field occupied by infringement to the owners of the mining right.

Due to the competition for oil resources between the local government and central enterprises, after the release of Document No. 1239, the local governments of Northern Shaanxi did not implement the document, but continued to attract investment for the oil resources within the region, and even made more efforts by offering more preferential terms. These efforts brought in large amount of private capitals again, and it was at this time that most farmers began to buy wells to exploit oil (Zhou Wenshui, 2005).

In September 2002, the former State Economic and Trade Commission and other departments required that Shaanxi Province shall immediately recover the ownership, management, and administrative rights, and right to yields concerning the oil wells developed by joint development through attracting investment. Shaanxi provincial government carried out material rectification on non-state-owned oil exploitation enterprises. However, Shaanxi provincial government began to take back non-state-owned enterprises' oil wells not merely to meet the requirements of the former State Economic and Trade Commission and other departments, but above all, to take the preemptive opportunities in the competition with CNPC for oil resources in Northern Shaanxi.

On March 13, 2003, the People's Government of Ansai County, Yan'an City released the *Circular on Taking back the Right to Yield of Individual Investment Oil Wells in Joint Ventures* (《关于收回原联营单位个人投资油井并益权的通告》), which stipulated that the oil wells, individually invested, shall be taken back completely from March 16 to 24 of the same year. But there were great disagreement between private enterprises and the government on the standard for compensation. And conflicts between oil well owners and the government occurred many times during the process. For instance, on May 12, 2013, the People's Government of Ansai County led by the Secretary of CPC Committee of the County gathered in total more than 300 people from public security, armed police, court, procuratorate, as well as hired armed organizations and confronted the related personnel of the local private enterprises operating crude oil and arrested more than 50 persons, among whom 8 persons were arrested for "open plunder of the state property and interference with public function" on May 28. The arrested oil investors were paraded through the main streets to warn the public. In late June of the same year, Yulin City organized a group composed of 1,600 cadres and a police group consisting of more than 400 policemen to disperse investors by force, and arrested more than 30 people.

With the competition between the great pressure from the local government and the resistance of private enterprises, in August 2003, the Northern Shaanxi authorities announced that the withdrawal work had already achieved a "complete victory" and 98% of oil wells had already been settled and redeemed. In fact, compensation and settlement for private enterprises whose oil wells were taken were far lower than the market value of such oil wells.

In the Northern Shaanxi Oilfield Incident, the compensation standard for oil wells taken back is one of the most important focal points of contradictions in the whole event. It was once explicitly stipulated in the 1999 Document No. 1239 that "the cooperative operators shall join Shaanxi Yanchang Petroleum Industrial Group by various methods such as transferring, acquisition, merger and asset shares, etc. according to their different conditions," that is, the oil wells are taken back for value. But in the withdrawal of oil wells conducted by county governments in Northern Shaanxi in 2003, it was initially emphasized that the withdrawal of oil wells was free. For example, on June 14, 2003, Yulin Municipal Government issued the *Emergency Notification on Yulin Municipal People's Government on Printing and Distributing the Minutes of the Dispatch Meeting on Taking back Three Rights of Oil Wells in the Whole City and Deputy Mayor WANG Bin's Speech at the Meeting* (《榆林市人民政府关于印发全市收回油井三权调度会议纪要和王斌副市长在会议上讲话的紧急通知》) (i.e., Document No. 55), which insisted that oil wells with investments for more than five years or negative profit and those with a daily output of less than 600 kg shall be taken back without compensation.

Since there were great discrepancies between the government and private capitals in the compensation of oil wells, the event and conflict also expanded, and municipal and county governments in Northern Shaanxi began to change free withdrawal to paid withdrawal, under the pressure. The whole process of withdrawing private oil wells can be divided into two stages. The first stage started from the last 10 days of June 2003. Local government unilaterally implemented the compensation standard calculated by daily output. For instance, Jingbian County, Yulin City compensated by RMB380,000 per ton by daily output, while Dingbian County compensated by RMB410,000 per ton by daily output (CCTV.com, 2003). According to statistics, only 39 among at least 1,000 oil wells did not get compensation by signature. The second withdrawal stage began in 2005, which only aimed at those oil wells not compensated in the first stage and the compensation standard was two to four times that in the first stage.

Most of oil wells in Northern Shaanxi Oilfield Incident were recovered in the first stage, and the actual compensation standard was

RMB380,000 per ton based on the daily output. So we took reference from the profit rate (34.7%) of crude oil exploration and exploitation in the annual report of SINOPEC for 2003, with the 20-year national debt treasury bonds return rate being 4% as the long-term risk-free return rate, in consideration of the conservative property of estimation, we assumed that the average exploitation term of oil fields is 20 years. We have estimated by the discounted cash flow method that the compensation standard should be RMB2.47 million per ton by daily output.

It can be observed that the actual compensation standard of RMB380,000 in the first stage is only 15.4% of the market value of oil wells. The compensation standard in the second stage is two to four times of that in the first stage, only 61.6%, even if calculated by the ceiling rate which is four times. Since the compensation standard for privately-operated oil wells in the Northern Shaanxi event was a standard unilaterally employed by the government, and there was no independent third-party assets appraisal institution, underestimation of the compensation standard occurred as a result.

VI. Damaging Consumers

1. The Petroleum Products Price has Long been on the High Side

Since the quality standard implemented domestically is inconsistent with that of European countries and the US, the comparability of the petroleum products prices at home and abroad reduces. Therefore, prior to the price comparison between petroleum products at home and abroad, it is essential to make necessary amendments to the quality standard and price of domestic petroleum products. Furthermore, among the executive standards for petroleum products at home, Beijing Standard is among the highest level in China, so we choose the petroleum products of Beijing as the subject to be compared with those abroad.

Within the time interval from 2006 to 2011 that we researched, Europe basically executed standards such as European Standard IV, European Standard V, and European Standard V+, while Beijing basically executed standards such as European Standard III, European Standard IV.

The executive standards of Beijing were one stage lower than those of Europe in the same period.

First, we have compared the executive standard of domestic petroleum products with that of Beijing (Figure 3.11).

From Figure 3.11, it can be observed that within the same period, the petroleum products standard of Beijing is obviously higher than the domestic standard, and that of Beijing is closer to that of Eupropean countries and the US. Our analysis emphasizes the comparison between Beijing standard and European standard (Figure 3.12).

Figure 3.12 shows that in order to make the prices of petroleum products in Beijing comparable with those in Europe and US, it is needed to convert the prices of petroleum products during the period from 2006 to 2008 to those under European Standard IV; to convert the prices of petroleum products during the period from 2009 to 2011 to those under European Standard V; and to convert the prices of petroleum products during the period from 2011 to 2012 to those under European Standard V+.

What is relevant is that in July 2005, in order to compensate the rise in oil refining cost caused by the petroleum products in Beijing executing

	2006	2007	2008	2009	2010	2011	2012
National executive standard	National Standard II					National Standard III	
Executive standard of Beijing	European Standard III			European Standard IV			

Figure 3.11. Comparison between Beijing Standard and National Standard of Petroleum Products (2006–2012)
Note: The national executive standard refers to the standard executed in regions except Beijing, Shanghai, Guangzhou, and Shenzhen.

	2006	2007	2008	2009	2010	2011	2012
Executive standard of Europe	European Standard IV				European Standard V		European Standard V+
Executive standard of Beijing	European Standard III			European Standard IV			

Figure 3.12. Petroleum Products Executive Standards and Beijing and Europe and Times of Implementation (2006–2012)

European Standard III, in the background, the retail prices per ton of gasoline and diesel were uniformly raised by RMB250 and RMB150 respectively, throughout the country (except Beijing), and the retail prices per ton of gasoline and diesel in Beijing were raised by RMB460 and RMB340, respectively. That is to say, the retail prices of gasoline and diesel in Beijing were respectively raised by RMB210 and RMB190 when the executive standard upgraded from European Standard II to European Standard III, in October 2008, in order to compensate the rise in oil refining cost caused by the implementation of European Standard IV on petroleum products. Beijing, alone, raised the retail prices per ton of gasoline and diesel by RMB200 and RMB290 respectively, after the end of May 2012, when Beijing began to execute Beijing Standard V (equivalent to European Standard V). The prices were not raised consequently (generally, the retail prices of petroleum products are raised after a new standard has been executed for half a year).

In order to make prices comparable, we add RMB200 and RMB290 respectively to the retail prices per ton of gasoline and diesel in Beijing during the period from 2006 to 2008, as necessary compensations to the upgrade from European Standard III to European Standard IV during that period. In the same fashion, according to the average value of price range raised for two oil quality upgrades in Beijing in 2005 and 2008, we respectively add RMB205 and RMB240 to the retail prices per ton of gasoline and diesel during the period from 2009 to 2011, as necessary compensations to the upgrade from European Standard IV to European Standard V in Beijing during that period. During the period 2011–2012, besides raising the retail prices per ton of gasoline and diesel by RMB205 and RMB240 respectively, as compensation for the upgrade from European Standard IV to European Standard V, we further raise the retail prices per ton of gasoline and diesel by RMB102 and RMB120 respectively as compensations for the upgrade from European Standard V to European Standard V+.

According to the adjustment principle aforesaid, we have adjusted the quality standard of petroleum products, in consideration of tax factor, made the comparison between the petroleum products price of Beijing and the international petroleum products price (see Tables 3.12 and 3.13). The foreign price is the weighted average of petroleum products prices of

Table 3.12.   Comparison between Domestic and Overseas Gasoline Prices (Pre-tax) (2006–2011, US$/gallon)

	2006	2007	2008	2009	2010	2011
Belgium	2.26	2.50	3.20	2.21	2.72	3.49
France	2.12	2.36	3.02	2.15	2.59	3.38
Germany	2.15	2.38	2.91	2.15	2.58	3.31
Italy	2.42	2.64	3.34	2.46	2.88	3.66
Netherlands	2.49	2.87	3.51	2.31	2.68	3.44
Britain	2.14	2.35	2.95	1.93	2.46	3.21
USA	2.40	2.62	3.15	2.19	2.63	3.36
Weighted average of foreign countries	2.30	2.57	3.06	2.18	2.64	3.38
China	2.07	2.26	2.80	2.72	3.22	3.92

Source: US Energy Information Administration; all previous price adjustment information of petroleum products was released in the website of the National Development and Reform Commission; the foreign price is the weighted average with the population of every country as the weight. The domestic price is calculated by deducting a consumption tax of RMB1/liter, deducting the actual value-added tax rate and adding the import crude oil added-value tax, about 8.62% according to the value-added tax data of SINOPEC from 2005 to 2011. For detailed discussion, see the appendix of Sub-Report I.

every country with the population of every country as the weight, so as to serve as the reference in comparison with the domestic petroleum products price. Meanwhile, we also have estimated the welfare transfer and losses caused by the difference between the domestic and overseas petroleum products prices (Table 3.12).

Due to the difference between domestic petroleum products and foreign average price, a total welfare loss of RMB839.6 billion was caused during the period 2006–2011.

In fact, the monopolistic high price became manifest after November of 2008 and showed interest rigidity; it revealed that the petroleum products price (pre-tax) was approximately 31% higher than the price (pre-tax) of petroleum products of the same quality of major countries during the same period. From 2009 to 2011, the consumer loss caused by monopoly prices was up to RMB11,980 (see Table 3.14).

Table 3.13. Comparison between Domestic and Overseas Diesel Prices (Pre-tax) (2006–2011, US$/gallon)

	2006	2007	2008	2009	2010	2011
Belgium	2.39	2.64	3.82	2.30	2.84	3.75
France	2.26	2.48	3.61	2.17	2.64	3.57
Germany	2.27	2.56	3.63	2.26	2.70	3.64
Italy	2.60	2.79	3.96	2.53	2.95	3.92
Netherlands	2.47	2.77	3.94	2.27	2.67	3.70
Britain	2.31	2.50	3.58	2.15	2.58	3.48
USA	2.22	2.43	3.39	2.00	2.54	3.36
Weighted average of foreign countries	2.33	2.54	3.50	2.13	2.64	3.52
China	2.15	2.44	3.03	2.95	3.51	4.25

Source: US Energy Information Administration; all previous price adjustment information of petroleum products was released in the website of the National Development and Reform Commission. The domestic price is calculated by deducting a fuel tax of RMB0.8/liter, deducting the actual value-added tax rate and adding the import crude oil added-value tax about 8.62% according to the value-added tax data of SINOPEC from 2005 to 2011. For detailed discussion, see the appendix of Sub-Report I.

Table 3.14. Welfare Loss Caused by Price Monopoly (2006–2011, RMB100 million)

	2006	2007	2008	2009	2010	2011
Gasoline	−385	−503	−454	971	1,177	1,169
Diesel	−537	−311	−1,395	2,635	3,179	2,849
Total	−922	−813	−1,850	3,607	4,356	4,018

Source: The sales data of gasoline and diesel come from annual reports on domestic sales data of gasoline and diesel of CNPC and SINOPEC over the years (2006–2011); the sales volumes of gasoline and diesel in SINOPEC petroleum products sales are calculated by 1:2.

2. Exporting Oil and Maintaining the High Price at Home

According to the statistics of related departments, China's real excess capacity of petroleum products was approximately 60 million tons in 2009; by 2015, the excess capacity may reach 220 million tons (International Finance News, 2011). The contradiction is mainly caused by irrational petroleum products pricing mechanism in that the new mechanism of petroleum products pricing adopts the crude oil cost plus method when the terminal price of petroleum products is higher, and the high profit will stimulate refineries to improve the rate of capacity utilization to increase the impulsion of crude oil import. In order to keep the monopolistic high price, the inventory pressure will be shifted to retail terminals, or will be relieved by export. For instance, from December 2009 to February 2010, China's export volume of petroleum products was higher than the import volume. The export of petroleum products is mainly through state-owned enterprises. According to the statistics of customs, in the first three quarters of 2009, the petroleum products exported by state-owned enterprises in China was 11.61 million tons, accounting for 68.1% of the total volume of petroleum products export of China in the same period.

Through export, oil monopoly group has maintained the petroleum products price on a level higher than the international market price for a long period. According to the import and export data of petroleum products from customs, it is estimated that China's import and export prices of petroleum products are far lower than the domestic price. In 2009, the export price of petroleum products was RMB2.72/liter and the price including tax was approximately RMB3.03/liter; but in June of the same year, within a period of less than one month, the government dramatically raised the petroleum products price twice and the price of No. 93 gasoline in Beijing was raised to RMB6.66/liter, which was more than two times the above-mentioned export price including tax. In 2012, the average export price of petroleum products was RMB4.42/liter and the oil price including tax calculated according to the tax bearing of SINOPEC was approximately RMB5.63/liter; in 2012, the price of No. 92 gasoline in Beijing was RMB7.31–8.33/liter (see Table 3.15).

VII. Causing Gasoline Shortages Frequently

1. All Previous Large-Scale Gasoline Shortages at Home

A gasoline shortage refers to a nationwide or regional acute shortage of petroleum products supplies resulting from various reasons. On the one hand, due to the monopoly feature of our national petroleum industry,

Table 3.15.   Import and Export of Petroleum Products in China (2008–2012)

	Import				Export			
	Qty (10,000 tons)	Amount (US$100 million)	Unit price (US$/ ton)	Unit price (RMB/ liter)	Qty (10,000 tons)	Amount (US$100 million)	Unit price (US$/ton)	Unit price (RMB/ liter)
2008	3,885	300.4	773	4.27	1,703	136.7	803	4.43
2009	3,696	169.8	459	2.49	2,503.8	125.5	501	2.72
2010	3,688	223.4	606	3.26	2,687.8	170.4	634	3.41
2011	4,060	327	805	4.14	2,570	207.7	808	4.15
2012	3,982	329.9	828	4.16	2,177	191.5	880	4.42

Note: The data of 2012 is for the period from January to November of the year. Converted according to the density of gasoline and diesel, 1 ton petroleum products are approximately 1,258 liters.
Source: The data is cacluated according to the data from General Administration of Customs.

including crude oil exploitation and petroleum products pricing, the petroleum products is in short supply on the whole; on the other hand, with the rapid development of economy in recent years, demand for oil consumption has gradually increased and this is also the background for the petroleum industry system and the overall economic. Generally speaking, after 2000, regional gasoline shortages, especially diesel shortages, occur almost every year and nationwide large-scale oil shortages are registered as follows:

(1) *2003 gasoline shortage.* The gasoline shortage beginning in November 2003 originated in Yangtze River Delta area, and then spread from the east to the west. An acute shortage of petroleum products supplies, especially an acute shortage of diesel supplies, occurred in Jiangxi, Chongqing, Hunan, and Hubei; later, it also occurred in Xi'an, South China Region, North China Region, and Northeast China Region. From December, the petroleum products prices began to rise on a national scale. For instance, from December 6 of the year, the petroleum products price in Beijing began to rise, with an average increase of 5.8%; the gasoline and diesel prices in Shanghai averagely increased by 5.5%; the gasoline price in Nanjing even rose by 8.3% (Wang Wen *et al.*, 2003). The price adjustment

Table 3.16.   Oil Price Adjustment Plan of SINOPEC Beijing Petroleum Branch

Oil grade	Prime price	Standard retail price after adjustment	Current price	Amount of increase
No. 90 gasoline	RMB2.83/liter	RMB2.77/liter	RMB2.99/liter	RMB0.16/liter
No. 93 gasoline	RMB3.02/liter	RMB2.96/liter	RMB3.20/liter	RMB0.18/liter
No. 97 gasoline	RMB3.22/liter	RMB3.15/liter	RMB3.40/liter	RMB0.18/liter
No. 0 diesel	RMB3.06/liter	RMB3.00/liter	RMB3.24/liter	RMB0.18/liter
No. −10 diesel	RMB3.06/liter	RMB3.00/liter	RMB3.24/liter	RMB0.18/liter
No. −20 diesel	RMB3.19/liter	RMB3.13/liter	RMB3.38/liter	RMB0.18/liter

Note: In 2003, the retail price of petroleum products floated up or down by 8% based on the standard price.
Source: Wang Wen *et al.* (2003).

information of petroleum products in Beijing, during the gasoline short-age in 2003, is shown in Table 3.16.

(2) *2005 gasoline shortage.* In the beginning of July 2005, the petroleum products in Guangdong Province entered the state of short supply; in the middle and late July, it had already evolved into a large area of short sup-ply. On July 23, the gasoline price rose by RMB0.25 per liter in Guangzhou, Shenzhen, Dongguan, and Foshan, but it did not relieve the tension. In order to ensure the supply of petroleum products, on August 23 of the same year, NDRC announced to raise the retail price of petroleum products throughout the country. On August 30, NDRC, jointly with the Ministry of Finance, the Ministry of Commerce, the State Administration of Taxation, and the General Administration of Customs, released the *Circular on Issues Concerning the Adjustment of Petroleum products Export Policy* (《关于调整成品油出口政策有关问题的通知》), which stipulated that from September 1, 2005 to December 31 of the same year, the petroleum products export shall be under control, and gasoline export rebates and processing trade contract of crude oil shall be suspended. The Guangdong Gasoline Shortage (also known as "South China Gasoline Shortage") was relieved after the NDRC took measures to raise petroleum products price and restrict the export of petroleum products.

(3) *2007 gasoline shortage*. In October 2007, shortages of diesel supplies arose in Guangdong, Shanghai, Beijing, and Nanning. According to the market report issued by the China Chamber of Commerce for Petroleum Industry, a continued shortage of supply occurred in the diesel market of Beijing, Shijiazhuang, Taiyuan, Rizhao, Nanjing, Hangzhou, Nanchang, Yunnan, and Xi'an, etc. On October 31 of the same year, NDRC announced that from November 1, it would raise petroleum products prices and the prices of gasoline, diesel and aviation kerosene would be raised by RMB500 or around 10% respectively, and retail prices of gasoline and diesel reached RMB5,458/ton and RMB5,020/ton respectively, after the rise in prices. The gasoline shortage was temporarily relieved, but it began to spread soon afterwards (Shi Zhongtian, 2008). NDRC continuously issued five documents during the period from August to November instructing CNPC and SINOPEC to ensure the supply of petroleum products. Influenced by the rise in petroleum products price and supporting measures, the spreading trend was curbed and the gasoline shortage was relieved.

(4) *2010 gasoline shortage*. In September 2010, diesel short supply occurred in Guangdong, Jiangsu, Zhejiang, and Beijing. CNPC and SINOPEC began to control wholesale and made terminal control over their self-run gasoline stations. However, the gasoline shortage was not put under control, but became even worse. In October of the same year, the gasoline shortage soon spread to Northeast China and Northwest China, which are traditional with surplus petroleum products to be transferred out. On September 8, 2010, just before the gasoline shortage, CNPC's 10 million tons oil refining project in Qinzhou, Guangxi costing RMB15.1 billion was officially put into operation and on Spetember 10, 2010, CNPC's 10 million tons oil refining project in Kunming was officially put into operation. In 2010, the 10 million tons oil refineries located in the South were Maoming Refinery Plant subordinate to SINOPEC, SINOPEC Guangzhou, Qinzhou Refinery Plant subordinate to CNPC and Huizhou Refinery Plant subordinate to CNOOC; the refining capacity of petroleum products in the South was unprecedented, and some oil sales enterprises even held sales promotion in early September prior to the gasoline shortage, but it was immediately followed by the gasoline

shortage. According to the statistics, due to the shortage of diesel supplies, traffic jams in Hanzhou–Ningqiang Expressway at the juncture between Sichuan and Shaanxi and Guazhou–Xingxingxia Section from Gansu to Xinjiang lasted several days with diesel vehicles' queuing in lines up to tens of kilometers waiting for diesel; in Guyuan, Ningxia, the 130 buses of the entire city came to a halt. However, contradictory to the gasoline shortage, the customs data in the first three quarters of 2010, showed that China's petroleum products export reached 21.02 million tons, increasing by 23.4% year-on-year. In September, when the gasoline shortage had just started, the petroleum products export reached 2.09 million tons and diesel export reached 368,100 tons, increasing by 25.3% year-on-year.

(5) *2011 gasoline shortage.* In October 2011, diesel shortage occurred in provinces including Jiangsu, Anhui, Zhejiang and cities such as Shijiazhuang, Jinan, Wuhan, and Chengdu in different degrees. On October 9, 2011, NDRC announced the fall in prices of gasoline and diesel, then the gasoline shortage followed. Seen from the supply and demand data of petroleum products, the domestic petroleum products supply was not obviously lower than the demand; from January 2011 to September of the same year, the domestic petroleum products production was 184.28 million tons, while the consumption was 184.03 million tons; moreover, the fall in domestic petroleum products tariff in July 2011 also promoted the import of petroleum products. In August of the same year, China's import petroleum products reached 3.41 million tons, increasing by 33.2% year on year, among which the growth of diesel imports even reached 61% (Wang Lu, 2011). In contrast to the petroleum products supply data, according to the statistics made by ICIS C1 Energy on nearly 300 social gasoline stations and nearly 350 main gasoline stations throughout the country, 18% of social gasoline stations made overpriced sales; 13% of social gasoline stations and 15% of main gasoline stations limited the fuel amount; 15% of social gasoline stations and 5% of main gasoline stations had fuel cut-off; 7% of main gasoline stations had the phenomenon of queuing up for oil; 56% of social gasoline stations, and 77% of main gasoline stations could ensure normal sales (Wang Lu, 2011b). Oil monopoly groups obviously were reluctant to sell out and limited sales after the fall in petroleum products price.

2. "Gasoline Shortages" Were Caused by Oil Monopoly Groups' Pursuit of their Own Interests

The domestic gasoline shortage is not just caused by a demand larger than supply as it appears to be. It is also related to the petroleum products pricing mechanism and interests of oil monopoly groups in China, due to which China's gasoline shortage has already exceeded the category of economic market, mostly shown as human factors.

(1) *Gasoline shortages and petroleum products pricing mechanism.* The price control over petroleum products in China includes the regulation on the difference between the wholesale price of petroleum products and the retail price at the time. For instance, in the *Circular on the SDPC on Improving Measures for Petroleum Price Link and Adjusting Petroleum Products Price* (《国家计委关于完善石油价格接轨办法及调整成品油价格的通知》) promulgated by the former SDPC in 2001, it is stipulated that "the rate of both wholesale prices and retail prices of gasoline and diesel of social gasoline stations outside the supply system of CNPC and SINOPEC shall not be less than 5.5%, ..."

In 2006, the government made an adjustment on the petroleum products pricing mechanism again, and still exercised management on difference in price. In the same year, the State Council promulgated the *Circular on the General Office of the State Council on the Transmission of the Comprehensive Supplementary Reform on Improving Petroleum Pricing Mechanism and Related Suggestions of the National Development and Reform Commission and Other Departments* (《国务院办公厅关于转发发展改革委等部门完善石油价格形成机制综合配套改革和有关意见的通知》), which stipulated that in regions exercising rationing system, the difference between the wholesale price and retail price shall not be less than RMB300 per ton. In regions not exercising rationing system, the difference between the wholesale price and retail price shall be reasonably determined by provincial price control sector, on the basis of considering freight and miscellaneous charges. The *Administrative Measures for Oil Prices (for Trial)* (《石油价格管理办法》) promulgated by the State Council on May 7, 2009, stipulates in Article 10 that "Petroleum products wholesale enterprises may, on the premise of not exceeding the highest wholesale prices of gasoline and diesel, determine the specific wholesale price through negotiation with retail enterprises. When the market retail price falls, the wholesale price shall also decrease correspondingly. Where rationing is required in contract, the difference between the wholesale price and retail price shall not be less than RMB300 per ton; where rationing is not required in contract, the difference between the wholesale price and retail price shall not be less than RMB300 per ton after deducting freight and miscellaneous charges."

However, in such management on wholesale prices and retail prices, on the one hand, market guide prices are adopted in the retail market of petroleum products; but on the other hand, it was monopoly groups' wholesale prices "fluctuating along with market changes." This led to "reversion of wholesale prices and retail prices"[6] of domestic petroleum products, due to which lots of private gasoline stations are unable to replenish stock. So it not only blew private gasoline stations, but also caused gasoline shortage, actually.

The "reversion of wholesale prices and retail prices" at home has already exceeded the simple meaning that the pure wholesale price is higher than the retail price. Against the backdrop that the retail price of petroleum products at home has already exceeded that abroad, the phenomenon that the wholesale price of petroleum products at home is still higher than the retail price during the time of gasoline shortage is somewhat related to the manipulation of monopoly groups. Here, we have compared the domestic and overseas situations of crude oil price, which is the prime cost of petroleum products and compared the retail prices of petroleum products at home and abroad (Figures 3.13 and 3.14).

With respect to the crude oil price constituting the prime cost of petroleum products, the overall trend of domestic price was basically consistent with that of the international average price. But with respect to the petroleum products as finished goods, the domestic price was obviouly lower than the international average price only in 2008, and after 2008, the domestic petroleum products price was not adjusted downwards at the same rate along with the fall in the international oil price and China's petroleum products price began to significantly exceed the international

---

[6] It refers to the phenomenon that the wholesale price of refined oil is higher than the retail price.

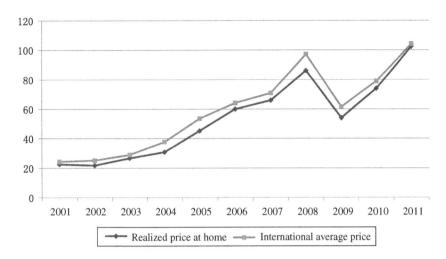

Figure 3.13. Tendency of Domestic and International Crude Oil Prices (2001–2011, US$/barrel)
Source: Annual reports of CNPC over the years (2007–2012), annual reports of SINOPEC over the years (2001–2011); the international average price of crude oil is the average of Dubai crude oil, Brent crude oil, and West Texas intermediate crude oil in BP's 2012 annual report.

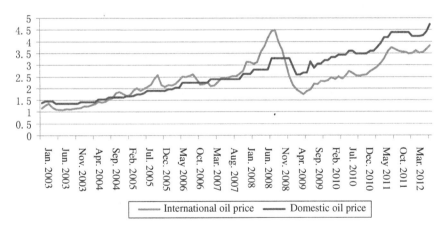

Figure 3.14. Comparison between Domestic and Overseas Prices of Petroleum Products (With the same quality, excluding tax, 2003–2012, US$/gallon)[7]
Source: The data are obtained from the data base of the Development Research Center of the State Council, the price adjustment information of petroleum products previously released on the website of NDRC, the website of Beijing Development and Reform Commission and the information on the website of US Energy Information Administration.

---

[7]To take the diesel price as an example here, the overall trend of gasoline price is the same as that of the diesel price.

average price, without too large changes in rate, which reflected interest rigidity.

From Figures 3.13 and 3.14, we know that the "reversion of wholesale prices and retail prices" in China's petroleum products market occurred in almost every gasoline shortage, even though the domestic crude oil price was slightly lower than the international price and the domestic petroleum products retail price was slightly lower or higher than the international average price at most times (except 2008). This also proved that "reversion of wholesale prices and retail prices" in previous large-scale gasoline shortages was not caused by the low retail price of domestic petroleum products, but the high domestic wholesale price, which have exceeded even the retail price of petroleum products overseas.

After 2009, the petroleum products retail price regulated by NDRC was higher than the foreign average price and higher than the domestic market price. For instance, the market transaction prices formed in various petroleum exchanges established by local governments were lower than the higher retail price regulated by NDRC. The market transaction prices of exchange basically revealed the market characteristic in that it fluctuated under the highest retail price regulated by NDRC. Even so, monopoly groups still set the wholesale price above the highest retail price during the gasoline shortage. But in operation, the characteristic that the wholesale price is difficult to be controlled also fostered the occurrence of "reversion of wholesale prices and retail prices."

(2) *Gasoline shortages and adjustment in price of petroleum products.* Due to the monopoly behavior of oil monopoly enterprises in China, the occurrence of gasoline shortages at home did not exclude the possibility that CNPC and SINOPEC imposed limitations on sales in consideration of increasing monopoly profits and compelled NDRC to raise the retail price of petroleum products. For instance, the 2003 gasoline shortage, 2005 gasoline shortage, 2007 gasoline shortage, 2010 gasoline shortage, as well as 2011 gasoline shortage, almost all, began with the fall in petroleum products retail price made by NDRC and ended with the rise in retail price of petroleum products.

From Table 3.17 and Figure 3.15, it can be seen that several larger gasoline shortages at home had direct relation with the NDRC's adjustment in petroleum products price. Table 3.17 provided information on

Table 3.17. Previous Large-Scale Gasoline Shortages and Related Adjustments in Price of Petroleum Products (2003–2011)

Previous large-scale gasoline shortages (Peak periods of previous gasoline shortages)	Time	Adjustment information of petroleum products
2003 Gasoline shortage (November 2003)	May 12, 2003	Gasoline price is reduced by RMB290/ton Diesel price is reduced by RMB260/ton
	July 1, 2003	Gasoline price is raised by RMB90/ton
	Dec. 8, 2003	Gasoline price is raised by RMB200/ton Diesel price is raised by RMB180/ton
2005 Gasoline shortage (Beginning of July 2005)	May 23, 2005	Gasoline price is reduced by RMB150/ton
	June 25, 2005	Gasoline price is raised by RMB200/ton Diesel price is raised by RMB150/ton
	July 23, 2005	Gasoline price is raised by RMB300/ton Diesel price is reduced by RMB250/ton
2007 Gasoline shortage (October 2007)	Jan. 14, 2007	Gasoline price is reduced by RMB220/ton
	Nov. 1, 2007	Gasoline price is raised by RMB500/ton Diesel price is raised by RMB500/ton
2010 Gasoline shortage (October 2010)	June 1, 2010	Gasoline price is reduced by RMB230/ton Diesel price is reduced by RMB220/ton
	Oct. 26, 2010	Gasoline price is raised by RMB230/ton Diesel price is raised by RMB220/ton
2011 Gasoline shortage (Middle of October 2011)	Oct. 9, 2011	Gasoline price is reduced by RMB300/ton Diesel price is reduced by RMB300/ton
	Feb. 8, 2012	Gasoline price is raised by RMB300/ton Diesel price is raised by RMB300/ton

Source: Arranged according to the previous adjustments information in petroleum products price on the website of NDRC.

adjustments in petroleum products price made by NDRC before and after every large-scale gasoline shortage at home.

Figure 3.15 shows the overall trend of changes in domestic petroleum products price and frequency of occurrence of previous large-scale gasoline shortages at home. Meanwhile, it shows that as the domestic petroleum products price steadily rose, large-scale gasoline shortages occurred

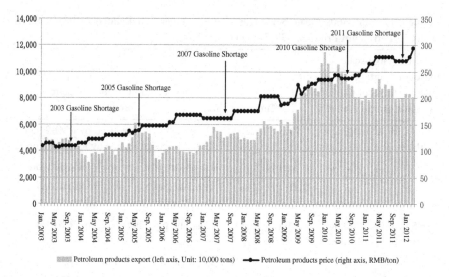

Figure 3.15. Previous Prices and Export Volumes of Chinese Petroleum Products and Gasoline Shortages (2003–2012, Unit: 10,000 tons, RMB/ton)
Source: Oil export data during 2001–2008 comes from the database of the Development Research Center of the State Council; oil export data during 2008–2012 comes from the website of the General Administration of Customs.

after the petroleum products price was brought down every time (the domestic petroleum products price was brought down during 2008–2009, but it did not give rise to a large-scale gasoline shortage at home. The reason was that the international oil prices experienced plunge under the influence of the international financial crisis at that time, and rebounded after 2009). During the period 2003–2011, the domestic petroleum products retail price had been brought down 9 times (raised 24 times). Excluding 2008 and 2009, due to the influence of the international financial crisis, the domestic petroleum products retail price had been brought down 5 times, respectively in 2003, 2005, 2007, 2010, and 2011, and these are the exact same years when the 5 large-scale gasoline shortages occurred in China.

On the one hand, CNPC and SINOPEC, as enterprises monopolizing the petroleum industry at the national level, were doing so at the cost of fair participation rights of private enterprises, and they transferred a large amount of land and fund resources, allocated for the purpose of ensuring stable oil supply to the country, for their own interests. From Table 3.16, it can be seen that NDRC's adjustment in petroleum products price not only followed the simple rule that "in 22 consecutive working days and the rate of rise and fall shall exceed 4%," it also contained the information of game pertinent to petroleum products price of every sector. The reasonability that oil monopoly enterprises exist and the ambiguity and operation goals are the root cause of gasoline shortages.

(3) *Gasoline shortages at home and petroleum products export.* The shortage of petroleum products supplies at home does not show purely as shortage in production, because it is mostly caused by the oil monopoly groups' sales limitation and export for their own interests. For instance, during almost all large-scale gasoline shortages at home, China's export volume of petroleum products did not decrease, but significantly increased. On a monthly basis, we have arranged the sorted-out average data of domestic petroleum products export in three months. See Figure 3.15.

From Figure 3.15, it can be observed that the high points of export volume of domestic petroleum products basically corresponded to the occurrence of gasoline shortages after 2000. And, sharp rises in export volume almost occurred about half a year prior to large-scale gasoline shortages. For instance, there was a sharp increase in export volumes half a year before 2003 gasoline shortage, 2005 gasoline shortage, 2007 gasoline shortage, as well as 2010 gasoline shortage (there was no sharp increase in the export volume before the gasoline shortage in the second half of 2011, because it was stipulated that diesel export shall suspend in principle in the *Circular on Ensuring Stable Supply to the Current Petroleum Products Market* (《关于保障当前成品油市场稳定供应的通知》) promulgated on May 12, 2011). The time lag between the increase in petroleum products export and gasoline shortages may have the following two reasons:

First, supply of petroleum products has tended to be tight all the time in China, so the sharp increase in export of domestic petroleum products will lead to decrease in inventory of domestic petroleum products and make it difficult to meet the domestic demand, resulting in or intensifying the occurrence of gasoline shortages. From Figure 3.15, it can be known that the time lag from the substantial increase in export of petroleum products to large-scale gasoline shortages was around half a year.

Second, upon the occurrence of large-scale gasoline shortages, national departments concerned would generally intervene in the petroleum products supply market and import and export market, and decrease export or stop export of petroleum products through administrative orders, and as a result, after the occurrence of gasoline shortages, domestic petroleum products export would decrease in comparison with that half a year before the occurrence of gasoline shortages. For instance, during the 2005 gasoline shortage, NDRC united with the Ministry of Finance, the Ministry of Commerce, the State Administration of Taxation, and the General Administration of Customs to release the *Circular on Issues Concerning the Adjustment of Petroleum Products Export Policy* (《关于调整成品油出口政策有关问题的通知》), which stipulated that from September 1, 2005 to December 31 of the same year, the export of petroleum products shall be controlled, and gasoline export rebates and processing trade contract of crude oil shall be suspended. During the 2007 gasoline shortage, NDRC had continuously issued five documents from August to November requiring that CNPC and SINOPEC ensure the supply of petroleum products; during 2011 gasoline shortage, NDRC also issued instructions that oil monopoly groups shall ensure supply.

If calculated by the oil of the same quality, as shown in Figure 3.15, during the period of 2003–2011, China's petroleum products price was lower than the international average price only in 2005, 2006, 2007, and 2008, and the margin was small, except in 2008; while in other periods, the petroleum products price was higher than the international average price. But domestic petroleum products were exported every year and the export volume increased rapidly in some years. For instance, the domestic petroleum products prices in 2003 and 2009 were both higher than the international average price, but petroleum products export sharply increased in both years. The high price of domestic petroleum products is achieved by monopoly groups through decrease in supply, which is also the most direct means adopted by common monopoly enterprises to get monopoly profits. Product price is raised through the control over supply volume, and then monopoly enterprises realize their benefit maximization. The increase in export is one of the channels to decrease domestic supply, while the higher price of domestic petroleum products is just the result of monopoly enterprises' "limitation on volume and increase in price" (限量提价).

Originally, in a society, overall monopoly rights come with overall obligations. In the case of oil monopolies in China, it's another story. Like the public utility of natural monopoly with obligations of "ceaseless services" and "universal services," oil monopoly enterprises should have obligations of "ceaseless services" and "universal services" in the oil field.

However, CNPC and SINOPEC have high monopoly rights without shouldering relevant obligations but putting pressure on control organs of the central government by implementing "interruption" and "discrimination." For instance, after an gasoline shortage occurred in October 2011, when being asked why they did not supply private gasoline stations with diesel at the wholesale price regulated by the government, a sales staff of SINOPEC said that "the company shall ensure the diesel supply of our own gasoline stations first; private gasoline stations are enterprises, while SINOPEC is also an enterprise. We are obliged to ensure market supply, but not obliged to ensure the supply of private gasoline stations." (Li Chunlian, 2011). This remark reveals that oil monopoly enterprises consider themselves as enterprises pursuing their own maximal benefit, and they have no obligations of "ceaseless services" and "universal services." For their own interests, they can cut off the supply to thousands of gasoline stations, regardless of social stability and national security. Therefore, oil monopoly enterprises threaten social stability.

VIII. Squeezing Interests of Local Governments and Causing Tensions and Oppositions between Local and Central Governments

1. Conflict of Interest in Oil Exploitation Field

The fight for interests related to oil resources between local governments and central enterprises has necessary connection with the land and petroleum management systems and benefit sharing system in China.

(1) *China's dual property right system separating oil from land.* Article 9 of the *Constitution of the People's Republic of China* (《中华人民共和国宪法》) stipulates that crude oil resources are owned by the state, that is, by the whole people, and the control power is exercised by the central

government. Article 3 of the *Mineral Resources Law of the People's Republic of China* (《中华人民共和国矿产资源法》) stipulates that the rights of State ownership in mineral resources are exercised by the State Council. Meanwhile, the land of China is in the period when the owner-ship by the whole people coexists with the collective ownership; in gen-eral, urban land belongs to the state and most of the land in villages and suburbs is subject to the collective ownership. Thus, there is inconsistency between land ownership and oil resources ownership, but land acquisition is inevitable in the exploitation of oil resources. In western countries like the US, the ownership of underground resources is subject to the land ownership.

(2) *China's sharing system of oil resources interests.* Crude oil extraction produces great destructive effects on the local environment and leads to environmental pollution, i.e., negative externality. So compensation must be made for the place where resources are located. The rents directly out of oil resources include resource tax, mineral resources compensation fee, and special oil gain levy. The resource tax falls into local tax category; the mineral resources compensation fee is usually split between the central and local governments in the proportion of 5:5 or 4:6; special oil gain levy belongs to non-tax revenue of the central government. But in practice, China's resource tax and mineral resource compensation level are very low. The sum of resource tax and mineral resource compensation exceeded 1% of the total annual sales only in 2011, while in foreign countries the oil resource rent is 10–50% (see Table 3.18).

Generally speaking, if there are oil and natural gas resources in a region, it should be a good fortune for that region. However, oil monopoly enterprises pay only approximately RMB24 as resource rent per ton in average, which is RMB300 to RMB400 lower than the mining royalty set by the market, and the special oil gain levy belongs to central tax. CNPC and SINOPEC, as central enterprises, make few contributions to local finance, though they occupy local land and cost local resources, and in fact, they seize large amount of wealth from the local areas, which leads to the distortion of fiscal relation between the central and the lcoal govern-ments (see Table 3.19).

Table 3.18. **Proportion of Paid Resource Tax and Mineral Resource Compensation of SINOPEC (2001–2011, RMB1 million, %)**

Year	Paid resource tax	Paid mineral resource compensation fee	Proportion in annual sales (in %)
2001	106	618	1.39
2002	96	595	1.38
2003	108	734	1.36
2004	114	859	1.35
2005	201	1,283	1.41
2006	789	1,741	1.83
2007	826	1,176	1.38
2008	817	1,200	1.11
2009	815	722	1.34
2010	1,274	711	1.30
2011	3,078	1,054	2.04

Note: Since the data in annual reports of SINOPEC are comprehensive, while some data of CNPC are not obtained as its listing time is relatively late, the table makes use of the previous data of SINOPEC and such data can represent the average situation of the whole industry.

Source: Arranged according to the data in the annual reports of SINOPEC over the years (2001–2011).

Table 3.19 shows that in terms of resource rent, during quite a long period, CNPC and SINOPEC only contributed hundreds of million to several billion yuan in RMB to local finance of the oil-producing regions every year. But in most countries, revenues from mineral resources, e.g., mining royalty, are divided between the central and the local governments. The local sharing proportion ranges from 50% to 100%. For instance, in Australia, the mining royalty of onshore oil and natural gas resources completely belong to state finance; in the US, the proportion is 50% (Wang Jiashan and Li Shaoping, 2005). In China, in April 2006, the State Council approved to carry out experiments of coal industry policies in Shanxi, and stipulated that stock mining right shall surrender revenues, which shall be shared by and between the central government and the Shanxi Provincial Government in the proportion of 2 : 8. Suppose that the sharing ratio between the central and the local is 3 : 7. If oil royalty is

Table 3.19. Amount of Lost Local Incomes Caused by Short-paid Mining Royalty of Oil Monopoly Enterprises (2001–2011, Unit: RMB100 million)

		2001	2002	2003	2004	2005	2006	2007	2008	2009	2010	2011	Subtotal
SINOPEC	Resource tax (land tax)	4	5	4	5	6	8	9	9	9	13	32	103
	Mining royalty collected by 10%	48	45	57	72	105	129	128	176	98	155	209	1,221
	Local allocation shared 70%	33	32	40	51	74	90	89	123	68	108	147	855
	Mining royalty loss acquired by the local government	29	27	36	46	67	82	81	114	60	95	115	751
CNPC	Resource tax (land tax)	17	17	17	17	18	34	32	43	63	98	198	553
	Resource tax collected by 10%	154	143	175	218	326	392	408	512	314	421	569	3,632
	Local allocation shared 70%	108	100	122	153	228	274	286	359	220	294	399	2,543
	Mining royalty loss acquired by the local government	91	84	105	136	210	241	253	316	156	196	201	1,989
Total mining royalty loss acquired by the local government		120	110	141	182	278	323	334	430	216	291	315	2,741

Note: The resource tax rate prior to 2004 is RMB8–24/ton, and by reference to the rate level of tax paid by SINOPEC, an intermediate value of RMB16/ton, which is a relatively conservative value, is used for calculating the resource tax amount paid by CNPC during the period 2001–2005. Other data are according to the annual reports of CNPC and SINOPEC.

collected by 10%, with the sharing ratio between the central and the local being 3:7, the local finance can additionally obtain tens of billion yuan in RMB per year. For details, see Table 3.19.

In other words, CNPC and SINOPEC seized tens of billion yuan per year from oil-producing regions. During the decade from 2001 to 2011, the mining royalty that was short paid by both CNPC and SINOPEC to the local finance, i.e., the wealth grabbed from the local regions, was up to RMB274.1 billlion. Undoubtedly, that distorted the revenue allocation of the central and the local finances and gave rise to the strained relation between them. It is worth stressing that the surplus income of oil monopoly enterprises' short-paid mining royalty was not transferred to the central finance, but occupied by oil monopoly enterprises.

Most oil-producing regions are central and western regions or ethnic minority areas. These regions are relatively poorer and need more financial support. The current practice of imposing too low resource tax on oil monopoly enterprises obviously violates the basic principle of income distribution, i.e., to cut the rich and to help the poor; on the contrary, it cuts the poor and helps the rich, because it distributes the income that should ideally be distributed among poor regions, to the oil monopoly enterprises. However, there are no external restrictions on payoff within such enterprises, so the income of such enterprises' employees is several times of the social average level and there is a large number of redundant employees in such enterprises.

A typical example is the Northern Shaanxi oilfield incident. In the whole incident, there were three major participants, i.e., central monopoly enterprises represented by CNPC, local government of Shaanxi Province, and investment entities introduced by the local government. The competition for oil resources between central enterprises and the local government is one of the main contradictions in Northern Shaanxi oilfield incident.

It was explicitly specified in the Document No. 1239 that Shaanxi Yanchang Petroleum Industrial Group shall, on the basis of acquiring drilling and exploitation companies of all counties, "actively create conditions and strive to enter in China National Petroleum Corporation as a whole."[8] If Northern Shaanxi oil fields are completely incorporated into

---

[8] See the *Investigation Report on Oil Exploitation Order in Northern Shaanxi.*

CNPC as required by the document, there is no doubt that CNPC will benefit the most from the Northern Shaanxi oilfield incident after the document was issued. The Shaanxi Provincial Government did not immediately recover related oil wells as required by the document, but accelerated the recovery for the interests of the local government in 2003, when it realized that CNPC would take up those oil wells. MA Lebin, the then Secretary of CPC Committee of Jingbian County, said at that time that "any enterprise can have management right so long as taxes and duties are paid to the local government." (Jiang Rong, 2004)

2. Conflict of Interest in Oil Refining Field

In the oil refining field, the oil monopoly system crushes the development of local state-owned oil refining enterprises and private oil refining enterprises by control over domestic supply and import of crude oil, because such enterprises directly compete with oil monopoly enterprises.

On the other side, since the domestic market is wide and has great demand and oil monopoly (administered) price is high, local governments and private enterprises still indomitably develop oil refining industry, even though their development is constrained. It is roughly estimated that by 2011, the scale of local oil refining enterprises (including private oil refining enterprises) had already reached 130 million tons of crude oil processing capacity. However, due to the restriction imposed on oil monopoly system over the import of crude oil, the actual crude oil processed was only 40 million tons. The operation rate of local oil refining enterprises in Shandong Province was only 45.7%.

The sharing proportion for enterprise value-added tax between the central government and the local government is 75%:25%, and the sharing proportion for income tax is 60%:40%. Therefore, when enterprises are owned by local governments or privately owned, 25% of value-added tax and 40% of income tax will be owned by the local government (at different levels); but when enterprises are owned by the central government, the part of tax will go to the central government. When the operation rate is insufficient because production capacities of local state-owned oil refining enterprises and private oil refining enterprises are constrained, the taxes obtained by local governments will also be constrained. See Table 3.20.

Table 3.20.   Sales and Tax to be Increased due to the Growth in Operation Rate of Local Oil Refining Enterprises

	Calculated by the petroleum products rate of CNPC (1)	Calculated by the petroleum products rate of SINOPEC (2)
Oil refining capacity of local oil refineries	130 million tons	130 million tons
Actually processed crude oil	40 million tons	40 million tons
Production capacity of petroleum products, in the case of operation rate of 85%	68.02 million tons	65.07 million tons
Actually short-produced petroleum products	46.11 million tons	41.52 million tons
Increasable sales	RMB367.5 billion	RMB330.9 billion
Increasable national tax	RMB74.5 billion	RMB66.5 billion
Increasable government rent	RMB12 billion	RMB10.8 billion

Notes: (1) The petroleum products rate of CNPC is 65.40%; (2) the petroleum products rate of SINOPEC is 58.89%; (3) the tax is calculated by the SINOPEC's proportion of tax in operation revenue; (4) the petroleum products price is in line with the weighted average pre-tax price of main countries, RMB8,134/ton.

Therefore, when local oil refining enterprises cannot fully operate as they are suppressed by the oil monopoly system, local governments' tax will approximately decrease by RMB10 billion to RMB12 billion per year, let alone the decrease in enterprise profits and employment and wages of workers.

It can also be observed that the fiscal revenue of the central government is also significantly reduced by the control over import of crude oil for the purpose of squeezing local oil refining enterprises and making them unable to operate fully.

IX. Violating the Constitutional Principle of the State

1. Enterprises' Arrogation of Public Power

In fact, CNPC and SINOPEC also have some administrative and regulatory powers, though they are enterprises.

For instance, in the *Circular on Strengthening Management and Rectification of Petroleum Products Market* (《关于加强成品油市场管理和整顿的通知》) and the *Circular on the General Office of the State Council on Carrying out Special Rectification on Gasoline Stations* (《国务院办公厅关于开展加油站专项整治工作的通知》) (G.B.F. [2002] No. 18) promulgated by SINOPEC and the State Administration for Industry and Commerce and the State Development Planning Commission in 1989, CNPC or SINOPEC was one of the main participants in management and implementation of rectification. For example, it is stipulated in the *Suggestions on Further Rectifying and Regulating Market Order of Petroleum Products* (《关于进一步整顿和规范成品油市场秩序的意见》) (Document No. 72) that "CNPC and SINOPEC shall actively cooperate with national department's concerned and local governments in work, and effectively clear and rectify related small oil refineries and petroleum products circulation enterprises." The participation in the "clearing and rectifying," as called by administrative department is to exercise functions and power of relevant competent authority of the industry to some extent.

To cite another example, the former State Economic and Trade Commission annouced in April 2002 that non-state-run quantitative trade quota of crude oil shall only be used for the processing of refineries of CNPC and SINOPEC. This means that an enterprise cannot import crude oil, even though it obtains non-state-run quantitative trade quota, if it is not listed in the production plan (production scheduling) of CNPC and SINOPEC. It is explicitly stipulated in the *Tie Yun Han* (铁运函) *No. 150 Decree* promulgated by the Ministry of Railways in 2003 that without the approval and seals of CNPC and SINOPEC, any railways bureau shall not accept transportation business of petroleum products. That is equal to granting CNPC and SINOPEC the power of controlling the entry into the industry.

2. Administrative Departments' Arrogation of Legislative Power

The main reason for the monopoly of oil and gas industry is that administrative departments arrogate legislative power. Document No. 38, Document No. 72, Document No. 18, and the *Tie Yun Han* (铁运函)

No. 150 Decree mentioned above are all only documents of administrative departments, so they have no legal effect, but they are used as the basis for the monopoly right of oil monopoly enterprises. In fact, that is a kind of arrogation of administrative departments.

The so-called Document No. 38, in particular, is only the *Suggestions on Clearing and Rectifying Small Refinery Plants and Regulating the Circulation Order of Crude Oil and Petroleum Products* (《关于清理整顿小炼油厂和规范原油成品油流通秩序的意见》) of the former State Economic and Trade Commission and several other departments transmitted by the General Office of the State Council. The General Office of the State Council is only a secretary institution for internal service of the State Council which does not have power to issue orders to the public, besides the document is called "Suggestions"; departments including the former State Economic and Trade Commission also did not follow the procedures in the *Legislative Law* (《立法法》). Therefore, such documents are even not "administrative rules" and since they are at the lowest level of regulations, they have no legal force.

The reason why Document No. 38, etc. was exercised is that such administrative departments exerted their law enforcement power to implement such documents, completely regardless of the fact that the documents themselves lacked legal effect and conflicted with the Constitution and other higher-level laws.

3. Monopoly towards Government and Putting Pressure on Government at a Crucial Time

In fact, the monopolistic behavior of monopoly enterprises not only aims at consumers and competitors, but also can be used for coping with government and control organs. If the central government has fewer negotiating counterparts in the oil field, the position of the central government in the negotiations will fall and monopoly enterprises may bargain with it by making use of its concerns, such like developing oil industry, ensuring oil supplies, avoiding the political unrest brought about by gasoline shortages, as well as stable oil supplies in the time of war. However, the re-occurrence of gasoline shortages shows that oil monopoly enterprises have already learned the ropes of the game with the central government, and they will, in the pursuit of their own interests, not consider the damages to the society and the state.

Similar things also happened in telecommunications industry once. Before the establishment of China Unicom, there was only one enterprise which integrated government administration with enterprise, i.e., the Ministry of Posts and Telecommunications — Directorate General of Telecommunications. In 1982, the central government instructed to develop the telecommunications industry, and the Ministry of Posts and Telecommunications — Directorate General of Telecommunications proposed a very high price, obtaining two "reversion of one to nine" (倒一九), that is, the preferential policy that income tax is only paid 10%, and non-trade foreign exchange earnings are only paid 10%. Afterwards, in 1986, it was approved that only 10% of principal and interest was paid for the loaning instead of allocating within the budget. The preferential policy of such three "reversions of one to nine" was cancelled in 1995, when China Unicom was established (Ke Ao and Wang Qiang, 2008). It can be seen that the central government has to make concessions when there is only one monopoly enterprise in the whole country, but its position in negotiations immediately rises when a competitor of the monopoly enterprise comes into being and will rapidly cancel its previously too-large concessions.

Therefore, we often see that spokesmen of CNPC and SINOPEC make some statement inconsistent with the position of enterprises. For example, after the central government made regulations on special oil gain levy, principals or spokesmen of CNPC and SINOPEC made complaints in the public (*Shanghai Evening Post*, 2011); and when the central government collected mining royalty by 5–10%, both monopoly groups expressed that the royalty was too high.

4. Impairing the Publicity of Administrative Departments of Government

On the whole, the existing system of oil and gas industry is completely established around the aim of establishing, maintaining, and strengthening the monopoly right of oil monopoly groups. In the perspective of social justice and efficiency, the administrative departments' excuses, to set straight monopoly rights, stand on shaky ground. It just reveals that for the interest of oil monopoly enterprises, related administrative departments take no consideration of superficial justice and economic rationality. They deny, even overturn, the publicity of administrative departments as a public organ of power, and become a tool used by oil monopoly enterprises to maintain their private ends.

5. Administrative Departments' Veto Power of Reform

When the existing monopoly system of petroleum industry produces a series of serious matters and leads to the dissatisfaction of consumers, private enterprises and the rest of the society, it will give rise to suggestions and calls for reform. But in China's existing institutional structure, the channels of public opinions are not well-maintained. Suggestions are often held back by related administrative departments, so it cannot drive the reform of oil system in effect.

For example, the All-China Federation of Industry and Commerce once put forward the proposal "on clearing and abolishing provisions of related documents and improving the private investment environment in petroleum industry" at the fifth session of the 11th National Committee of the Chinese People's Political Consultative Conference. That proposal was transmitted to the National Energy Administration under NDRC and was basically denied a reply by the Administration. And their reasons are as follows: on the one hand, the existing system basically has no problems; on the other hand, the reform will involve every aspect, so it is essential to make overall arrangements. Therefore, the reform is indefinitely postponed.

Fundamentally, the procedures of the reform are wrong. First, the organs which establish and maintain oil monopoly right are just related administrative departments, so it is impossible for them to overturn their own previous decisions. Second, administrative departments are only departments enforcing laws, they have no legislative power. They have no decision-making power on the basic economic systems, e.g., the decision-making power on whether or not to establish monopoly right. Nor do they have veto power on related proposals on the reform of oil monopoly system.

In fact, it is the Chinese society that has the decision-making power on whether or not to reform the oil monopoly system, and the legal institution which can make them institutionalized is the legislative body, i.e., the People's Congress of the People's Republic of China. Therefore, it is an expression that monopoly interest groups influence and distort channels of public opinion and the decision-making mechanism of institutional reform under the real institutional structure of China in that reform proposals were submitted to related administrative departments through the National Committee of the Chinese People's Political Consultative Conference (CPPCC) and were denied by them.

X. Summary

1. The oil monopoly system has brought about a great efficiency loss in the whole society. It is estimated that the welfare loss in the petroleum industry reached as high as RMB3.477 trillion from 2001 to 2011.

2. The system also distorts the income distribution and violates the principle of fairness. From 2000 to 2011, the short-paid profits of three monopoly petroleum companies reached RMB1.4701 trillion. But the incomes of the employees of these companies are far higher than the social average level. The per capita salary of the CNOOC in 2010 was about RMB340,000, about 10 times of the social average.

3. The system violates the market rules. It enables oil monopoly enterprises to become unfair competitors. From 2001 to 2011, the short-paid land rent of CNPC reached RMB395.8 billion in total. From 2001 to 2011, the short-paid resource rent of petroleum enterprises totally reached about RMB307.9 billion. From 2001 to 2011, the short-paid financing cost of petroleum enterprises totally reached about RMB287.8 billion.

4. Since administrative departments arrogate laws to establish monopoly right and restrict the entry of competitors, making an originally competitive market a monopolized one, it is impossible to set prices in competitive form. But the monopolists' pricing will be a monopolistic high price deviating from the equilibrium price, so the price can only be set through government regulation. See the aforesaid petroleum pricing mechanism.

5. But the pricing mechanism of government regulation has very low efficiency. So the price set by the mechanism will deviate from the price determined by the market, which will inevitably bring about welfare losses. Meanwhile, it makes monopolists reduce their production and supply when the price is low, but conduct overproduction or oversupply when the price is high, and influence prices by production and inventory.

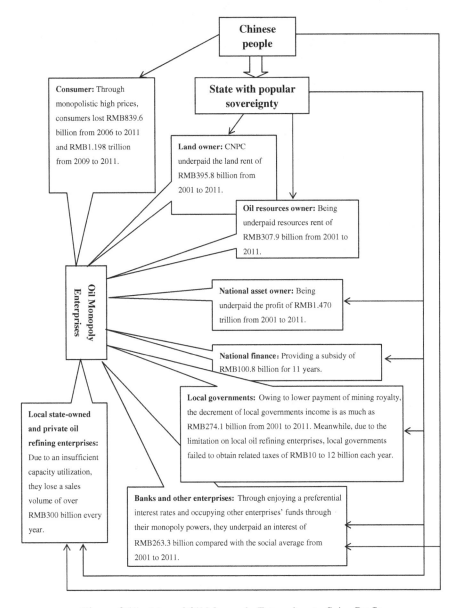

Figure 3.16   Map of Oil Monopoly Enterprises to Seize Profit

6. The system also directly damages other competitors, including private enterprises, in the following aspects: (1) To prohibit other competitors from entering or to force out those who have already entered into the oil exploitation and sales field; (2) to impose restrictions or discriminations on competitive enterprises that have already entered the petroleum industry; (3) to cooperate with local governments and rejects competitors through administrative powers; (4) to directly violate the property rights of private enterprises, etc.

7. The control on crude oil import has resulted in serious insufficiency of capacity utilization of other oil refining enterprises outside oil monopoly enterprises, so a total loss of sales reached more than RMB300 billion every year.

8. From 2006 to 2011, the losses of consumers caused by the high monopoly (administered) price of petroleum products were as high as RMB839.6 billion; from 2009 to 2011, the monopoly (administered) price (pre-tax) of petroleum products in China was about 31% higher than the average price of main countries, so the losses of consumers reached as high as RMB11,980.

9. The aforesaid oil monopoly enterprises trespass against the whole society, including the state and other interest groups and this is shown in Figure 3.16.

10. The system also damages national security and influences social stability. It provides the conditions and excuses for oil monopoly enterprises to create "gasoline shortages," resulting in the tension and opposition between the central government and local governments and damages the interests of central and western regions and ethnic minority areas. Meanwhile, monopoly enterprises blackmail the government at a crucial time.

11. Finally, the system itself violates the framework of Chinese constitutionalism. Monopoly enterprises arrogate the public power and exercise administrative power or quasi-administrative power. Administrative departments arrogate legislative power and abuse their law enforcement power to put the monopoly and control stipulated in administrative documents in force.

12. Therefore, it is a system with significant problems, which should be reformed fundamentally.

Chapter 4

Basic Concept of Reform in Petroleum Industry System

I. Constitutionality, Validity and Economic Rationality of the Reform in Petroleum Industry System in China

To sum up, fundamental reform is necessary for the oil and gas industry in China, as it is constitutional, legally valid, and economically rational.

1. Constitutionality of Reform in the Petroleum Industry System

As mentioned before, the existing monopolistic oil and gas industry system violates the constitution.

First, it violates the basic constitutional principles. As stipulated in Article 15 of the *Constitution* "the state practices socialist market economy ...," the basic principle of market economy is fair competition. Apparently, monopoly and competition march in the opposite direction.

Second, monopoly results in unfair income distribution, for the enterprise income acquired by monopoly is shifted into individual income of staff according to unfair distribution principle in their enterprise, free from external restraint, which leads to unfairness not only in income quantity but also in income distribution principle, violating the spirit in the *Constitution* that all citizens are equal.

Third, monopoly right setting in oil and gas industry stands against the due procedures as specified in the *Constitution* and *Legislative Law*. The *Legislative Law* stipulates that all laws involved with major economic systems shall be legalized by the National People's Congress of the People's Republic of China. Granting monopoly right to some enterprises is apparently involved with major economic system and therefore, should be determined by the legislative body. However, the current monopoly right supporting oil monopoly enterprises is just set up by administrative departments through issuing administrative documents, and therefore, unconstitutional.

For these reasons, abolishing monopoly right in oil and gas industry, specifically, cancelling the monopoly rights of CNPC, SINOPEC Group, and CNOOC, is constitutional, or in another word, an action upholding the *Constitution*.

2. Validity of Reform in Petroleum Industry System

First, the administrative documents comprising the monopoly system in the oil and gas industry are "illegal" due to non-compliance of due procedures of law upon setting up. According to Article 87 of the *Legislative Law*,

"Any law, administrative laws and regulations, local laws and regulations, autonomous regulations, specific regulations or rules with one of the following circumstances shall be amended or cancelled by related organs in accordance with the authority stipulated in Article 88 of the *Legislative Law*:

(I) Beyond authorities;
(II) Breaching the provisions in upper-level law as a lower-level law;
..."

Accordingly, it is legal to cancel these administrative documents constituting monopoly rights in oil and gas industry.

Second, the monopoly system in oil and gas industry violates the *Anti-Monopoly Law* (《反垄断法》), for its monopolistic conducts belong to the following by abusing their market dominant positions prohibited in Article 17 of the *Anti-Monopoly Law* (《反垄断法》):

(I) "Selling commodities at unfairly high prices or buying commodities at unfairly low prices," namely, oil monopoly enterprises since 2009, have been selling their petroleum products at the price apparently higher than equilibrium price in a competitive market while using state-owned land with payment apparently lower than rent ratio in the land market and mining oil and natural gas with the market rental rate (mining royalty and market price of mining right) obviously lower than that for oil and natural gas resources.

(III) "Refusing to enter into transactions with trading counterparts without justifiable reasons," namely oil monopoly enterprises refuse to sell their crude oil or petroleum products to some oil refineries and gasoline stations.

(IV) "Forcing their trading counterparts to make transactions exclusively with themselves or with the operators designated by them without justifiable reasons," namely oil monopoly enterprises and relevant administrative departments required that petroleum importers shall only sell crude oil and petroleum products to themselves.

(VI) "Discriminating between trading counterparts of the same qualifications with regards to price or other transaction terms without justifiable reasons;" namely, the price, paying methods, and paying terms for subordinate wholesale business and gasoline stations and other wholesale business and gasoline stations applied by oil monopoly enterprises are distinctly different.

Thus, it is legal to fundamentally reform monopoly system pursuant to the *Anti-Monopoly Law*.

3. Economic Rationality of Reform in Petroleum Industry System

As stated in Chapter 3, the existing system in oil and gas industry leads to significant efficiency loss and distribution distortion, which are directly expressed as loss incurred by consumers, competitors, surrounding residents, local government and the mass, as well as the unfair distribution phenomenon of income of staff in oil monopoly enterprises far higher than social average level. Fundamental reform of the system may eliminate these problems and restore economic rationality.

(1) *Improve overall social efficiency and obviously increase social wealth.* We can anticipate the reduction of annual loss up to RMB600–700 billion (or an increase of social wealth up to RMB600–700 billion) if the monopoly and corresponding improper control in oil and gas industry is eliminated and a system featuring the market system is established.

(2) Petroleum products price will drop to the level equivalent to that of the same quality in major countries across the world, exempting

consumers from the annual loss up to RMB300–450 billion caused by the high price of petroleum products.

(3) Competitors will benefit from released oil refining production capacity available; local oil refining enterprises will increase annual sales up to over RMB300 billion, contributing over RMB60 billion of taxation to central government and RMB10–12 billion tax revenue to local government every year; benefits are available for consumers as well.

(4) More mining royalty sharing will be available for oil-producing regions, particularly central and western regions and minority areas, and oil production enterprises will provide over RMB30 billion of mining royalty for local finance.

(5) Logistics industry will embrace faster development and the whole society will benefit from reduced transaction expense.

(6) Gasoline shortages will be alleviated, and then disappear.

(7) There will be an increase by over RMB50 billion from rent of land for the country every year.

(8) There will be an increase by over RMB20 billion from mining royalty of oil resources for the country every year.

(9) Excessive income in oil monopoly enterprises will be inhibited.

(10) Dramatic reduction of personnel redundancy in oil monopoly enterprises.

The general static effect of reform in petroleum industry system based on analysis in Chapter III and data in 2011, is shown in Figure 4.1.

All in all, the overall reform of oil and natural gas system will bring about significant benefits to China.

II. General Framework of the Reform in Petroleum Industry System in China

1. To Establish a System of Oil and Gas Industry Based on the Market Institutions

Since oil and natural gas have the nature of private goods, due to their competitive nature of production, the market system of oil and gas industry is a fundamental system. Enterprises can have free access to the industry. Enterprises in the industry have equal rights; it is prohibited that some

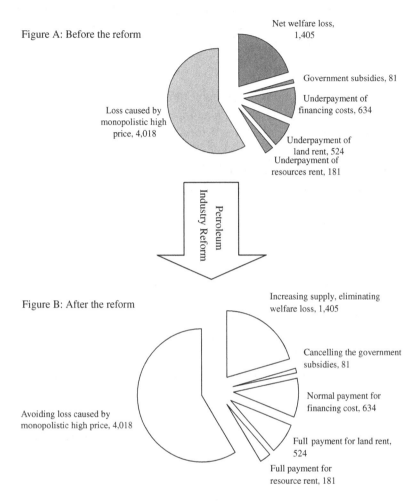

Figure 4.1. Diagram on the Static Effects of the Reform in Petroleum Industry System (Unit: RMB100 million)

enterprises have monopoly right or enjoy preferential prices upon acquisition of resources; the government, in principle, shall not intervene in prices, production, or the number of enterprises of the industry.

In such a market system, government shall first do well in its own work, i.e., to protect property rights, maintain market order and make fair decisions on disputes. It goes without saying when behaviors violating market rules occur, government shall stop them and impose punishments. For example, monopoly behavior and unfair competition behavior shall be stopped and be punished by law.

2. To Form a Fair and Effective Competitive Pattern Involving the Upstream, Midstream, and Downstream Sectors of Oil and Gas Industry

(1) *Exploration and exploitation stage*: Enterprises can obtain exploration right and mining right through competitive bidding and carry out exploration.

(2) *Transportation stage*: Since oil pipelines have some natural monopoly nature, exploitation companies can form an oil pipeline joint-stock company so as to constrain monopoly, or an independent company may engage in related operations and government regulatory departments control oil transportation prices.

(3) *Oil refining stage*: Enterprises have free access and may participate in competition; but since oil refining has to demonstrate economies of scale, the final market structure encourages effective competition among several large enterprises.

(4) *Wholesale and retail*: Enterprises have free access and may participate in competition; government makes regulations in the aspect of safety.

(5) *International trade*: Enterprises have free access and may participate in competition; government makes regulations in the aspect of safety.

3. The Government Represents the State to Grant the Mining Rights of Oil and Natural Gas in a Competitive Manner

According to Chinese law, oil and natural gas mineral resources belong to the state. The government shall represent the state to grant the mining rights of oil and natural gas to enterprises in a competitive manner. In the bidding process, the highest bidder wins.

4. The Government shall Impose Limited Control Only in Special Fields at Specific Times

Particularly, as market failures still exist in the oil and gas industry and this industry bears characteristics of public goods, government has to take some control measures in particular, links, periods, and regions. Such measures include:

(1) When the fluctuation in prices is abnormal, it seriously affect social stability and industry survival, and government may regulate prices within a defined period.
(2) In the time of war, governmemt may control prices of oil and natural gas products and implement allocation system.
(3) Government may collect gasoline tax corresponding to economic rent (scarcity).
(4) Government may establish oil reserve system.

5. Basic Reform Measures

If the above-mentioned reform goals are to be achieved, basic reform measures shall include the following:

(1) To cancel the administrative protection for the monopoly position of several oil monopoly groups and recover the administrative power granted to several oil monopoly groups;
(2) To establish impartial and neutral regulatory institutions of energy industry to make supervisions on safety, technology, environmental protection, and quality;
(3) To abandon the control over every field of oil and gas industry, so that enterprises can have free access;
(4) To cancel the price regulation.

III. Summary

1. The oil and gas industry in China needs a fundamental reform. The reform has constitutionality, validity, and economic rationality.
2. Fundamental objectives of the reform in petroleum industry system:

   (1) To establish a system based on the market institutions for the oil and gas industry;

(2) To form a fair and effective competitive pattern involving the upstream, midstream and downstream sectors of oil and gas industry;

(3) The government represents the state to grant the mining right of oil and natural gas in a competitive way;

(4) The government shall impose limited control only in special fields at specific times.

3. Basic measures for the reform in petroleum industry system:

(1) To abolish the monopoly powers and parts of administrative powers of the oil monopoly enterprises;

(2) To establish an impartial and neutral regulatory organization for the energy industry;

(3) To open all fields of the oil and gas industry;

(4) To cancel the price control.

Chapter 5

Solutions for Reform on Opening the Market of Crude Oil and Petroleum Products

I. Importance of Opening the Market of Crude Oil and Petroleum Products for the Reform in Petroleum Industry System

It is a strategic move for a society to carry out the all-round reform of petroleum industry system mentioned in Chapter 4. It will give rise to material social changes and meet strong resistance. From the point of strategy, it is essential to choose a proper point of penetration and break-through point so as to make the overall reform start easily, rapidly show results, and have the approval and support from the majority of people, so as to promote the next round of reforms.

We propose that the point of penetration or breakthrough point shall be the relaxation of control over crude oil and petroleum products markets. The reasons are as follows:

1. In History, Significant Changes Began with the Field of Transaction

Historically, any remarkable institutional change is the result of a change in the production system structure. The reason is that the system change resulted in larger changes in production modes and production technology and brought about significant growth in people's welfare and social wealth. But that is always the result of the institutional change in the field of transaction.

Professor Douglass C. North pointed out that "the industrial revolution as I know begins with the expansion of market size" (North, 1994, p. 188).

The expansion of market size is due to the increase in transaction volume, which is the system or technology reform in the field of transaction, resulting in the fall in transaction expense.

Therefore, the reform in the field of oil and natural gas shall also begin with the field of transaction. The reasons are as follows:

(1) *In comparison with fundamental system changes, the reform of transaction mode costs less and is more flexible.* Professor Douglass C. North divided institutional changes into fundamental institutional changes and secondary institutional changes. The former can be understood as changes of legal system; and the latter can be understood as changes of transaction modes (North, 1994).

In general, the reform of transaction mode can be realized as long as both parties of the transaction agree; thus, the cost is very low and the reform is very flexible. And it can lead to significant and in-depth institutional changes. For instance, the production of currency is caused by the reform of transaction mode. But the reform of law system shall wait until a certain social change has run up to a certain degree, it shall go through public selection, so it lags behind, and needs high costs. It has to be agreed by the majority of people and go through legal procedures.

(2) *The reform of transaction mode may give rise to the reform of production mode.* The reform of transaction mode will lead to a fall in transaction expense and an expansion of market size, which will provide conditions for mass production and in-depth and specialized division of labor. And mass production and in-depth division of labor will decrease production cost (Sheng Hong, 1992). On the contrary, the reform of production mode does not always lead to the reform of transaction mode. Therefore, the reform of transaction mode usually has much more profound significance.

(3) *The reform of transaction mode will not directly give rise to the conflict of redistribution of income, so it can reduce the cost of reform.* Since transaction reform is subject to the consent of both parties of the transaction, both parties will be satisfied with the income distribution resulting from the reform, so there exists no dissatisfaction or conflict about redistribution of income, which may bring about social cost to reform and

impede the progress of reform. For instance, the collapse of slavery in some countries depended on the fact that slaves redeemed themselves in currency.

(4) *The reform of transaction mode may give rise to further reforms by reform of economic variables such as price.* Though the reform of transaction mode needs very low cost and has small fluctuations, it will cause changes in prices and other economic variables. For instance, in the beginning of the 1980s reform in China, a double-track price system occurs in some industrial product markets, among which one track is planned price, and the other track is market price. The occurrence of market price gave rise to the development of lots of enterprises outside the system, especially township enterprises. The challenge of township enterprises promoted the reform of state-owned enterprises.

2. The Reform on Opening the Markets of Crude Oil and Petroleum Products is the Supporting Point and Lever of Reform in Oil and Natural Gas System

Let's go back to the reform of crude oil and petroleum products markets. The reform includes two important aspects. One is the relaxation of market control; the other is the relaxation of price control.

The so-called "relaxation of market control" means to cancel the ban on other enterprises' against entering into crude oil and petroleum products markets and give free access to any enterprise. If it is necessary to make control over the access due to some reasons, it is essential to propose reasons to related regulatory departments and the access control shall not be set without the consent of legislative body. The access control shall be equal to all enterprises without discrimination.

The so-called "relaxation of price control" refers to the market price formed through the competition among multiple enterprises, after the control over the crude oil and petroleum products markets and the price of crude oil and petroleum products are relaxed.

The relaxation of crude oil and petroleum products markets is a reform in the field of transaction, so it has various characteristics and advantages described in Section 1.

(1) *In comparison with other reforms in oil and natural gas field, the reform on opening the crude oil and petroleum products markets is more flexible and with lower costs.* The reforms of other aspects in oil and gas industry, such as exploration, exploitation, and refining, all will affect related laws, e.g., the *Mineral Law*, or involve the core part of the current administrative monopoly right. But the reform on opening crude oil and petroleum products markets only involves the matter of letting enterprises enter the market, and though there also exist administrative documents impeding entry of market (e.g., Document No. 38), they rank lower in importance in the eyes of law, thereby, making it easy to achieve a breakthrough.

(2) *The reform on opening the crude oil and petroleum products markets will drive the reform of production fields such as crude oil exploitation and refining.* After the opening of crude oil and petroleum products markets, it will form a market price in a competitive way. And the price will squeeze the high price among monopoly prices currently controlled, so as to reduce the nominal profits of monopoly enterprises, thus it will promote the reform breaking the monopoly. On the other hand, with the increase in crude oil supplies, private oil refining enterprises and other oil refining enterprises also will grow.

(3) *During the early days of opening crude oil and petroleum products markets, original monopoly enterprises suffer no direct damage.* There is no sharp difference between the current crude oil and petroleum products prices and international oil prices, the entry of new enterprises will not lead to large changes in prices in the short term, so the immediate interests of original enterprises in the market will not directly reduce sharply. Thus, they will have less resentment toward the reform on opening crude oil and petroleum products markets, the reform will be promoted more easily.

(4) *The reform on opening the crude oil and petroleum products markets will give rise to the reform in other aspects of oil and natural gas field, like a lever.* Since the reform on opening the crude oil and petroleum products markets will finally form a domestic market of crude oil and

petroleum products, it will change prices of crude oil and petroleum products in Chinese market, give correct price signals, promote the growth of non-monopoly petroleum enterprises, as well as change domestic total supply and demand of crude oil and petroleum products in China, even change the world energy structure.

(5) *The reform on opening the crude oil and petroleum products markets will also promote closer cooperation with China's economic cooperation partner and the integration of trade and economy.* Since China's main trade and economic partners such as US, Europe and Japan, mostly adopt free-trade system and policy of crude oil and petroleum products, once China relaxes control over the import and export market of crude oil and petroleum products, we will be in line with the international system in oil field, which will greatly facilitate trade and other economic cooperation between the enterprises in these countries and China, expand China's international market, and establish China's pricing power in the oil business.

In the long term, the reform on opening the crude oil and petroleum products markets will finally lead to the marketization of the whole oil and gas industry in China. In the market system, China's energy industry will have more in-depth and professional division of labor. The development of energy conservation and emission reduction technology will be promoted, and the R&D and production of new energy will be accelerated.

II. Framework of Reform Solutions for Opening the Markets of Crude Oil and Petroleum Products

Unlike the market of other products, crude oil market shall be a unified market or a market linking the markets of different regions. Due to the existence of countries, the market can be divided into domestic and international market. For a country, "international market" is an import and export trade linking domestic market with international market. The division becomes clearer due to China's existing control over the market access. As mentioned above, the access control over import and export of crude oil shows as establishing qualification of special permission and regulating import quota. The control over the domestic market access of crude oil is the control over the entry into crude oil exploitation and the control over the exploited crude oil by monopoly enterprises.

Similarly, the petroleum products market can also be divided into domestic market and international market. As for the import and export trade of petroleum products linking the international market, the existing system restricts the number of enterprises entering and the enterprise type by establishing enterprise qualification of petroleum products import. In the domestic market, since oil monopoly enterprises accounts for 80% of the market share in the output, the market is in fact, controlled by them.

The reform on opening crude oil and petroleum products markets relaxes the control not only over the crude oil market, but also over the petroleum products market. It not only relaxes the domestic market, but also abandons the access control and quota control over import and export trade.

The reform has two basic goals. The first one is to give enterprises free access to the market of the two products, so as to make the market of crude oil and petroleum products a competitive one. The other goal is to form prices of crude oil and petroleum products through competition, so as to cancel the pricing system of setting the domestic petroleum products price by reference to the foreign exchange price.

The specific reform plan for opening crude oil and petroleum products markets covers four aspects below: (1) The reform on opening crude oil import and export markets; (2) the reform on opening the domestic market of crude oil; (3) the reform on opening the import and export market of petroleum products; and (4) the reform on opening the domestic market of petroleum products.

As for the order of the reform, on the international and domestic dimension, the reform on opening the import and export market shall go first, and then the reform on opening domestic market follows; on the dimension of crude oil and petroleum products, the reform on opening crude oil market control shall be implemented first, and then the reform on opening petroleum products market.

III. Reform Solutions for Opening the Import and Export Trade of Crude Oil

1. Existing Procedures for the Control over the Import Trade of Crude Oil

In the existing system, if a non-state-owned enterprise wants to engage in the import business of crude oil, in accordance with the *Interim Methods for Operation and Management on State-run Trading and Importing of Crude Oils, Petroleum Products and Chemical Fertilizers* (《原油、成品油、化肥国营贸易进口经营管理试行办法》) (Decree of the Ministry of Foreign Trade and Economic Cooperation of the People's Republic of China, 2002, No. 27), China's import of crude oil and petroleum products exercise state-run trade management and it is allowed that non-state-run trading enterprises engage in part of import.

The Ministry of Commerce issues the *Total Allowable Import Quantity, Application Conditions and Application Procedures for Crude Oil of*

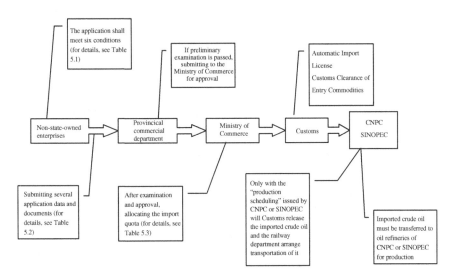

Figure 5.1. Flowchart of Application for Qualification for Import Operation Right of Crude Oil and Quota of Non-state-owned Enterprises

Table 5.1.   Conditions for Applying for Import License of Crude Oil

1. Having the right to use water transportation port for crude oil with a capacity beyond 50,000 tons (or a railway port with annual reloading capacity of 2 million tons), and the use right of a crude oil storage tank with capacity no less than 200,000 cubic meters.

2. Foreign trade dealers with registered capital no less than RMB50 million, and bank credit line no less than US$20 million.

3. Having professionals (at least two persons) engaging in international trade of oil.

4. Enterprises shall have no record of smuggling, tax evasion, evasion of foreign currency or arbitrage of exchange.

5. Import performance of crude oil in recent two years.

6. Other factors needing consideration.

Table 5.2.   Data and Documents for Applying for Import Licensing Operation Right of Crude Oil

1. The documentary evidence for line of credit issued by banks. It is essential to produce the original of official documents issued by headquarters or immediate branches of every bank.

2. Application letter, which shall include basic company information, description for meeting application conditions, application reason, specific programs concerning crude oil procurement, production use or sales and introduction to professionals engaging in oil international trade.

3. Copies of *Duplicate of Business License of Enterprise Legal Person* passing annual inspection with the signature of the legal representative, copies of *Registration Form for Foreign Trade Dealers* or *Qualification Certificate of Import and Export Enterprises* or *Business Certificate of Foreign-Funded Enterprise* or *Clearance and Registration Certificate of Consignee and Consigner of Imported and Exported Cargoes* and *Organization Code Certificate* with the seal for registration affixed.

4. Produce the originals of use agreements for facilities such as crude oil port (or railway port) and storage tank; copies of documentary evidence for loading and unloading capacity and storage tank capacity of the port (or railway port) issued by prefecture-level (or above) department in charge of investment (or others such as environmental protection department and fire department).

5. 2011 crude oil import performance certification. Self-operated import shall produce copies of customs declaration and proxy agent import shall produce agency agreements or related service invoices.

6. The evidentiary material proving there was no tax evasion, foreign exchange evasion and arbitrage issued by tax administration and foreign exchange department.

Table 5.3. Allocation Basis for Import Quotas of Crude Oil of Non-state Trading Enterprises

1. The allowable quantity of import of crude oil of non-state trade was 29.1 million tons in 2012.

2. If the total applying quantity of enterprises meeting conditions is not more than 29.1 million tons, it will be allocated according to the applying quantity of enterprises.

3. If the total applying quantity of enterprises meeting conditions is more than 29.1 million tons, it will be allocated with the import actual performance of every enterprise as cardinal number.

4. Production, operation, and sales status of the applying enterprise and other factors needing consideration.

Non-state-run Trade (《原油非国营贸易进口允许量总量、申请条件和申请程序》) annually, which requires that the crude oil import of non-state-owned enterprises must be handled according to the conditions and procedures as follows, and they do not vary too much every year, with changes mainly in quota. Now we take the *Total Allowable Import Quantity, Application Conditions and Application Procedures for Crude Oil of Non-state Trade in 2012* (《2012年原油非国营贸易进口允许量总量、申请条件和申请程序》) and other related provisions an example (see Figure 5.1):

The flow and requirements for conditions almost have no rationality. Their real function is to exclude enterprises other than oil monopoly enterprises from importing crude oil by harsh terms and arbitrariness of examination results.

For example, the requirement for registered capital is a judgment on the enterprise credit and strength and it shall be checked by other enterprises which have transactions with the enterprise, but it is not something the government would be concerned about.

And whether having the use right of a port and an oil tank shall not serve as a condition. On the contrary, under the conditions of market economy, as long as crude oil is imported, it is possible to rent the use right of ports and oil tanks.

For another example, "having professionals (at least two persons) engaging in international trade of oil" also seems unnecessary. Any enterprise will hire related professionals once it engages in some business, so it is not necessary for the government to make relevant regulations at all.

In addition, whether having any "record of smuggling, tax evasion, evasion of foreign currency and arbitrage of exchange" is a very ridiculous term. Because such acts as smuggling, tax evasion, evasion of foreign currency, and arbitrage of exchange are prohibited, even not applying for the import right of crude oil. Such unlawful acts shall be punished on any occasion. Judicial organs have functions and powers in such aspects; the Ministry of Commerce seems to have no occasion to administer such things which are beyond its authority.

In fact, most important of all, the application flow on the surface is not of criterion doctrine, that is, control organs must approve as long as conditions are met, but of approval doctrine, that is, control organs have non-accountable and arbitrary power to make decision on whether to approve the application.

Moreover, even if a quota is obtained, the import of crude oil must have the consent of CNPC and SINOPEC, i.e., even if an enterprise imports crude oil, it is not allowed to refine the imported oil at its own discretion. This is equal to putting all the import rights of crude oil in the hands of CNPC and SINOPEC. Two barrels of oil (referring to CNPC and SINOPEC), as enterprises, have the functions of administrative examination and approval at the same time, which a situation integrating government administration with enterprise.

Thus, the flow has no value to justify its existence, but costs lots of public resources, violates market rules and makes enterprises and consumers suffer severe losses.

2. To Cancel the Entry Control over Import Trade of Crude Oil

Therefore, the reform of import trade field of crude oil is to cancel the above-mentioned application flow for entering the field and to cancel the limitation on the import quantity of crude oil of non-state-run trade so as to make the import and export trade of crude oil very simple (see Figure 5.2).

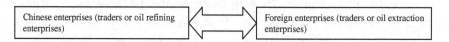

Figure 5.2. Schematic Diagram for Opening the Import Trade of Crude Oil

Specifically, it is essential:

(1) To cancel Article 2 in the *Interim Methods for Operation and Management on State-run Trading and Importing of Crude Oils, Petroleum Products and Chemical Fertilizers* (《原油、成品油, 化肥国营贸易进口经营管理试行办法》) (Decree of the Ministry of Foreign Trade and Economic Cooperation of the People's Republic of China, 2002, No. 27) promulgated by the former Ministry of Foreign Trade and Economic Cooperation, which stipulates that "the state implements state-run trading management on the import of crude oil, petroleum products and chemical fertilizers."

(2) To take China's commitment concerning oil trade upon entry of WTO, that from 2002, China will issue annual non-state-run trading quota and allow non-state-run trading enterprises to engage in part of crude oil import, with the quota increasing with years as a baseline commitment, without taking the promised amount as the upper limit of the import quantity of crude oil of non-state-run enterprises.

(3) To stop implementing and cancel Article 3 "to further strengthen the allocation management of crude oil" in the *Suggestions on Clearing and Rectifying Small Refinery Plants and Regulating the Circulation Order of Crude Oil and Petroleum products* (《关于清理整顿小炼油厂和规范原油成品油流通秩序的意见》) (Document No. 38) transmitted by the General Office of the State Council, i.e.:

> The crude oil produced by CNPC and SINOPEC, the crude oil sold by CNOOC at home and the crude oil produced by SINOPEC Star Petroleum Co. Ltd., and local oil fields, as well as imported crude oil are subject to the national uniform allocation and shall not be sold without authority. …"

IV. Reform Solutions on Opening the Domestic Market of Crude Oil

1. Flow for Entry Control over the Domestic Market of Crude Oil

Under the existing system, if an enterprise other than the oil monopoly enterprises wants to enter the domestic market of crude oil, it has to go through the following application procedures (see Figure 5.3).

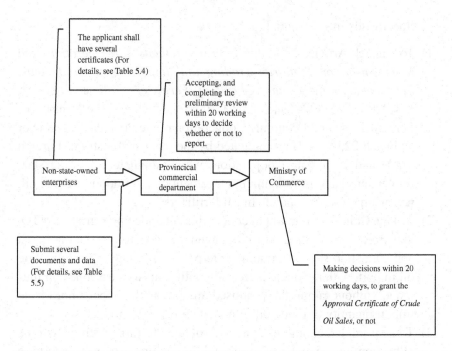

Figure 5.3. Flowchart of the Application for Operation Right in the Domestic Market of Crude Oil

Table 5.4. Certificates and Documents for Application for Operation Right in the Domestic Market of Crude Oil

Development and reform department	Approval document for oil depot project
Industrial and commercial administrative department	*Business License* (duplicate) or *Notification on Pre-approval on Enterprise Name*
Department of land and resources	*State-owned Land Use Certificate* or *Approval Certificate of Construction Land*
Planning department	*Construction Land Use Permit* and *Planning Permit of Construction Engineering*
Construction department	*Builder's License of Construction Engineering* and *Registration Form for Completion Acceptance of Construction Projects*

(*Continued*)

Table 5.4. (*Continued*)

Fire department	*Opinions on Fire Control Acceptance of Construction Engineering*
Environmental protection department	Reply document to environmental protection acceptance upon the completion of oil depot projects
Meteorological department	*Building Lightening Protection Security Detection Certificate*
Quality and technology supervision department	*Calibration Certificate* of measuring instruments through variable inspection
Safety supervision and management department	*Dangerous Chemicals Business Permit* (duplicate) and *Safety Qualification Certificate* of legal representative (principal)

Besides the above-mentioned unreasonable requirements for registered capital, capacity of oil tank, and so on, the absurdity of the flow is that it reverses cause and effect. For example, the requirements for "a crude oil supply agreement signed with an oil supply enterprise for at least one year, which is in line with its business scale" and "having secular, stable and legal marketing channel of crude oil." In the existing system, how can a rational enterprise sign agreements with other enterprises and have long-term marketing channels, before it obtains operation license of crude oil sales. And the absurdity behind the intention of such entry control is proved. It is not to guarantee the market order, but to obviously stop other enterprises from entering the domestic market of crude oil; so it is a means for maintaining the interests of oil monopoly enterprises.

In fact, like the examination and approval on the import operation right of crude oil, most important of all, the application flow on the surface is not of criterion doctrine, but of approval doctrine. Therefore, they are just a decoration.

Some reasonable items in those conditions are the requirements of the *Dangerous Chemical Business Permit*. But those requirements shall not be required by the entry control, but by the environmental protection and the control organ shall be environmental protection department.

Table 5.5.   Documents and Certifications for Application for Operation Right in the Domestic Market of Crude Oil

Applicant	Manufacturing enterprise of crude oil	Import enterprise of crude oil	Resale enterprise of crude oil	Branch of a Chinese enterprise legal person
Application materials	*Manufacturing enterprise of crude oil*: It shall submit *Oil Mining License* within the term of validity issued by department of land and resources and documentary evidence for the real output of self-produced crude oil in the last year.	*Import enterprise of crude oil*: It shall submit documentary evidence for having the import operation qualification of crude oil and documents such as customs declaration and customs statistical certification proving the import quantity of crude oil to be more than 500,000 tons in recent 2 years	*Resale enterprise of crude oil*: It shall submit a crude oil supply agreement signed with a manufacturing enterprise or import enterprise of crude oil for at least 1 year, which is in line with its business scale	If the applying entity is a branch of a Chinese enterprise legal person, it shall also submit the identification document of the principal of the enterprise, written document proving the parent company's approval on its application, the *Approval Certificate of Sales Operation of Crude Oil*, and documentary evidence for registered capital or capital verification report

Application documents.

Approval documents of the aforesaid administrative departments.

Documentary evidence or capital verification report for registered capital of RMB100 million at least issued by a legal capital inspection organ.

Legal documentary evidence for having the ownership of oil pipeline for loading and unloading petroleum products or railway special line or highway facilities for receiving and sending oil or a water transport port of at least 10,000 tons for petroleum products.

Documentary evidence for the property right in oil depot and related supporting facilities.

(Continued)

Table 5.5. (*Continued*)

Legal documentary evidence for wholly owning or holding more than 50% (exclusive) shares in a petroleum products depot with capacity of 200,000 cubic meters above and meeting the development planning for oil depot.

As for the land use right of oil depot gained by invitation to bid, auction, and listing, it is also required to produce the pre-approval document for approving the applicant's bid or bidding issued by government competent department and confirmation document for the auction, bid and listing of the use right of state-owned land approved and issued by Ministry of Land and Resources.

Identification paper of the legal representative and related documentary evidence.

1. Oil refineries wholly-owned or with more than 50% (exclusive) of shares constructed upon the state's approval according to law, meeting the national industry policy, with primary processing capacity of crude oil no less than 2 million tons; or	2. A crude oil sales agreement signed with an oil refining enterprise which is constructed upon the state's approval according to law and meets the national industry policy, with primary processing capacity of crude oil no less than 5 million tons for at least 1 year and the related documentary evidence of the oil refinery.

Other documents required by the approval organ.

2. To Cancel the Entry Control over the Domestic Market of Crude Oil

The reform on opening the domestic market of crude oil is to cancel the control over enterprise entry, so that enterprises can freely make crude oil transaction at home as shown in Figure 5.4.

Specifically, it is essential:

(1) To stop implementing and cancel Article 3 "to further strengthen the allocation management of crude oil" in the *Suggestions on Clearing and Rectifying Small Refinery Plants and Regulating the Circulation Order of Crude Oil and Petroleum Products* (Document No. 38) transmitted by the General Office of the State Council, i.e.:

> "The crude oil produced by CNPC and SINOPEC, the crude oil sold by China National Offshore Oil Corporation at home and the crude oil produced by SINOPEC Star Petroleum Co. Ltd., and local oil fields, as well as imported crude oil are subject to the national uniform allocation and shall not be sold without authority. ..."

3. To Establish a Trading Market of Crude Oil

After the entry control over the import and sales of crude oil is cancelled, it is essential to establish a trading market of crude oil in proper places, such as port cities of crude oil import, so as to form the crude oil price of the domestic market in China and guide the resource allocation of enterprises.

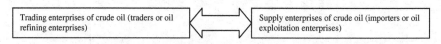

| Trading enterprises of crude oil (traders or oil refining enterprises) | | Supply enterprises of crude oil (importers or oil exploitation enterprises) |

Figure 5.4.   Schematic Diagram for Opening the Domestic Market of Crude Oil

V. Reform Solutions on Opening the Domestic Market of Petroleum Products

1. Entry Control over the Domestic Market of Petroleum Products

Under the existing system, if an enterprise outside the oil monopoly enterprises wants to enter the domestic market of petroleum products, it shall go through the following application procedures.

(1) Flow for entering the wholesale and operation business of petroleum products (Figure 5.5).

(2) Flow for retail operation business of petroleum products (Figure 5.6).

Similar to the entry control of crude oil market, for the entry control concerning petroleum products, registered capital, supply channel, capacity of oil depot, transportation facilities and technical security of gasoline

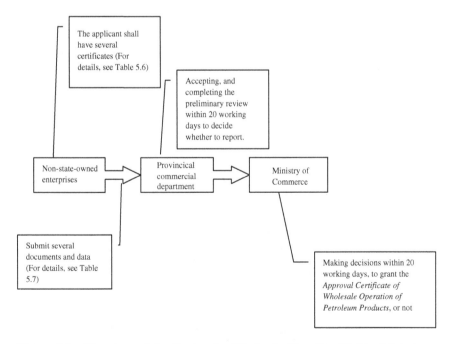

Figure 5.5. Flowchart of Application for Wholesale Operation Right of Petroleum Products

Table 5.6. Certificates and Documents for Application of Wholesale Operation Right in the Domestic Market of Petroleum Products

Development and reform department	Approval document for oil depot project
Industrial and commercial administrative department	*Business License* (duplicate) or *Notification on Pre-approval on Enterprise Name*
Department of land and resources	*State-Owned Land Use Certificate* or *Approval Certificate of Construction Land*
Planning department	*Construction Land Use Permit* and *Planning Permit of Construction Engineering*
Construction department	*Builder's License of Construction Engineering* and *Registration Form for Completion Acceptance of Construction Projects*
Fire department	*Opinion on Fire Control Acceptance of Construction Engineering*
Environmental protection department	Reply document to environmental protection acceptance upon the completion of oil depot projects
Meteorological department	*Building Lightening Protection Security Detection Certificate*
Quality and technology supervision department	*Calibration Certificate* of measuring instruments through variable inspection
Safety supervision and management department	*Dangerous Chemicals Business Permit* (duplicate) and *Safety Qualification Certificate* of legal representative (principal)

stations, etc. are not reasons for establishing entry control. It can be seen that the main purpose of the set of entry control is to restrict the entry of enterprises outside oil monopoly enterprises (see Table 5.9).

Moreover, the application flow is of approval doctrine, rather than of criterion doctrine.

However, it is necessary to keep the entry control concerning the operation of hazardous chemicals and the entry regulation concerning safety and firefighting of gasoline stations. But such entry controls are for the purpose of public safety, not restricting other enterprises to enter, so they have nothing to do with the current entry regulation organs and they shall still be implemented by the regulation organs of safety production.

Table 5.7. Data and Documents for Application for Wholesale Operation Right of Petroleum Products

Applicant	Enterprise with oil refineries	Import enterprise of petroleum products	Enterprise signing a petroleum products supply agreement with a domestic wholesale enterprise	Enterprise signing a petroleum products supply agreement with an import enterprise of petroleum products	Branch of China enterprise legal person
Application materials	Enterprise with oil refineries: It shall submit documentary evidence for having oil refineries constructed upon the state's approval according to law, meeting the state industry policy, with primary processing capacity of crude oil more than 1 million tons and with annual output of gasoline and diesel meeting the national product quality standard reaching at least 500,000 tons.	Import enterprise of petroleum products: It shall submit documentary evidence for having the import operation qualification of petroleum products.	Enterprise signing a petroleum products supply agreement with a domestic wholesale enterprise: It shall submit copies of the Approval Certificate of Wholesale Operation of Petroleum products of the wholesale enterprise of the petroleum products, documentary evidence of annual operation quantity of petroleum products more than 200,000 tons (legal documentary evidence provided by a tax department or an accounting firm), and a petroleum products supply agreement signed by both parties for at least 1 year in line with respective operation scale.	Enterprise signing a petroleum products supply agreement with an import enterprise of petroleum products: It shall submit the import operation qualification certification of the import enterprise, customs declaration of petroleum products annual import quantity of 100,000 tons above, customs statistical certification, and a petroleum products supply agreement signed by both parties for at least 1 year in line with respective operation scale.	It shall also submit identification document of the principal of the enterprise, written document proving the parent company's approval on its application, the Approval Certificate of Wholesale Operation of Petroleum Products, and documentary evidence for registered capital or capital verification report.

(Continued)

Table 5.7. *(Continued)*

Application documents.

Approval documents of the aforesaid administrative departments.

Documentary evidence or capital verification report for registered capital of RMB30 million at least issued by a legal capital inspection organ.

Legal documentary evidence for having the ownership of oil pipeline loading and unloading petroleum products or railway special line or highway facilities for receiving and sending oil or water transport terminal with a capacity of at least 10,000 tons for petroleum products.

Documentary evidence for the property right in oil depot and related supporting facilities.

Legal documentary evidence for wholly-owned or having more than 50% (exclusive) shares in petroleum products depots with capacity of 10,000 cubic meters above and meeting the development planning for oil depot.

As for the land use right of oil depot gained by invitation to bid, auction and listing, it is also required to produce the pre-approval document for approving the applicant's bid or bidding issued by government competent department and confirmation document for the auction, bid, and listing of the use right of state-owned land approved and issued by Ministry of Land and Resources.

Identification paper of the legal representative and related documentary evidence.

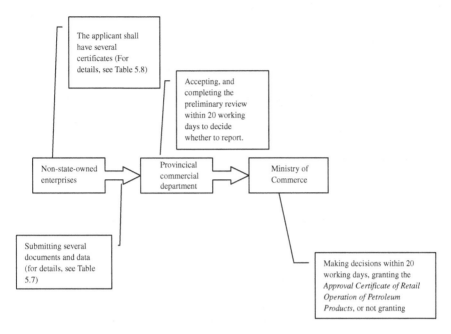

Figure 5.6. Flowchart of Application for Retail Operation Right of Petroleum Products

2. To Cancel the Entry Regulation over the Domestic Market of Petroleum Products

The reform on opening the domestic market of petroleum products is to cancel the entry control over the wholesale and retail of petroleum products implemented by the Ministry of Commerce, but to maintain the security control implemented by the supervision department of safety production and the public security and fire departments. Such controls are not only entry controls, but also conventional controls, treating all enterprises equally without discrimination, no matter state-owned or private enterprises. Based on the premise, enterprises can have free access to the wholesale and retail field of petroleum products. See Figure 5.7.

To carry out the reform, it is essential:

(1) To stop implementing and cancel Article 4 "to implement centralization of wholesale of petroleum products" in the *Suggestions on Clearing and Rectifying Small Refinery Plants and Regulating the*

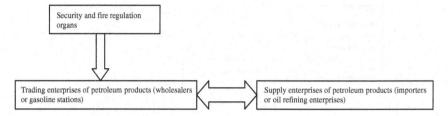

Figure 5.7. Schematic Diagram of Opening and Regulation of Domestic Market of Petroleum Products

Circulation Order of Crude Oil and Petroleum Products (Document No. 38) transmitted by the General Office of the State Council:

> "(I) All petroleum products (gasoline, kerosene, diesel, similarly hereinafter) produced by all domestic oil refineries shall be completely handed over to wholesale enterprises of CNPC and SINOPEC, while other enterprises and units shall not wholesale and every oil refinery shall not sell through their own channels.
>
> For oil refineries which sell petroleum products by violating regulations, the crude oil supply to such refineries shall be stopped.
> ..."

And Article 5 "To regulate the retail market of petroleum products":

> "We will carry out clean-up and rectification on various gasoline stations (sites) operating gasoline and diesel. ...... Meanwhile, we will gradually carry out centralzied distribution and chain operation mode of petroleum products in the process of petroleum products retail."

(2) To stop implementing and cancel Article 1 "To strictly investigate construction and operation of gasoline stations violating laws and rules" in the *Suggestions on Further Clearing, Rectifying and Regulating the Market Order of Petroleum Products* (Document No. 72) promulgated by the State Economic and Trade Commission etc.:

> "(I) All gasoline stations not obtaining the *Approval Certificate of Retail Operation of Petroleum Products* and business license and those already established but not meeting the planning requirements and involving illegally occupying land and construction against rules and regulations shall be banned according to law."

Table 5.8. Certificates or Approval Documents for Application for Retail Operation Right in the Domestic Market of Petroleum Products

Development and reform department	Approval document
Industrial and commercial administrative department	*Business License* (duplicate) or *Notification on Pre-approval on Enterprise Name*
Department of land and resources	*State-owned Land Use Certificate* or *Approval Certificate of Construction Land*
Planning department	*Construction Land Use Permit* and *Planning Permit of Construction Engineering*
Construction department	*Builder's License of Construction Engineering* (Note 1) and *Registration Form for Completion Acceptance of Construction Projects*
Fire department	Opinion on Fire Control Acceptance of Construction Engineering
Environmental protection department	*Reply of Application Form for Environmental Protection Acceptance upon Completion of Gasoline Station Project*
Meteorological department	*Building Lightening Protection Security Detection Certificate*
Quality and technology supervision department	*Verification Certificate* for the oiling machine passing the measuring inspection and oiler work license
Safety supervision and management department	*Dangerous Chemicals Business Permit* (duplicate) and *Safety Qualification Certificate* of legal representative (principal)
Tax department	*Tax Registration Certificate* or *Register tax registration certificate*
Water supervision department (Note 2)	*Review Opinions on Operation Conditions of Refueling Ship*

Note 1: Generally, it is specified that the certificate may not be provided in the case of investment of less than RMB300,000 or construction of less than 300 square meters.

Note 2: Only for enterprises engaging in marine gasoline stations (vessels), but not other enterprises.

Table 5.9. Data and Documents for Application for Retail Operation Right of Petroleum Products

Applicant	Gasoline station enterprises built in rural areas and only sell diesel	The rest enterprises engaging in retail business of petroleum products
Application materials	Submitting data in accordance with the conditions established by commercial competent department at the provincial level	Application document
		Approval documents of the aforesaid administrative departments
		Construction acceptance material of gasoline station construction, and qualification certifications of professional and technical personnel with regards to the inspection, metrology, firefighting and safe production of petroleum products
		Copies of a supply agreement of petroleum products signed with a petroleum products wholesale enterprise which passes annual inspection for 3 years above in line with the business scale and the *Approval Certificate of Wholesale Operation of Petroleum Products* of the enterprise
		Documentary evidence for the property right in oil depots and gasoline stations (sites) and related supporting facilities
		Where an enterprise obtains the land use right of gasoline stations (sites) by invitation to bid, auction, and listing, it shall also produce the pre-approval document for approving the applicant's bid or bidding issued by government competent department of commerce and the *Sales Confirmation* for the auction (bid and listing) of the use right of state-owned land approved and issued by the Ministry of Land and Resources.
		Identification paper of the legal representative and related documentary evidence.
		Other documents required by the approval organ.

And Article 2 "To implement strict access to the petroleum products market and further control the order of petroleum products market":

"(I) To strictly control the newly-built gasoline stations, regulate the approval procedures for newly-built gasoline stations. As of the issue date of the Suggestions, all newly-built gasoline stations in every region shall be uniformly constructed by CNPC and SINOPEC as their wholly-owned or holding subsidiaries; ..."

(II) Petroleum products shall be subject to the centralized wholesale of CNPC and SINOPEC. ..."

(3) To cancel the *Measures for Management of Petroleum Products Market.*
(4) To retain the access control over "dangerous chemicals business permit" and the access control and conventional control over related safety and fire protection.

3. To Establish Free Trading Market of Petroleum Products

Under the circumstance that enterprises can have free access to the domestic market of petroleum products, encourage and assist enterprises to establish free trading market of petroleum products, so as to improve transaction efficiency and form domestic market price.

4. To Cancel the Price Control over Petroleum Products

After the establishment of domestic petroleum products market and the formation of market pricing mechanism, cancel the government's formulation and control of petroleum products price.

VI. Reform Solutions on Opening the Import and Export Trade Markets of Petroleum Products

1. Procedures for Entering the Import and Export Markets of Petroleum Products under the Existing System

According to Article 4 in the *Measures for the Administration of the Petroleum Products Market* (《成品油市场管理办法》), the term "petroleum products" as mentioned below refers to gasoline, kerosene, diesel and other alternative fuels which satisfy the product quality standards of the state and for the same purposes, such as ethanol gasoline and bio-diesel oil, excluding fuel oil.

Under the existing system, a non-state-owned enterprise cannot engage in the import business of petroleum products, but can only import fuel oil. According to the *Interim Methods for Operation and Management on State-Run Trading and Importing of Crude Oils, Petroleum Products and chemical fertilizers* (《原油、成品油、化肥国营贸易进口经营管理试行办法》) (Decree of the Ministry of Foreign Trade and Economic Cooperation of the People's Republic of China, 2002, No. 27), China's fuel oil import is also subject to the state trading management, and non-state trading enterprises are allowed to engage in part of import.

The Ministry of Commerce will promulgate the *Total Allowable Import Quantity, Application Conditions, Allocation Principle and Related Procedures for Petroleum Products (Fuel Oil) of Non-state Trade* (《成品油（燃料油）非国营贸易企业进口允许量申领条件、分配原则和相关程序》) annually, and in accordance with those provisions, the fuel oil import of non-state-owned enterprises must be handled according to the conditions and procedures as follows, and they do not vary too much every year, with changes mainly in quota. Now take the *Total Allowable Import Quantity, Application Conditions, Allocation Principle and Related Procedures for Petroleum Products (Fuel Oil) of Non-state Trade in 2012* (《2012 年成品油 (燃料油) 非国营贸易企业进口允许量申领条件、分配原则和相关程序》) as an example:

The import quantity of fuel oil allowed in 2012 implements the allocation mode of "first come, first served."

Enterprises meeting the application conditions for fuel oil import of non-state-run trade and obtaining the allowable quantity of fuel oil import in 2011, can apply for the allowable quantity for fuel oil import in 2012, according to relevant provisions.

The application and operation procedures for the rest enterprises are shown in Figure 5.8.

The entry control over import and export market of petroleum products is similar with other entry controls except slight differences. They also have conditions such as amount of registered capital, transportation equipment conditions, storage equipment conditions, and bank credit which originally can be examined by the transaction makers in the market, serving as conditions for market access, and other permit application procedures which are generally regulated by judicial authorities, show no reason for being subject to government control and belong to approval doctrine rather than criterion doctrine. Therefore, such conditions are also just decorations. **The purpose for setting market access is to prevent other enterprises from entering.**

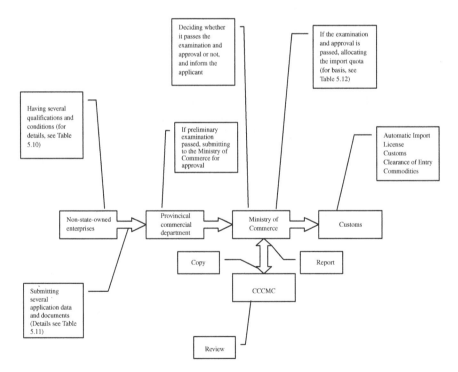

Figure 5.8. Schematic Diagram of Application and Operation Procedures for Import and Export Operation Right of Petroleum Products

Table 5.10. Qualifications and Conditions for Application for Import and Export Operation Right of Petroleum Products

1. Having ownership or use right of loading and unloading facilities such as import port or railway special line (limited to border land transportation enterprises) for petroleum products with a capacity of at least 10,000 tons.

2. Having ownership or use right of a storage tank or an oil depot for petroleum products with a capacity of at least 50,000 cubic meters.

3. Bank line of credit of at least US$20 million.

4. Without behaviors violating national laws and regulations.

5. Production-oriented foreign-funded enterprises shall follow the existing regulations.

6. Other factors needing to be considered.

Table 5.11. Data and Documents for Application for Import and Export Operation Right of Petroleum Products

Applicant	Non-state trading enterprise
Application materials	• The documentary evidence for line of credit issued by banks. It is essential to produce the original of official documents issued by headquarters or the immediate branches of every bank. A subsidiary company of central enterprises may supply the certification of collective credit extension of the head office. • Application letter, which shall include basic company information, description for meeting application conditions, application reason, specific programs concerning crude oil procurement, production use or sales, and introduction to professionals engaging in oil international trade. • Copies of *Duplicate of Business License of Enterprise Legal Person* passing annual inspection with the signature of the legal representative, copies of *Registration Form for Foreign Trade Dealers* or *Qualification Certificate of Import and Export Enterprises* or *Business Certificate of Foreign-Funded Enterprise* or *Clearance and Registration Certificate of Consignee and Consigner of Imported and Exported Cargoes* and *Organization Code Certificate* with the seal for registration affixed.

(Continued)

Table 5.11. (*Continued*)

- Produce the original of use agreements for facilities such as crude oil port (or railway port) and storage tank, copies of documentary evidence for handling capacity and storage tank capacity of the port (or railway port) issued by prefecture-level (or above) department in charge of investment (or others such as environmental protection department and fire department).

- 2011 crude oil import performance certification. Self-operated import shall produce copies of customs declaration, and proxy agent import shall produce agency agreements or related service invoices.

- The evidentiary material proving that there was no tax evasion, foreign exchange evasion and arbitrage issued by tax administration and foreign exchange department.

Table 5.12. **Initial Allowable Quantity of Import**

1. For an enterprise which already gained an allowable import volume for fuel oil of 400,000 tons (inclusive) and above in 2011, its initial allowable import volume is 200,000 tons in 2012.

2. For an enterprise which already gained an allowable import volume for fuel oil of 160,000–390,000 tons (inclusive) and above in 2011, its initial allowable import volume is 150,000 tons in 2012.

3. For an enterprise which already gained an allowable import volume for fuel oil of 60,000–150,000 tons (inclusive) in 2011, its initial allowable import volume is 100,000 tons in 2012.

4. For a new enterprise which obtains an allowable import quantity of fuel oil of 50,000 tons (inclusive) below in 2011 and meets the conditions for non-state import trade, its initial allowable quantity of import is 50,000 tons in 2012.

2. To Cancel the Entry Control over Import and Export Market of Petroleum Products

To carry out the reform of relaxation of petroleum products import market control, it is essential to cancel the above-mentioned access control over the import and export market of petroleum products, so as to make enterprises freely access the market. Meanwhile, it is essential to maintain the control of government departments concerned over the safety and fire fighting in petroleum products operation. And such control should be equal to all enterprises, no matter state-owned or private, with no discrimination. Based on this premise, enterprises can freely access the import and export market of petroleum products. See Figure 5.9.

To achieve the goal, it is essential:

(1) To cancel Article 2 in the *Interim Methods for Operation and Management on State-Run Trading and Importing of Crude Oils, Petroleum Products and chemical fertilizers* (《原油、成品油、化肥国营贸易进口经营管理试行办法》) (Decree of the Ministry of Foreign Trade and Economic Cooperation of the People's Republic of China, 2002, No. 27),

> "the state implements state trading management on the import of crude oil, petroleum products and chemical fertilizers. ..."

(2) To cancel the *Announcement on Application Conditions, Application Materials, and Application Procedures for Enterprise Qualification Registration of Non-state-Run Trading and Importing of Crude Oils, Petroleum Products and chemical fertilizers* (《关于原油、成品油、化肥非国营贸易进口经营企业资格备案申请条件、申报材料和申报程序的公告》); (Annoucement of Ministry of Foreign Trade and Economic Cooperation, 2002, No. 19).

(3) To cancel the *Total Quota, Allocation Basis and Application Procedures for Import of Petroleum products in 2003* (《2003 年成品油进口配额总量、分配依据和申请程序》) (Announcement of the State Economic and Trade Commission, 2002, No. 51).

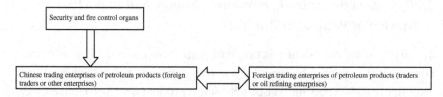

Figure 5.9. Schematic Diagram of Opening and Regulation of Import and Export of Petroleum Products

(4) To retain the access control over "dangerous chemicals business permit" (危险化学品经营许可) and the access control and conventional control over related safety and fire protection.

VII. Basic Measures of the Reform Solutions

China's reforms since the 1980s, imply a specific kind of reform modes or means. That is, to drive the reform by administrative departments and to adopt administrative means. For example, whether to open a certain market or whether to allow other enterprises to enter the former monopoly field (e.g., China Unicom's entry into telecom field) is decided by administrative departments, who also are responsible for related implementation.

Under the system background today, administrative documents are not the impetus of reform any longer, but the resistance against reform or even the object to be reformed. If the reform means after the 1980s, such as the All-China Federation of Industry and Commerce are still used today, it would not deliver the same effects achieved in those years. Thus, the means of our reform should be more tridimensional and effective.

Basically, our reform shall take legislative, judicial, and administrative means.

1. Legislative Means for the Oil System Reform

We have already known that a series of documents concerning oil monopoly right are promulgated by administrative departments. For instance, the administrative documents laying foundations for oil monopoly right, i.e., Document No. 38 and Document No. 72, were promulgated by several administrative departments led by the State Economic and Trade Commission at that time, so they have no legal effects. Therefore, we can submit proposals to the National People's Congress of the People's Republic of China or the standing committee of the People's Congress for changing or cancelling such administrative documents.

Article 87 of the *Legislative Law* stipulates that:

Any laws, administrative laws and regulations, local laws and regulations, autonomous regulations, specific regulations or rules with one of the following circumstances shall be amended or cancelled by related organs in accordance with the authority stipulated in Article 88 of the Law:

(I) Beyond authorities;

(II) Breaching the provisions in upper-level law as a lower-level law;

...

(V) Violating legally prescribed procedures.

Obviously, Document No. 38 and Document No. 72 are formulated by administrative departments beyond authorities, which violate the basic principle and specific provisions in higher level laws such as the *Constitution* and the *Anti-Monopoly Law et al.*, and legal procedures, so they can be amended and cancelled by submitting applications to related organs.

Article 88 of the *Legislative Law* stipulates that "The authorities for amending or cancelling a national law, administrative regulation, local decree, autonomous decree or special decree, and administrative or local rule are as follows:

(I) The National People's Congress of the People's Republic of China has the authority to amend or cancel any inappropriate national law enacted by its Standing Committee and to cancel any autonomous decree or special decree approved by its Standing Committee in violation of the *Constitution* or the provision of Section 2 of Article 66 hereof;

(II) The Standing Committee of National People's Congress of the People's Republic of China has the authority to cancel any administrative regulation which contravenes the *Constitution* or any national law, and to cancel any local decree which contravenes the *Constitution* or any national law or administrative regulation, and to amend or cancel any autonomous decree or special decree approved by the Standing Committee of the People's Congress of any province, autonomous region, or municipality directly under the central government in violation of the *Constitution* or the provision of Section 2 of Article 66 hereof;

...."

That is, the People's Congress and its standing committee can amend and cancel the administrative documents setting oil monopoly right according to the provisions of Article 87 of the *Legislative Law*.

In terms of specific operations, 10 members of the standing committee of People's Congress can submit the *Proposal on Cancelling the Administrative Laws and Regulations Establishing and Maintaining Oil Monopoly Right* (《关于撤销设立和维护石油垄断权的行政法规的议案》) through joint signature according to the provisions of Article 32 of the *Organic Law of the People's Congress* (《人民代表大会组织法》). It is possible that it will be listed in the agenda of standing committee of People's Congress.

The administrative documents concerning oil monopoly right, especially those stopping free access to crude oil and petroleum products markets, that are to be listed in the *Proposal* include:

Suggestions on Clearing and Rectifying Small Refinery Plants and Regulating the Circulation Order of Crude Oil and Petroleum Products (《关于清理整顿小炼油厂和规范原油成品油流通秩序的意见》) (G.B.F. [1999] No. 38);

Suggestions on Further Clearing, Rectifying and Regulating the Market Order of Petroleum Products (《关于进一步清理整顿和规范成品油市场秩序的意见》) (Document No. 72);

Implementation Suggestions on Clearing and Rectifying Circulation Enterprises of Petroleum Products and Regulating the Circulation Order of Petroleum products (《关于清理整顿成品油流通企业和规范成品油流通秩序的实施意见》) (Document No. 637, 1999);

Circular on Strict Control over Problems of Newly-built Gasoline Station (《关于严格控制新建加油站问题的通知》) (Document No. 543, 2001).

Interim Methods for Operation and Management on State-Run Trading and Importing of Crude Oils, Petroleum Products and Chemical Fertilizers (《原油、成品油、化肥国营贸易进口经营管理试行办法》);

Announcement on Application Conditions, Application Materials, and Application Procedures for Enterprise Qualification Registration of Non-state-run Trading and Importing of Crude Oils, Petroleum Products and Chemical Fertilizers (《关于原油、成品油、化肥非国营贸易进口经营企业资格备案申请条件、申报材料和申报程序的公告》);

Measures for Management of Petroleum Products Market (《成品油市场管理办法》).

...

In consideration of strategy or priority, it is essential to first cancel Document No. 38 and Document No. 72 or articles setting monopoly right of crude oil and petroleum products therein.

However, almost all such administrative documents are just administrative rules promulgated by ministries of the State Council, even just "suggestions," so they cannot reach the level of "administrative laws and regulations." In accordance with the *Legislative Law*, "administrative laws and regulations" refer to the administrative documents which are drafted by the State Council and promulgated by way of a State Council order signed by the Premier. However, what supports such administrative rules or suggestions is the *Decision on the State Council on Establishing Administrative License for the Administrative Examination and Approval Items Really Necessary to be Retained* (《国务院对确需保留的行政审批项目设定行政许可的决定》) promulgated by the State Council in 2004, where Item 183 maintains "the examination and approval of wholesale, storage and retail operation qualification of oil and petroleum products."

Therefore, the main content of the *Motion on Cancelling the Administrative Laws and Regulations Establishing and Maintaining Oil Monopoly Right* (《关于撤销设立和维护石油垄断权的行政法规的议案》) is to cancel Item 183 of the *Decision on the State Council on Establishing Administrative License for the Administrative Examination and Approval Items Really Necessary to be Retained* (《国务院对确需保留的行政审批项目设定行政许可的决定》) and other license approval items that shall be cancelled, it shall also be proposed that "the standing committee of the National People's Congress shall instruct the State Council to clear and cancel Document No. 38 and Document No. 72 and other documents setting monopoly right by the way of passing a resolution."

2. Judicial Means for the Oil System Reform

Since the establishment of oil monopoly right and the acts of enterprises having monopoly right obviously violate the *Anti-Monopoly Law*, judicial actions can be imposed on such acts. Such actions include:

(1) To ask **anti-monopoly law enforcement agency to carry out anti-monopoly investigation on the state-owned monopoly in**

petroleum industry and to institute a public prosecution against oil monopoly enterprises after the verification of monopoly practices.

(2) **To institute legal proceedings against oil monopoly enterprises.**

However, it is generally held that the oil monopoly enterprises are exempt from the restrictions of the *Anti-Monopoly Law* as Article 7 of the *Law* provides that "The state shall protect the lawful business activities of those operators from the industries of vital importance for economic or national security which hold positions of control in the state-owned economy or the industries which are specialized providers of particular products or services ...." But the "lawful" mentioned in the "The state shall protect the lawful business activities" shall refer to laws and regulations within the scope specified by the *Constitution* and the *Legislative Law*, including the laws made by the National People's Congress and "administrative laws and regulations" made by the State Council, as well as "administrative rules" made by departments of the State Council. However, Document No. 38 and Document No. 72 serving as the basis for the monopoly right of oil monopoly enterprises are not included in the above-mentioned scope, so the monopolistic practices of oil monopoly enterprises are not "legal business activities" and hence, the article does not apply.

Thus, in accordance with Article 17 of the *Anti-Monopoly Law* which stipulates that "Operators who hold a dominant market position shall be prohibited from engaging in the following practices which may be classified as an abuse of such position." including:

(I) Selling commodities at unfairly high prices or buying commodities at unfairly low prices;

(III) Refusing to enter into transactions with trading counterparts without justifiable reasons;

(IV) Forcing their trading counterparts to make transactions exclusively with them or operators designated by them without justifiable reasons;

(VI) Discriminating between trading counterparts of the same qualifications with regards to price or other transaction terms without justifiable reasons;

We can ask anti-monopoly law enforcement institution to carry out an anti-monopoly investigation on oil monopoly enterprises.

Or, in the name of individual consumers, we can file a lawsuit against CNPC or SINOPEC for "selling commodities at unfairly high prices." Because we currently hold hard evidence which proves that for the long term, at least since 2009, the price of the petroleum products supplied by CNPC and SINOPEC to the public has been significantly higher than the market equilibrium price (with the average price of main states in the world as the standard).

For another example, it is feasible to consider directly adopting measures of entering crude oil and petroleum products markets. When related administrative departments make intervention, a lawsuit can be field to a court. If the court accepts it, and cites the aforesaid administrative rules which establish the monopoly right, it is allowable to apply for an investigation on the validity of such administrative rules.

3. Administrative Means for the Oil System Reform

Since it were administrative rules that constitute the monopoly system of oil industry, in accordance with Paragraph 3 of Article 88 in the *Legislative Law* that "The National People's Congress has the authority to amend or cancel any inappropriate administrative rule or local rule," and Article 20 of the *Administrative License Law* (《行政许可法》) that "The organ that establishes the administrative license shall periodically evaluate the administrative license it set. If it considers that an already established administrative license can be solved through any of the methods listed in Article 13 of the *Law*, it shall modify the provisions for the establishment of the administrative license or abolish it without delay. The executive organ of an administrative license shall evaluate the information of the implementation of the administrative license and necessity of its existence, and shall report the relevant opinions to the establishing organ of the administrative license. The citizens, legal persons, or other institutions may put forward opinions and suggestions about the establishment and implementation of the administrative license to the organs establishing or implementing such license."

The new government can announce to carry out further clear-up on unreasonable administrative licenses, and China Chamber of Commerce for Petroleum Industry (CCCPI), as a non-governmental organization representing private oil enterprises, may apply to the State Council for including the administrative licenses (market access limitations) that violate the principle of market economy of the *Constitution*, the *Anti-Monopoly Law* and related policies including the 36 articles for the development of non-public-owned economy in the scope of clearing up of the new government.

It is possible to directly submit the *Suggestions on Cancelling Administrative Rules Establishing and Maintaining Oil Monopoly Right* (《关于撤销设立和维护石油垄断权的部门规章的建议》) to the State Council and urge the State Council to clear and cancel the following administrative rules:

Suggestions on Clearing and Rectifying Small Refinery Plants and Regulating the Circulation Order of Crude Oil and Petroleum products (《关于清理整顿小炼油厂和规范原油成品油流通秩序的意见》) (G.B.F. [1999] No. 38);

Suggestions on Further Clearing, Rectifying and Regulating the Market Order of Petroleum Products (《关于进一步清理整顿和规范成品油市场秩序的意见》) (Document No. 72);

Implementation Suggestions on Clearing and Rectifying Circulation Enterprises of Petroleum Products and Regulating the Circulation Order of Petroleum Products (《关于清理整顿成品油流通企业和规范成品油流通秩序的实施意见》) (Document No. 637, 1999);

Circular on Strict Control over Problems of Newly-Built Gasoline Station (《关于严格控制新建加油站问题的通知》) (Document No. 543, 2001);

Interim Methods for Operation and Management on State-Run Trading and Importing of Crude Oils, Petroleum Products and Chemical Fertilizers (《原油、成品油、化肥国营贸易进口经营管理试行办法》);

Announcement on Application Conditions, Application Materials, and Application Procedures for Enterprise Qualification Registration of Non-State-Run Trading and Importing of Crude Oils, Petroleum Products and Chemical Fertilizers (《关于原油、成品油、化肥非国营贸易进口经营企业资格备案申请条件、申报材料和申报程序的公告》);

Measures for Management of Petroleum Products Market (《成品油市场管理办法》);

…

Certainly, it is essential to cancel Document No. 38 and Document No. 72 at first.

In fact, in terms of specific operations, the State Council has already taken actions to some extent and it just lack more powerful drive. For instance, it is put forth in the *Several Suggestions of the State Council on Encouraging and Guiding the Development of Individual and Private Economy and Other Non-Public Sectors of the Economy* (《国务院关于鼓励与引导个体私营等非公有制经济发展的若干意见》) promulgated in 2005 that "to relax the market access control over non-public sectors of economy" and the specific policy measures include "to implement the principle of equal access and fair treatment." It is required that "related national departments and local people's department shall complete the clearing and amend laws, regulations and policies on restricting the market access to non-public sectors of the economy as soon as possible." And it is explicitly stipulated that "non-public capital is allowed to enter the monopolized industries and fields." "We will accelerate the reform of monopolized industries, and further introduce market and competitive mechanisms to such industries and fields as power, telecommunications, railway, civil aviation and oil."

It is stipulated in the *Several Suggestions of the State Council on Encouraging and Guiding the Healthy Development of Private Investment* (《国务院关于鼓励和引导民间投资健康发展的若干意见》)   (G.F. [2010] No. 13) promulgated in 2010, that " the setting the investment access threshold shall be standardized and a market environment of equal competition and access shall be created. The market access standards and the preferential and supportive policies shall be open and transparent; various types of investment entity shall be equally treated, and no additional conditions shall be individually set for private capitals." And it is explicitly stipulated that private capitals are encouraged to participate in the construction of oil and natural gas. And private capitals are encouraged to enter the field of oil and natural gas exploration and development, and to carry out cooperation with state-owned petroleum enterprises in oil and natural gas exploration and development. Private capitals are supported to have participation in construction of storage and pipeline transportation facilities and network. Therefore, it is required that "Regulations, policies and provisions against the development of private investment shall be cleared and amended, so as to effectively protect the legal rights of private investment, cultivate and maintain the investment environment of equal competition. When formulating the laws, regulations, and policies concerning private investment, it is essential to listen to the opinions and suggestions of related chambers of commerce and private enterprises, so as to fully reflect the reasonable requirements of private enterprises.

Although the policies have been promulgated for many years, related departments are still negative toward the relaxation of oil industry market access and take no action in that aspect. Thus, with the impetus of change in the term of office of government, and the driving force in legislative and judicial aspects, it is possible to make the State Council complete the "final step" for clearing the administrative documents that set oil monopoly right in violation of the *Constitution* and laws.

VIII. Implementing Steps and Possible Effects of the Reform Solutions

1. Implementation Steps

The reform plan for opening crude oil and petroleum products markets shall proceed in the following order:

(1) Reform on opening the import and export market of crude oil;
(2) Reform on opening the import and export market of petroleum products;
(3) Reform on opening the domestic market of petroleum products;
(4) Reform on opening the domestic market of crude oil.

2. General Analysis on the Effects of Reform on Opening Markets of Crude Oil and Petroleum Products

Once the reform on opening crude oil and petroleum products markets is realized, oil refining enterprises outside the monopoly system will have great development and new oil refining enterprises will enter the market, thus the petroleum products supply will have a large increase and the monopoly (administered) price will be broken to fall to the market price level.

Thus, though the opening of crude oil and petroleum products markets is just a breakthrough for the oil system reform, it brings about most revenues of the reform of the overall oil system (see the Figure 5.10). Except

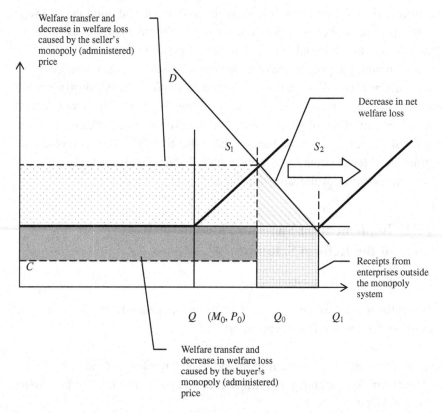

Figure 5.10   Schematic Diagram of Effects of Reform on Opening Markets of Crude Oil and Petroleum

Note: After the opening of crude oil and petroleum products markets, oil refining enterprises outside the monopoly system develop on a large scale and enter the market in a large number, which makes the supply curve move from S_1 to S_2, and even return to S_0 in theory. At this time, the price falls from the monopoly (administered) price P_1 to P_0; consumers reduce losses amounting to the dotted rectangle part in the figure; since the equilibrium supply and demand increase from Q_0 to Q_1, consumers increase the consumers' residual welfare amounting to the diagonal triangle part; meanwhile, enterprises also increase incomes amounting to the latticed rectangle part, including worker income, enterprise interests and government tax revenue.

for the oil monopoly enterprises' obtainment of production factors for free or at a low price, it brings about three parts of reform benefits. One part is the price of petroleum products that consumers less pay according to the current consumption quantity; one part is the consumption increased by consumers because of the lower price, the increased supply and the consumer surplus brought about thereof; and one part is the income of enterprises outside the monopoly system, including worker income, enterprise interests and government tax revenue.

3. Possible Effects of the Reform on Opening the Import and Export Market of Crude Oil

Once enterprises have free access to the import and export market of crude oil, they will provide lots of domestic local oil refining enterprises "on short commons" with sufficient raw materials, and increase the supply of petroleum products. Since the current local oil refining enterprises approximately account for about 20% of the market shares of petroleum products, and there is still 60% of refining capacity idled, once the crude oil supply is sufficient, it is possible to increase the market shares up to 40% or even 50% within a very short time. At this time, the former monopoly of CNPC and SINOPEC over the domestic market of petroleum products will be broken and as a result:

The price of petroleum products will fall to the international level of the petroleum products of the same quality, which will benefit consumers. According to the data during the period 2009–2011, the prices of both diesel and gasoline in China will be reduced by about 31%. So if the consumption is the same as that of 2011, consumers could pay RMB401.8 billion less each year.

Even according to the price of petroleum products trading center outside the current monopoly system in China, the price will also decrease after the markets of crude oil and petroleum products are opened. See Figure 5.11. The price of No. 93 gasoline in the petroleum products trading center of the Yangtze River Delta is about 13% lower than the administered price set by the National Development and Reform Commission.

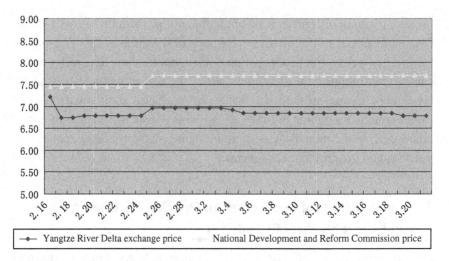

Figure 5.11. Comparison between Gasoline Price (No. 93) in Yangtze River Delta Trading Center and that Set by NDRC (February 16, 2013–March 21, 2013)

Source: Yangtze River Delta Petroleum Products Exchange provides a reference retail price of No. 93 gasoline. The NDRC administered price adopts the average value of retail prices of every place, except Beijing, Shanghai, Guangdong, Shenzhen, Hainan, and Tibet.

The price of Yellow River Delta exchange is 18% lower than the NDRC price. See Figure 5.12. It reflects that once the control of crude oil import is released, the supply of petroleum products will have a large increase and promote the price trend of petroleum products to downside.

In addition, since more petroleum products are consumed, there will be an increase in the consumer surplus of approximately RMB140 billion for consumers.

(1) With sufficient supply of crude oil, if calculated on the basis that the current local oil refining enterprises' annual processing capacity of crude oil is 130 million tons, the operation rate will increase from 45% to 85%, and, if calculated by the current market price of petroleum products, there will be an increase of approximately RMB300 billion in sales, thus the central finance and local finance will obtain additional tax revenues of over RMB60 billion and over RMB10 billion respectively every year. Dynamically, the opening of the import market of crude oil will enable local oil refining enterprises and private oil refining enterprises to have greater development.

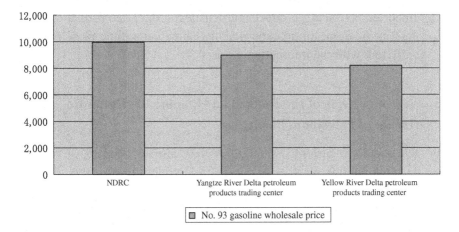

Figure 5.12. Comparison of Three Gasoline Wholesale Pricres (Februry 16, 2013–March 21, 2013, Unit: RMB/ton)

Source: Wholesale prices of No. 93 gasoline provided by Yangtze River Delta Trading Center and Yellow River Delta Trading Center. The NDRC wholesale price is estimated by deducting RMB500/ ton from the administered retail price released by it.

(2) CNPC and SINOPEC will experience a tendency of sharp decrease in profit due to their higher internal cost and lower efficiency.

(3) CNPC and SINOPEC and part of local or private oil refining enterprises will increase the export of petroleum products.

(4) Domestic crude oil output will fall to a certain extent.

4. Possible Effects of the Reform on Opening the Import and Export Market of Petroleum Products

After the import and export market of crude oil is opened, the supply of domestic petroleum products will have a large increase, and the refined oil price will be formed in the market competition among more competitors, significantly lower than the upper limit of the government administered price. Therefore, the opening of the import and export market of petroleum products will not bring about too serious impacts and the results may be that

(1) Petroleum products export increases, that is, the net import of petroleum products decreases;

(2) Imported petroleum products participates in the price formation process in the domestic market, making China's domestic price organically link with the international price.

5. Possible Effects of the Reform on Opening the Domestic Market of Petroleum Products

In fact, under the current system, there have already been lot of trading centers and tangible markets of petroleum products all over the country. Such markets mainly involve the petroleum products produced by local oil refining enterprises and private oil refining enterprises and have formed market prices of petroleum products fluctuating below the upper limit of government administered price. After the import and export market of crude oil and petroleum products is opened, and based on the existing partial domestic petroleum products market, the opening of the domestic market of petroleum products is likely to produce the following results:

(1) The cancellation of entry control will lead to a rapid increase in the number of traders in the existing local petroleum products market and the transaction scale will rapidly expand;

(2) A national trading center will be formed and the price of the center will be deemed as the standard of petroleum products price of the whole country;

(3) The original monopoly enterprises will also enter the transaction market of petroleum products, forming a really unified national market.

6. Possible Effects of the Reform on Opening the Domestic Market of Crude Oil

After the opening of import and export market of crude oil, the opening of domestic market of crude oil is likely to produce the following effects:

(1) Increasing the domestic supply of crude oil;

(2) Forming a domestic price of crude oil;

(3) Monopoly enterprises of vertical integration will take the domestic crude oil price as a reference for the assessment of internal cost, which may result in the separation of oil refining part from oil exploitation part.

7. Possible Effects of Several Reforms

Overall, after the opening of the markets of crude oil and petroleum products, a uniform market of oil will be formed in China, and the basis system of petroleum industry will be transformed into market system. Under the system, even if the original monopoly enterprises do not abandon their monopoly right in oil exploitation field, take a dominant position in oil refining field and continue to enjoy the privilege of obtaining production factors freely or at low prices, their original dominant position of monopoly will shake and thus, their monopoly profits originally supported by monopoly prices will disappear.

On the other hand, since both crude oil price and petroleum products price are set by the market, all domestic enterprises will get correct signals to make more effective allocation of resources, and consequently the enterprises other than the monopoly ones will develop and rapidly expand.

Seen from the point of the entire society, there will be a reduction up to over RMB400 billion every year in the consumers's expenditure in petroleum products; as a result, the loss to the whole society will also decrease by hundreds of billion yuan every year; China's petroleum industry will develop faster on the whole and other enterprises will, at the time of getting more domestic market shares, expand overseas and thus, bring more overseas oil resources to China.

IX. Summary

The analysis of this chapter shows that the reform on opening the crude oil and petroleum products markets is a supporting point and lever of the whole oil system reform, which involves fewer aspects, and is less rigid compared to the reform that touches the vested interest of the upstream industries of oil monopoly enterprises, such as oil exploitation and oil refining stages, while would yield twice the result with half the effort.

Table 5.13.   Static Effects of the Reform on Opening Markets of Crude Oil and Petroleum Products

Year	Net welfare loss	Government subsidy	Financing costs	Land rent	Resource rent	Loss caused by monopolistic high prices	Total	Percentage of reform effects
2011	1,405	81	634	524	181	4,018	6,843	79

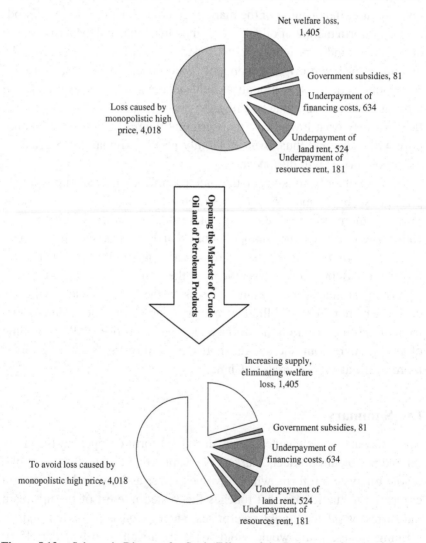

Figure 5.13.   Schematic Diagram for Static Effects of the Reform on Opening Markets of Crude Oil and Petroleum Products (Unit: RMB100 million)

On the one hand, the reform on opening crude oil and petroleum products markets can obtain most of benefits quickly from the breakup of monopoly, that is, it can eliminate the losses of consumers caused by monopolistic high prices, and will eliminate the net loss of social welfare caused by the limitation on enterprise entrance. According to welfare loss caused by the monopoly in 2011, the reform will obtain 79% or four fifths of effects of oil system reform (as shown Table 5.13 and Figure 5.13); moreover, it will increase a total sales volume of RMB300 billion every year due to the increase in the operation rate of local oil refining enterprises.

On the other hand, the market-oriented reform in the trading field will have significant effects on the upstream production field and will promote the final completion of the oil system reform in China.

Thus, it is a reform at very low cost, but with very high benefits.

Chapter 6

Incentives for and Strategies of the Reform — Political Economy and Transitional Economy for the Oil System Reform

I. Analysis on the Structure of Incentives of Reform

Oil system is a significant issue affecting the whole Chinese society . It is inevitable that the oil system reform will affect interest groups; some interest groups will benefit from the reform, while some will be impaired. So, it is natural that those impaired interest groups will resist the reform, which increases the cost of reform. When the cost of reform is quite high, the reform may fail. Therefore, if we want to push forward toward success, it is essential to make a serious analysis on the structure of reform impetus first.

1. The Monopoly is Unpopular

Oil monopoly enterprises have great economic strength and political resources, and their employees' incomes are enviable. Such high income-levels are obtained through exercising their monopoly rights and other privileges. The monopoly right inflicts damages to others' interests, so it is inevitable that it will bring about common dissatisfaction and grudges.

What's more, monopoly is considered a negative phenomenon which is criticized and condemned by all — from advocates of the traditional Chinese culture to modern economics. For instance, Mencius once called monopolists "mean fellows"; modern economics proves that monopoly will bring about not only efficiency loss, but also unfairness.

In recent years, China also has promulgated the *Anti-Monopoly Law*, which defines monopolistic behaviors and specifies that such monopolistic behaviors are illegal.

Therefore, in China today, monopoly enterprises are actually despised by everyone.

2. The Existing Oil Monopoly System Lacks Constitutionality and Justice

As analyzed above, the administrative documents, on which the current oil system depends, were formed without following the rules stipulated in both the *Constitution* and the *Legislative Law*, so they are not the "laws and regulations" admitted by the *Constitution* or the *Legislative Law*, and consequently they have no legal force. Actions of administrative departments such as bypassing due legal procedures, are backed strongly by monopoly enterprise's interest groups, and will be strongly questioned by the society. Thus, monopoly enterprises lack constitutionality.

On the other hand, the evil consequences of monopoly prove that it is a great injustice to make the whole society suffer from losses of RMB600 billion to RMB700 billion every year, i.e., to make the citizens and the state suffer losses in every aspect as consumer, land owner, oil resource owner, national asset owner, bank asset owner, bank creditor, enterprise owner, administrator or employee, and taxpayer of national finance — just for the interests of one or two monopoly enterprises.

Thus, it is in the interests of constitutionality and justice to thoroughly eradicate the unjust monopoly system that violates the basic principle of constitution. Such an action will be supported by the majority of people.

3. The Ruling Party and the Central Government have the Incentives to Reform

Oil monopoly enterprises function in an inefficient and unjust manner. In the name of "eldest son of the republic" (共和国长子) and the "ruling foundation" (执政基础) of the ruling party, they blame the ruling party and the central government for efficiency losses and infringe upon interests of all sectors of the society. Such act of their overturns the ruling foundation and brings shame on the political reputation of the ruling party. Undeterred, the oil monopolists seize and enjoy the ill-gotten wealth. The ruling party and the central government do not obtain any benefits from the existence of oil monopoly enterprises, but become scapegoats.

Moreover, oil monopoly enterprises constantly cause gasoline shortages for their own interests. In some important social issues, such as special oil gain levy, increase in mining royalty and improvement in the quality of petroleum products, they threaten the central government and become a social destabilizing factor. Thus, the central government providing social stability and public goods has the impetus to break up the oil monopoly system.

Breaking the oil monopoly can also bring about significant benefits to a wide circle of people, such as consumers, private enterprises, other enterprises, local governments and bank depositors; the ruling party and the central government will win high political reputation if they can promote the reform and break up the oil monopoly system.

Once the ruling party and the central government clearly see the harms inflicted by oil monopoly enterprises upon the ruling legitimacy and the huge benefits that would be brought to the society by breaking up oil monopoly, they will become the leading force in firmly pushing forward the reform of the oil sector.

4. Consumers have Incentives to Break Up the Oil Monopoly System

Consumers are on the opposite side of oil monopoly enterprises and have clear and definite information concerning the price fluctuations of crude oil. They have direct dissatisfaction with the situation where oil monopoly enterprises rapidly raise prices while rarely dropping them. The monopolists even raise prices against the trend of falling oil price in the international market by making use of the price released by the NDRC. The consumers will become more dissatisfied when they know that the domestic petroleum products price (pre-tax) is significantly higher than that of other countries. So, they have a strong motivation to ask for reform to break up the oil monopoly system.

Consumers exist in large numbers. In China, the vehicle fleet has already reached 220 million, and the private car fleet has already exceeded 100 million. A major consumer group of petroleum products is in the middle class — a huge and widespread group with continuous and stable consuming behavior. It is also an important nucleus in the society. Thus, from a political viewpoint, this consumer group carries heavy political weight.

From another aspect, even though consumers are numerous, according to the theory of Olson, everyone's interest share is very small, so rarely does an individual consumer have the impetus to push forward the reform; but when the consumers unite, the cost will be very high. So, the actual strength is not high, though there are lots of consumers.

A means to save the situation is to rely on the existing consumer organizations, e.g., the Consumers' Association, and some newly established organizations, such as the Consumers' Association of petroleum products and organize them to oppose oil monopoly.

5. Private Enterprises in the Petroleum Industry Ask for Reform

Private enterprises in the petroleum industry, including private enterprises in such sectors as oil extraction, oil refining, wholesale, retail, storage and transportation, have been suppressed by oil monopoly enterprises for a long time, with their right to enter the petroleum industry damaged and interests infringed. Once the oil monopoly is broken, the deprived private enterprises will directly benefit upon their entry into the market; so they have great impetus to support and promote the reform.

Private enterprises in the petroleum industry are less in numbers compared to consumers, however, the interest of an individual enterprise is larger, so they have the impetus and conditions to unite with each other for the purpose of propelling the reform in the petroleum industry. Private enterprises in the oil industry have already established the China Chamber of Commerce for Petroleum Industry and made efforts in promoting the reform.

6. Other Central State-Owned Enterprises and Local State-Owned Enterprises

In addition to the private enterprises, quite a few central state-owned enterprises also have been thinking highly of the oil industry, and have already invested to enhance the production capacities of oil refining. For instance, ChemChina has 9 oil refineries, and its annual processing capacity of crude oil reaches 25 million tons (the website of ChemChina, http://petro.chemchina.com/youqi/cpyfw/A0703web_1.htm), but its production capacity cannot be fully applied due to the restrictions on its crude oil import. Such kinds of central state-owned enterprises can obtain some import quotas of crude oil by lobbying senior leaders, but that cannot go on for long. If such restrictions on the crude oil import can be cancelled through reform, then the crude oil issue can be solved for good. So such enterprises will support the reform on breaking up monopoly.

Some local state-owned enterprises, like Shandong Local Oil Refining Enterprise, are also faced with the same problem with ChemChina. By 2012, the oil refining quantity of Shandong Local Oil Refining Enterprise reached 82.7 million tons (China Competition Information Center, http://www.askci.com, 2013). Since there is no suffcient import of crude oil, 60% of the processing capability of crude oil was idled. Therefore, such kinds of local state-owned enterprises also have the impetus to support the reform on breaking up monopoly and particularly to support the cancellation of restrictions on the import of crude oil.

7. Local Governments

As previously mentioned, neither CNPC nor SINOPEC bring about any benefit to the local finance, they bargain with the central government by virtue of their monopoly position, which usually is at the cost of local losses. For example, if both the monopoly enterprises pay mining royalty, according to the industry practice, local governments will obtain additional revenue of RMB30 billion every year. Therefore, local governments also have the impetus to support the reform on breaking up monopoly.

In another aspect, as their asset attributions are different, central state-owned enterprises, local state-owned enterprises and private enterprises pay 25% of their value-added tax and 40% of their corporate income taxes to different financial authorities. The two oil monopoly enterprises shall pay such expenses to the central government, while local oil refining enterprises and private oil refining enterprises shall pay such expenses to local governments. If Shandong Local Oil Refining Enterprise has enough raw materials to make full use of its production capacity, it will generate much more sales and added value, which will also promote a substantial increase in the fiscal revenue of Shandong local government, up to RMB6 billion to RMB7 billion per year. Therefore, from this point, local governments will have the impetus to support the reform on breaking up monopoly.

8. Administrative Departments Irrelevant to the Oil Monopoly System

A large number of administrative departments are presently irrelevant to the oil monopoly system. A civil servant, consumer or bank depositor — they all are disgusted with oil monopoly enterprises at their behavior of infringing upon the interests of others. Therefore, they also will support the reform.

9. Administrative Departments Relevant to the Oil Monopoly System

Those administrative departments participating in the establishment of monopoly right in petroleum industry, and those carrying out specific monopoly measures, such as some bureaus of the NDRC, the Ministry of Commerce, the Ministry of Railways, customs, and so on, may strongly oppose the reform on breaking up the monopoly, for they do not want to admit the errors in the system, or because they can obtain the benefits of rent-seeking when controlling the entry or prices.

Since they are in the center of the system and have the real capability to implement, they may offer the biggest resistance to the reform.

However, in the inner layers of such administrative departments, there are also officials who place the interests of the whole society above everything else, pursue overall efficiency and justice for society, and such officials will support the reform.

10. Management and Employees of Oil Monopoly Enterprises

Seemingly, the management and employees of oil monopoly enterprises benefit the most from the oil monopoly system, because their incomes are significantly higher than the social average level. So they will oppose the reform on breaking up the monopoly.

In 2011, the three monopoly enterprises, i.e., CNPC, SINOPEC, and CNOOC, totally had 2.79 million employees, and shall have more than 8 million persons if the family members are included. In the view of the whole society, their excessive incomes are ill-gotten wealth, but in their view, such incomes are deserved. Therefore, the reform will affect the interests of quite a large group, and may produce greater resistance.

However, it should also be seen that there are also people in favor of the reform inside the oil monopoly enterprises. One group is those with entrepreneurial ability and engineering technology capacity. Under the monopoly system, enterprises make no attempt to make progress, but place more emphasis on securing their own interests by virtue of main-taining and expanding their monopoly right, so they do not emphasize true entrepreneurial ability and engineering technology capacity. Therefore, the real ability of that group of employees cannot be appraised. Even if someone is put in an important position, he/she will not be able to truly display his/her ability due to the existence of the monopoly right. Such people hope to carry out a reform. They firmly believe that under a com-petitive system, their abilities can be enhanced and deployed suitably without causing a dip in their income-levels.

The other group comprises a large number of ordinary employees. Oil monopoly enterprises follow unfair rules in the distribution of wealth, and that practice will inevitably be transmitted in such enterprises; thus, the income of an employee depends more on his relationships than on his contributions. Therefore, quite a few employees feel dissatisfied with the existing system and ask for reform.

II. Reform Strategies

1. Seeking a Least Cost Reform Road

According to "transitional economics," the success of a reform depends on its cost; and the latter depends on whether the reform plan can change the pattern of income distribution or not at the time of change, and how many changes the reform will bring, how many persons' interests are affected, as well as the degree of damages. The more persons the reform affects, and the larger the degree of damages, the larger the strength opposing the reform, and the higher the cost of the reform, and success of the reform will be more difficult to achieve (Sheng Hong, 1994).

Therefore, when choosing the plan for the reform on opening crude oil (plan for the oil system reform) and petroleum products markets, we shall choose a reform road of least cost.

2. Effective Reform Strategies for China

One of the reasons why China's reforms over the past thirty odd years are successful is that we chose a proper road and plan for the reforms which avoided great conflicts and reduced the cost of reform. Such reform strategies include the following:

(1) *Reform outside the system.* That is, to carry out a reform outside the current state-owned system. This practice can not only steer clear of the predicament of the complicated system and implement new rules outside the system, but also indirectly affect the current interests inside the system. The development of township enterprises in the 1980s to 1990s is a case in point of the reform outside the system.

(2) *Incremental reform.* That is, it is possible to implement old rules on the stocking part within the current system, but new rules on the incremental part. As the saying goes, "veterans have old methods, while newcomers have new methods" (老人老办法，新人新办法).

(3) *Local reform.* That is, to experiment with reforms in part, like the reform in special economic zones including Shenzhen. The cost will be much lower when the reform at a national-level is promoted after the local reform demonstrates success of its reform program.

(4) *Subsidy reform.* That is, when the reform plan will inevitably impair the interests of a group of persons so as to achieve great reform goals. It is essential to offer compensations to such an affected group. Thus, it will eliminate, or at least reduce, the conflicts between the government and the affected group. For instance, at the time of cancelling the food allocation of planned price for urban residents, i.e., at the time of cancelling the food coupon, government gave corresponding subsidies to urban residents.

(5) *Transaction of the right to plan.* That is, under the premise of admitting the rights and obligations specified during the planned economy period, let economic entities make transactions on planned rights among them, which can eliminate planned rights themselves and realize marketization change. For instance, in the early 1990s, China once set foreign exchange quota transaction, which is a typical example for the transaction of planned right and the foreign exchange quota finally died out due to the result of that transaction (Sheng Hong, 1995; 1996).

The strategies of reforms over the past three decades still have practical significances today.

3. Strategies for the Reform on Opening Crude Oil and of Petroleum Products Markets

As discussed above, since the overall reform of the oil system moves to a large extent with profound influence and a wide range of involvement, if a reform is first carried out on opening crude oil and petroleum products markets, the cost of reform will be reduced and the related economic variables will be changed, thus giving rise to further reform and more profound changes in the production field.

To think further, what are the strategies for the reform on opening crude oil and petroleum products markets?

(1) *Gradual opening.* As described above, the markets shall be opened in the order as follows: the import market of crude oil, import and export markets of petroleum products, the domestic market of petroleum

products and the domestic market of crude oil. The time interval of several openings may range from half a year to one year. Thus, the impacts from the relaxation of markets can be relieved.

(2) *Reform outside the system.* While opening crude oil and petroleum products markets, retain the existing monopoly enterprises' institutional arrangement for the import and export of crude oil and petroleum products, including import and export determining mechanism and pricing mechanism and let other enterprises, including private enterprises, central state-owned enterprises and local state-owned enterprises, freely enter crude oil and petroleum products markets. This way, the existing oil monopoly enterprises will be allowed to adopt the existing operation mode over a long period.

(3) *Gradual entry.* In the process of opening markets, it is possible to consider letting other enterprises enter group by group. For instance, to let several enterprises with strong oil refining capacity, such as ChemChina, Shandong Dongming Petrochemical, Panjin North Asphalt Fuel and Lijin Petrochemical whose processing capacity of crude oil is more than 5 million tons and then let small scale enterprises enter.

(4) *Incremental reform.* The control over the incremental part of transaction can also be relaxed inside the existing oil monopoly enterprises. For instance, wholesale companies and gasoline stations of petroleum enterprises may buy petroleum products from other enterprises at the market price after completing their stocking task.

(5) *Subsidy reform.* When a reform leads to market competition, causes petroleum products price to fall to the market equilibrium price, other oil refining enterprises to expand on a large scale and oil monopoly enterprises to shrink due to low efficiency, lots of workers will be laid off or be out of work. At this time, other expanding enterprises will absorb most part of laid-off and unemployed employees of original monopoly enterprises. Even though there may be some employees of the original monopoly enterprises who cannot be re-employed, the government can establish an employment fund for the petroleum industry so as to award enterprises which employ laid-off employees, or directly subsidize the older.

(6) *Transactions of the planning rights.* For the oil monopoly enterprises, the government can abolish the price control on the selling of petroleum products in exchange of their acceptance on opening the markets of crude oil and petroleum products. Of course, the reform on opening markets does not have to be accepted by the monopoly enterprises; however, such a statement may eliminate or contradict their possible complaints.

If the above reform strategies are adopted, the reform cost will be further reduced, thus ensuring that the reform on opening crude oil and petroleum products markets would proceed smoothly and achieve success.

4. Discussion on Special Issues

In the reform on opening crude oil and petroleum products markets, the biggest issue possibly is that oil monopoly enterprises cannot withstand the competition with other enterprises, which will cause losses and shrinkage. That leads to a significant reduction in the incomes of the management and employees and possibly a number of laid-off or unemployed employees. This may give rise to a social turmoil.

For example, the Daqing Incident is an event of great influence. In 2002, lot of workers whose service years were bought out asked to return to their posts by way of petitions, processions and appealing to the higher authorities in Beijing for help because they felt they had suffered losses as the incomes of the in-service workers had increased by a large margin. Finally, the central government decided to resolve the incident at all costs and those agitating workers returned to their former posts, consequently.

However, after careful analysis, we know that the background at that time was quite different from the present scenario. Around the year 2000, the crude oil price slumped to US$10–20 per barrel; and it was just from the year of 2000 that China's oil monopoly system was gradually established. Since then, oil price surged from US$10 to 20 per barrel to even more than US$100 per barrel. Synchronously, the monopoly rights of the three petroleum enterprises become stronger and stronger. In that background, the income of petroleum enterprises had a substantial increase and the income of in-service workers increased significantly. Such circumstances will naturally bring psychological imbalance to laid-off workers.

By now, crude oil price has already risen to a quite high level. Now there is a significant increase in the proved reserves of world crude oil and the reserve and production ratio has already reached a new peak of 55, so it is difficult to imagine that the price can increase by a larger margin. On the other hand, the reform on breaking up monopoly is to weaken, even to remove the monopoly right of oil monopoly enterprises; therefore, it is impossible that the newly increased monopoly profits caused by the enhancement of monopoly right will arise. Therefore, under the background of the reform on breaking up monopoly, cases like the Daqing Incident will not occur any more.

After experiencing more than three decades of market-oriented reforms, the people of China, including workers of state-owned enterprises, all have gradually admitted the authority of the market. Generally, people can accept the losses caused by the market price development, like losses from investment in stocks. But, workers of state-owned enterprises cannot accept governments or enterprises to directly change their income levels as a result of market price development. If enterprises cut down incomes due to the market price development and their weaker competitiveness, workers can accept the fact to the extent that some capable employees may resign their positions with low pay and find a better job, while some employees with poor skills will not mind leaving enterprises which have difficulty in paying wages. Such circumstances have been proved by most of state-owned enterprises in the competitive field.

Finally, the reform in China has proved that when state-owned enterprises cannot absorb so many workers thus leading to large number of unemployed workers, non-state-owned enterprises will become the main force in providing job opportunities. For example, from 2008 to 2011, in all new employments, non-state-owned enterprises provided 96% of employments (according to the data from the State Statistics Bureau, 2012). Therefore, if market-oriented reform can be successful, it will rouse the prosperity of non-state-owned enterprises and create numerous job opportunities, which will be certainly more than the decrease in job opportunities in state-owned enterprises.

III. International Background and Opportunity of the Reform

It is better to carry out the reform on opening crude oil and petroleum products markets in an environment with adequate supply and unstrained relation between supply and demand.

Since the early 21st century, oil supply has been relatively strained, and oil demand has rapidly increased, so prices of oil products have climbed all the way. By now, crude oil price has already risen to a quite high level. On the other hand, the reserve and production ratio has already reached a new peak of 55; the "Shale Revolution" carried out by US at first will give rise to a strategic increase in oil supply. Natural gas has gradually become a leading energy source of the new era. Measures such as the Shale Revolution will result in a substantial increase in the supply of energy sources such as oil. Under the circumstance that the growth rates of China and India slow down gradually, the supply and demand relations of oil, even of energy, in the world market would relax relatively, so it is probable that the market price of oil will begin to slow down little by little.

In such an international background, if China opens crude oil and petroleum products markets to let more enterprises participate in the competition, and cancel the control over petroleum products price, then the oil market price formed in China will synchronize with the price in the world oil market, irrespective of other factors. Thus, the reform on opening crude oil and petroleum products markets will have fewer risks and more easily obtain the support of the majority of people.

Thus, 2013 would have been a very good occasion to begin the reform.

IV. Time Sequence of the Reform

1. In 2013, to relax the control over the crude oil import right of oil refineries of over 5 million tons;

2. In 2014,

    (1) to allow all enterprises to freely enter the import market of crude oil;

    (2) to open the domestic market of petroleum products, to establish and develop trading centers of petroleum products and form a national trading center;

    (3) to cancel the control over petroleum products price and make the price fixed in the market;

3. In 2015,

    (1) to open the import and export markets of petroleum products, under the conditions of establishing safety and fire control standards;

    (2) to allow subordinate enterprises of former original oil monopoly enterprises to directly enter the domestic market of petroleum products;

4. In 2016, to open the domestic market of crude oil.

V. Summary

1. The analysis on the reform motivation structure indicates that most people in China will support the oil system reform. Since the monopoly is unpopular and the current oil monopoly system lacks constitutionality and justice, the governing party and the central government have the desire to carry out the reform. Meanwhile, consumers and private enterprises are asking for a reform; other central enterprises, local state-owned enterprises and local governments also support the reform. Only those administrative departments related to the oil monopoly system and the managements and employees of oil monopoly enterprises may oppose the reform, however, among these groups a majority of them also support the reform.

2. When we select the scheme for the reform on opening the markets of crude oil and of petroleum products, we shall choose a way with the lowest cost.

3. The strategies for the reform on opening the markets of crude oil and of petroleum products are as follows:

    (1) *Gradual opening.* As described above, the markets shall be opened in the order as follows: the import market of crude oil, import and export markets of petroleum products, the domestic market of petroleum products and the domestic market of crude oil;

    (2) *Reform outside the system.* At the time of opening crude oil and petroleum products markets, to retain current institutional arrangements for the monopoly enterprises in importing and exporting of crude oil and petroleum products;

    (3) *Gradual entry.* During the process of opening the markets, it is possible to consider letting other enterprises enter the markets group by group;

    (4) *Subsidy reform.* For a possible situation where the oil monopoly enterprises may have laid-off or kept workers unemployed, the government can establish the employment fund for the petroleum industry, if other petroleum enterprises cannot absorb all such workers;

    (5) *Transactions of planned rights.* For the entire oil monopoly enterprise, the government can abolish the price regulation on the selling of petroleum products to exchange their acceptance on opening crude oil and petroleum products markets.

4. China's reform has proved that when state-owned enterprises cannot absorb so many workers including a large number of unemployed workers, non-state-owned enterprises will become the main force in providing job opportunities. For example, from 2008 to 2011, in all newly increased employments, non-state-owned enterprises provided 96% of job opportunities (according to the data from the State Statistics Bureau, 2012). Therefore, as long as the market-oriented reform can be successful, it will rouse the prosperity of non-state-owned enterprises and create numerous job opportunities, which will be certainly more than the decrease in job opportunities of state-owned enterprises.

5. Because the oil reserve and production ratio rises to 55, "Shale Revolution" will lead to a strategic growth in oil and natural gas supply, natural gas will become the dominant energy in the new period; in addition, as the growth rate slows down in China and India, the supply and demand relations will become relatively loose in the world oil markets, which is conducive to the reform on opening crude oil and petroleum products markets (see Figure 6.1).

6. Time sequence of the reform.

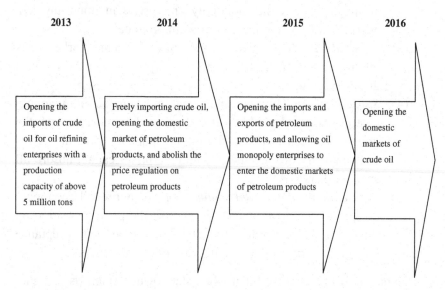

Figure 6.1. Sequence Diagram of the Reform on Opening Markets of Crude Oil and Petroleum Products

Economic Analysis on Administrative Monopoly in Petroleum Industry

I. Economic Analysis on Monopoly

Provided that petroleum industry is a fully competitive industry, there are lots of petroleum enterprises in the market, their cost functions are the same and the cost is of invariance. Furthermore, provided that at a certain time, administrative departments set entry barriers and regulations so that the oil market can only be operated by M_0 enterprises designated by them ($M_0 < X_0$, M_0) is a positive integer; X_0 is the number of enterprises when the perfectly competitive market is in a long-term equilibrium state), the economic analysis on the welfare of oil administrative monopoly can be conducted according to the Figure 1.

D is a market demand curve; horizontal line S_0 represents the industry supply curve in perfectly competitive market; crossing point E_0 is a market equilibrium point; the equilibrium price is P_0; the equilibrium output is Q_0 provided that marginal cost (MC) = average cost (AC) = equilibrium price (P_0). When oil market has administrative monopoly and the quantity of goods provided by M_0 enterprises is more than Q_2, the marginal cost will rise, and the supply curve will become the broken line P_0DS_1. At this time, the market equilibrium point is E_1; the equilibrium price is P_1; the equilibrium output is Q_1.

Based on the analytical framework in the Figure 1, welfare losses in petroleum industry include three parts: the welfare loss and transfer caused by the seller's monopoly price, the welfare loss and transfer caused by the buyer's monopoly price, and net social welfare loss (DWL, deadweight loss).

The DWL of social welfare refers to the absolute value between the decrease in consumer surplus and the increase in producer surplus in

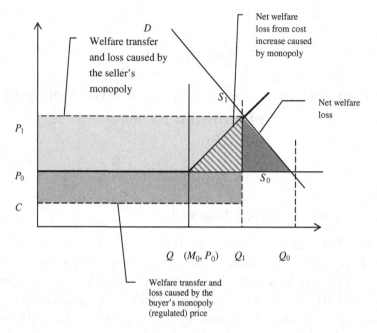

Figure 1. Economic Analysis on Welfare Loss and Transfer in Petroleum Industry[1]

Note: S_0 is the long-term average cost curve of the industry and it is formed by connecting the lowest average cost points on the long-term average cost (LAC) curve of several enterprises; S_1 is the marginal cost curve of the industry when the number of enterprises is M_0. P_0 is a competitive market price; P_1 is an administrative monopoly price; Q (M_0, P_0) is the maximum output when the number of enterprises entered is M_0 and the selling price is P_0; Q_0 is the equilibrium output in the competitive market; Q_1 is the equilibrium output in the case of administrative monopoly (Research Group of Unirule Institute of Economics, 2012). For more details, see Sub-Report I.

The welfare losses caused by the administrative monopoly in petroleum industry include: (1) Net welfare losses caused by monopoly (dark grey part in the figure); (2) underestimated cost, i.e., welfare transfer and welfare losses caused by the buyer's monopoly (administered) price (grey part in the figure); (3) welfare transfer and welfare losses caused by the seller's monopoly (administered) price (light grey part in the figure (including bar part), Research Group of Unirule Institute of Economics, 2012); (4) net welfare losses of cost increase caused by monopoly (bar part in the figure). The monopoly profit is the difference between the welfare transfer caused by the seller's monopoly price and the net welfare losses from cost increase caused by monopoly (light grey part in the figure).

---

[1]Model reference, Zhao Nong and Liu Xiaolu (2007).

comparison with a perfectly competitive market, it is a kind of direct and complete dissipation of social welfare. The DWL of social welfare, corresponding to the deep grey triangle part, also called Harberger Triangle, refers to the part of decrease in output when the actual output is compared with the output in the perfect competition, due to the existence of monopoly and the direct vanishing of that part output causes the DWL of social welfare. Fundamentally, the DWL of social welfare refers to the part of total social welfare which vanishes because monopoly manufacturers restrict output.

The welfare transfer caused by the seller's monopoly refers to the light grey rectangle part in Figure 1, which represents the part of social welfare transferring from consumers to producers due to higher monopoly price; the welfare transfer and loss caused by the buyer's monopoly, corresponding to the dark grey rectangle part in the Figure 1, refers to the transferring of social welfare from owners of production factors to monopoly manufacturers because monopoly manufacturers pay lower prices for some production factors. In a strict sense, the seller's monopoly and the buyer's monopoly first give rise to social welfare transfer, but not loss. But in the view of production, the transferred welfare is not directly used in production activity, but is mostly used in behaviors such as rent-seeking. Rent-seeking behaviors have huge opportunity costs and quantitatively equal to the sum of wealth produced by equal resources invested in production activities by the optimal production efficiency. So in this sense, the seller's monopoly and the buyer's monopoly also belong to a kind of DWL of social welfare. Meanwhile, the transferred part of social welfare also causes unfair distribution of social income, further distorts the compensation and remuneration deserved by all production factors, and distorts price signals, resulting in wrong allocation of resources.

II. Calculation of Welfare Losses

1. Harberger Triangle

The deep grey triangle part in Figure 1 is the Harberger Triangle and the calculation formula is $\int_{Q_1}^{Q_0} D(x)\mathrm{d}x - (Q_0 - Q_1) \times P_0$, which can be approximately estimated by the formula $\mathrm{DWL} = \frac{1}{2}(P_1 Q_1 - P_0 Q_1)$ (Cowling and Mueller, 1978).

If calculated according to the data of exploitation and processing industry of oil and natural gas in the *China Statistical Yearbook* (2001–2011), during the 11 years from 2001 (inclusive) to 2011, the DWL of social welfare of Harberger in oil and gas industry reached RMB1.5452 trillion, averaging RMB140.5 billion per year (see Table 1).

2. Welfare Transfer and Loss Caused by the Buyer's Monopoly Price

The buyer's monopoly refers to that monopoly manufacturers obtain production factors at lower prices so as to transfer social welfare. In petroleum industry, it mainly involves various financial aids provided for oil monopoly enterprises by the government, financing cost lower than that in the market and the absence of land rent and resource rent. It amounts to the grey part in Figure 1.

Table 1.   Profits of Petroleum Industry (Unit: RMB100 million)

Time	Profits of oil and natural gas extraction industry	Profits of oil processing and coking industry
2001	978	−12
2002	1,170	51
2003	1,221	123
2004	1,745	293
2005	2,958	−119
2006	3,652	−312
2007	3,535	216
2008	4,601	−1,003
2009	1,903	931
2010	3,027	1,221
2011	4,300	423
Total	29,091	1,813

Source: The website of National Bureau of Statistics of China.

(1) *Government subsidies*

CNPC and SINOPEC are "the most profitable companies" at home, but they often need various fiscal subsidies from the state. For instance, in 2008, CNPC and SINOPEC obtained national subsidies of RMB50.3 billion and RMB16.914 billion respectively, for the excuse that "such government subsidies are to make up the inversion between the domestic petroleum products price and crude oil price and losses caused in the corresponding year by the group in taking measures to meet the supply of domestic petroleum products market." (Annual report of SINOPEC for the year of 2008, 2009) But in that year, CNPC and SINOPEC generally made profits, and the net profits attributable to the parent company were respectively RMB113.798 billion and RMB29.689 billion. According to the statistics, CNPC and SINOPEC both obtained national fiscal subsidies of RMB100.795 billion during the period of 2001–2011. See Table 2.

(2) *Financing costs*

The banking industry-oriented financial system at home and the monopoly characteristic of domestic banking industry determine the scarcity of financial resource as a production factor. The scarcity results in the planning of domestic financial resources allocation and the allocation favoring state-owned enterprises, which gives rise to the inefficiency and distortion of financial resource allocation. At the economic operation level, it shows that under the premise that state-owned enterprises are not better than non-state-owned enterprises in terms of overall benefit, the scale and cost of bank credit funds that they obtained are obviously lower than those of non-state-owned enterprises. For instance, in 2007, the proportion of the total sales and that of total employment figure of part of non-state-owned enterprises in manufacturing industry exceeded 90%, but 80% of bank credit funds flowed to state-owned enterprises over the previous one more decade (Liu Xiaoxuan and Zhou Xiaoyan, 2011).

Though large enterprises usually gain a certain favorable interest rate in credit and loan activities, the three petroleum enterprises, as

Table 2. National Fiscal Subsidies Gained by SINOPEC and CNPC over the Years (Unit: RMB100 million)

Year	SINOPEC	CNPC
2001	—	—
2002	—	—
2003	—	—
2004	—	—
2005	94	4
2006	52	6
2007	49	12
2008	503	169
2009	—	11
2010	11	16
2011	14	67
Total	722	286

Source: Annual reports of CNPC and SINOPEC over the years.

mega central enterprises, have been "favored" by the financial resource plan allocation, and their financing cost is significantly lower than the market rate and that of large private enterprises. For instance, in 2011, the interest rates for the financing of CNPC, SINOPEC, and CNOOC were 1.18%, 1.03%, and 0.42%, respectively. However, in 2011, the actual interest rate for the financing of ENN Energy, as one of largest private enterprises in energy industry at home, was 5.05% (Liu Xiaoxuan and Zhou Xiaoyan, 2011). During the period 2000–2007, among the industrial enterprises above designated size, the actual interest rate for financing of state-owned enterprises was 1.6%, while that of private enterprises was 5.4%. Fundamentally, such wrong allocation of financial resources is to subsidize oil monopoly enterprises using national savings. We have given the financing costs of CNPC, SINOPEC, and CNOOC over the years and the market interest rate of

Table 3.   Financial Expenses of CNPC over the Years (Unit: RMB100 million)

Year	2001	2002	2003	2004	2005	2006	2007	2008	2009	2010	2011
Total liability	1,792	1,765	1,901	1,955	2,344	2,475	2,790	3,485	5,426	6,464	8,350
Actual interest rate (in %)	2.23	0.0217	0.0103	0.0078	0.0032	0.0053	0.0103	0.0067	0.0096	0.0093	0.0118
Paid financial expense	40	38	20	15	8	13	29	23	52	60	98
Payable financial expense	84	83	89	91	110	116	131	163	254	303	389
Short-paid financial expense	44	44	69	76	102	103	102	140	202	242	291

bank capital and short-paid financial expenses of the three oil monopoly enterprises in Tables 3–5. As for the market interest rate of capital, by calculating the weighted average of the actual interest rate of every manufacturing enterprise with reference to the data of manufacturing enterprises (excluding state-owned enterprises) from 2000 to 2007, we get the market interest rate of 4.68% (Research Group of Unirule Institute of Economics, 2011).

According to statistics, if calculated by the market rate, the short-paid financial expenses of the three oil monopoly groups during the period 2001–2011 are RMB287.8 billion in total (see Table 6).

(3) *Land rent*

• Land rent for industrial land of CNPC

It is stipulated in the lease contract of land use right signed by and between CNPC Company Limited and CNPC in 2000 that CNPC leases a land of approximately 1.145 billion square meters to CNPC Company

Table 4.　Financial Expenses of SINOPEC over the Years (Unit: RMB100 million)

Year	2001	2002	2003	2004	2005	2006	2007	2008	2009	2010	2011
Total liability	1,878	1,978	2,012	2,425	2,756	3,242	4,000	4,306	4,790	5,448	6,372
Actual interest rate (in %)	1.91	2.19	2.05	1.79	1.91	1.78	1.22	2.12	1.46	1.26	1.03
Paid financial expense	36	43	41	43	53	58	49	91	70	68	65
Payable financial expense	88	93	94	114	129	152	187	202	224	255	298
Short-paid financial expense	52	49	53	70	76	94	138	110	154	186	233

Table 5.　Financial Expenses of CNOOC over the Years (Unit: RMB100 million)

Year	2001	2002	2003	2004	2005	2006	2007	2008	2009	2010	2011
Total liability	—	89	268	374	412	475	455	464	683	1,122	2,595
Actual interest rate (in %)	—	2.15	1.73	1.18	0.23	3.86	4.47	0.89	0.78	0.69	0.42
Paid financial expense	—	2	5	4	1	18	20	4	5	8	11
Payable financial expense	—	4	13	17	19	22	21	22	32	52	121
Short-paid financial expense	—	2	8	13	18	4	1	18	27	45	111

Table 6.　Short-paid Financial Expenses of the Three Oil Monopoly Groups (Unit: RMB100 million)

Year	2001	2002	2003	2004	2005	2006	2007	2008	2009	2010	2011
Short-paid financial expense	96	96	130	160	197	200	241	268	383	474	96

Limited for 50 years, with the rent expense of annually RMB2 billion. The unit land rent is RMB1.75/m² per year, which is far lower than the market price level of industrial land and CNPC does not pay the rent to the state.

In accordance with the fixed-base index number for industrial land stipulated by the Ministry of Land and Resources[2], the annual rental price for industrial land is calculated by 3% of the industrial land price. After calculation, during the period from 2001 to 2011, the short-paid land rent of CNPC reached RMB166.83 billion in total. But that estimate may be an underestimated value, because the land leased by CNPC is commercial land in part, rather than pure industrial land. See Table 7.

- Rent of land for gasoline stations of CNPC and SINOPEC

The domestic state-owned land use system roughly experienced the land assignment system before 1990, the system combining land assignment with agreement grant from 1990 to 2002, as well as the land leasing system with bid, auction, and listing as the core after 2003. In terms of

Table 7.   Land Rent Payout Status of CNPC (2001–2011)

	2001	2002	2003	2004	2005	2006	2007	2008	2009	2010	2011
Industrial land price (Unit: RMB/m² a year)	453	466	493	502	511	524	608	604	617	662	697
Payable land rent (Unit: RMB100 million)	156	160	169	172	175	180	209	207	212	227	239
Short-paid land rent (Unit: RMB100 million)	136	140	149	152	155	160	189	187	192	207	219

Source: The industrial land price is obtained from the website of the Ministry of Land and Resources.

---

[2]The fixed-base index number for industrial land takes the average price for the national industrial land in 2000 as the base, and the index number is the ratio between annual acutal average price for industrial land and the average price for industrial land in 2000.

national laws and regulations, the *Interim Regulations of the People's Republic of China Concerning the Assignment and Transfer of the Right to the Use of the State-owned Land in the Urban Areas* (《中华人民共和国城镇国有土地使用权出让和转让暂行条例》) promulgated in 1990, determines the transition from free allocation system of land to negotiating transfer system. The *Regulations for Bid, Auction and Listing Transfer of the Right to the Use of the State-Owned Land* (《招标拍卖挂牌出让国有土地使用权规定》) promulgated in 2002 determined the bid, auction, and listing system for the state-owned land, in the same year, as a supplementary to the *Circular on the General Office of the State Council on the Transmission of the Suggestions of the State Economic and Trade Commission and Other Departments Concerning Further Rectifying and Regulating Market Order of Petroleum Products* (《国务院办公厅转发国家经贸委等部门关于进一步整顿和规范成品油市场秩序意见的通知》) (i.e., Document No. 72), the Ministry of Land and Resources promulgated the *Circular on Effectively Strengthening the Management on the Land for Gasoline Stations* (《关于切实加强加油站用地管理的通知》), which stipulated that the land for gasoline stations shall be included in the project with restricted land supply, and that the land for gasoline stations shall be uniformly subject to the paid use system, invitation to bid and auction shall be conducted according to regulations.

We suppose that the price formed in land bid, auction, and listing is the market price and the bid, auction, and listing system was practised on the land for gasoline stations at home from 2003. But from 1990 to 2002, land assignment system coexisted with agreement grant system and the land rent is underestimated, since the land price negotiated is significantly lower than the market price. We give the quantity of self-run gasoline stations of SINOPEC during the period 1999–2011, as shown in Table 8.

In 1998, CNPC industry changed separate operation to mixed operation. Meanwhile, in order to cope with the impact on the interests of monopoly groups from gasoline stations invested by foreign capitals in China, after the access to WTO, CNPC, and SINOPEC began to rapidly expand the number of gasoline stations at home and the speed was extremely rapid during the period 1999–2000. From Table 4, we can know

Table 8. Quantity of Self-run Gasoline Stations of SINOPEC over the Years (Unit: stations)

Year	1999	2000	2001	2002	2003	2004	2005	2006	2007	2008	2009	2010	2011
Quantity	11,374	20,259	24,062	24,000	24,506	26,581	27,367	28,001	28,405	28,647	29,055	29,601	30,106

Source: Annual reports of SINOPEC over the years.

that the growth of SINOPEC's gasoline stations exceed 78%. During the period from 2000 to 2011, SINOPEC's annual average speed of growth in gasoline stations was 3.67%, with stable growth rate. We take that as the growth rate of domestic gasoline stations in ordinary years (except the period 1999–2000), and estimate the quantity of annually newly-built gasoline stations of both CNPC and SINOPEC before the year 2000. On the other side, since state-owned land was subject to the free assignment system before 1990, in consideration of the conservation of the estimation of short-paid land rent of oil monopoly groups, we assume that domestic gasoline stations grow at the rate of 3.67% per year with the year of 1990 as the base period. For instance, provided that the number of SINOPEC's gasoline stations in 1990 was 8,225, by the year 1999, the number would increase to 11,374 at the rate of 3.67% per year. We estimate the quantity of newly-built gasoline stations of CNPC and SINOPEC per year during the period of 1990–2002 with that method, and estimate the area of newly-built gasoline stations according to the average area of gasoline stations of 2,500 m² stipulated in SINOPEC's construction standard for gasoline stations.[3] See Table 9.

During the period 1990–2002, assigned land coexisted with land granted through agreement, and the former decreased year on year, while the latter increased year on year. In 1992, assigned land accounted for 97.2% of the total land supply (Wang Yonghong, 2009), while by 2003, assigned land accounted for one-fourth of land granted through agreement (Research Group of Unirule Institute of Economics, 2011). Based on such

---

[3] It is calculated from the average of areas of gasolines stations of urban type, high-speed type, provincial highway type, and township type stipulated in SINOPEC's construction standard for gasoline stations in 2008, i.e., 2,583 m², while 2,500 m² is taken to be prudent.

Table 9.   Estimation of Quantity of Newly-Built Gasoline Stations of Both CNPC and SINOPEC Per Year (Unit: stations)

Year	1990	1991	1992	1993	1994	1995	1996	1997	1998	1999	2000	2001	2002
CNPC	3,127	115	119	123	128	132	137	142	148	153	5,367	369	879
SINOPEC	8,225	302	313	324	336	348	361	374	388	403	8,885	3,803	−62
Total	11,352	416	432	447	464	481	498	517	536	556	14,252	4,172	817
Area (Unit: 10,000 m^2)	2,838	104	108	112	116	120	125	129	134	139	3,563	1,043	204

Source: The data of SINOPEC during the period of 1999–2002 is from annual reports of SINOPEC over the years; the data of CNPC during the period of 2000–2002 is from annual reports of CNPC over the years; the data of other years are estimated values.

conditions, we have assumed that the proportion of assigned land in the transferred land in that very year decreases progressively from 100% in 1990 at the rate of 12.25%, to the proportion of newly-granted land of 25% by 2002, while the proportion of land granted through agreement in the newly-supplied commercial land every year increases from 0% in 1990 to 75% in 2002. Based on the assumption, we have estimated the average rent of commercial land per year during the period of 1990–2002. See Table 10.

The price of land granted through agreement is calculated by the average price of agreement grant of RMB443/m^2 during the period of 2003–2008 (Research Group of Unirule Institute of Economics, 2011), and calculated by 5% of the price, the annual rent is RMB22.15/m^2. And the annual average rent is the product of rent of agreement grant and the proportion of land granted through agreement in the newly-supplied commercial land.

We have determined that the annual rent of land for gasoline stations constructed by both CNPC and SINOPEC during the period 1990–2002 is RMB9.66/m^2 according to the weighted average of the quantity of newly-built gasoline stations per year in Table 10.

Meanwhile, we have provided the annual rent data of commercial land (with the year 2000 as the base period) according to the data of the fixed-base index number of commercial land from the Ministry of Land and Resources, which is also the market rent of commercial land,

Table 10. Estimation on Average Rent of Land for Gasoline Stations of Both CNPC and SINOPEC Per Year (Unit: RMB/m²)

Year	1990	1991	1992	1993	1994	1995	1996	1997	1998	1999	2000	2001	2002
Proportion of assigned land (in %)	100	89	79	71	63	56	50	45	40	35	31	28	25
Proportion of land granted through agreement (in %)	0	11	21	29	37	44	50	55	60	65	69	72	75
Rent of land granted through agreement	22.15	22.15	22.15	22.15	22.15	22.15	22.15	22.15	22.15	22.15	22.15	22.15	22.15
Annual average rent	0.00	2.42	4.57	6.49	8.20	9.72	11.08	12.28	13.36	14.32	15.17	15.93	16.61

Table 11.   Payable Rent of Land for Gasoline Stations of Both CNPC and SINOPEC Per Year (Unit: RMB/m²)

Year	2003	2004	2005	2006	2007	2008	2009	2010	2011
Fixed base index of commercial land	120	128	134	140	154	156	165	184	202
Land price	4,263	4,547	4,760	4,973	5,471	5,542	5,862	6,537	7,176
Land rent	213	227	238	249	274	277	293	327	359

Table 12.   Estimation on Short-Paid Rent of Land for Gasoline Stations of Both CNPC and SINOPEC[a] (Unit: RMB100 million)

Year	2003	2004	2005	2006	2007	2008	2009	2010	2011
Payable land rent	186	199	208	217	239	242	256	285	313
Paid-in land rent	8.44	8.44	8.44	8.44	8.44	8.44	8.44	8.44	8.44
Short-paid land rent	178	190	199	209	231	234	248	277	305

[a] There exists a gasoline station leasehold relation between SINOPEC Corp. and SINOPEC Group; since the rent collected by the Group is not paid to the state, the quantity of SINOPEC's gasoline stations we counted includes the quantity of gasoline stations that SINOPEC leased from the Group, that is, both SINOPEC Corp. and Sinopec Group are considered as a whole. For details, see annual reports of SINOPEC Corp. over the years.

serving as the payable rent of both CNPC and SINOPEC per year. See Table 11.

Based on the information in Tables 10 and 11, and the information on the area of gasoline stations of both CNPC and SINOPEC before 2003, we have estimated the short-paid land rent of both CNPC and SINOPEC during the period 2003–2011. See Table 12.

According to the estimation, the short-paid rent of land for gasoline stations of both CNPC and SINOPEC during the period 2003–2011 was RMB206.981 billion in total.

(4) *Resource rent*

Oil and natural gas resource taxes, mineral resource compensation fee, mining royalty, and special oil gain levy constitute the resource taxation and fee system in oil and gas industry of China. The resource taxation and fee represent the resource rent collected by owners of resources, and they can be divided into absolute land rent and differential rent. Resource tax, mineral resource compensation fee, and mining royalty belong to absolute land rent and the rent produced from that part shall be included in the cost of products; special oil gain levy refers to the rent collected for the excess portion when crude oil price exceeds a certain amount, and it belongs to differential rent.

In accordance with the *Provisional Regulations of the People's Republic of China on Resource Tax* (《中华人民共和国资源税暂行条例》)promulgated by the State Council in December 1993, the resource tax for crude oil and natural gas adopts quantity-based collection method and the resource tax for crude oil was RMB8–24/ton. From July 1, 2005, with the changes in resource tax rate, the resource tax for crude oil was adjusted to RMB14–30/ton, and the resource tax for natural gas was RMB7–15/kilo cubic meters. On June 1, 2010, the resource tax for crude oil and natural gas in Xinjiang was changed from specific tax to ad-valorem tax, with a rate of 5%. From December 1, 2010, the resource tax for crude oil and natural gas in 12 provinces and cities in the western regions were changed to ad-valorem tax, with a rate of 5%. Afterwards, the ad-valorem collection method for oil and natural gas was popularized in the whole nation. In accordance with the *Decision on Amending the Provisional Regulations of the People's Republic of China on Resource Tax* (《关于修改<中华人民共和国资源税暂行条例>的决定》) of the State Council, it was decided to levy the resource tax for crude oil and natural gas with the ad-valorem collection method on units or individuals extracting crude oil and natural gas in the territory and administered sea area of China, with a tax rate of 5–10%, and that will be implemented from November 1, 2011. Afterwards, in the *Implementing Rules for the Provisional Regulations of the People's Republic of China on Resource Tax* (《中华人民共和国资源税暂行条例实施细则》) promulgated by the State Council, it was stipulated that applicable tax rate for crude oil and natural gas is 5%.

The change in the collection of resource tax for crude oil and natural gas from the volume-based collection method to the ad-valorem collection method is a progress, and with oil resource becoming increasingly scarcer and with the increase in price, the rights and interests of resource owners can be better reflected and guaranteed. However, on the whole, China's resource tax is still on the low side, and if calculated according to the data disclosed in annual reports of CNPC and SINOPEC, the resource tax paid by petroleum industry within the computation period of this report is lower than 1%, significantly lower than the overseas tax rate level of resource tax, and the rights and interests of resource owners are not fully reflected and guaranteed. Although the resource tax rate of 5% began to be exercised from November 2011, it is still obviously lower than the overseas level. Overseas mining royalty is often collected at 10–20% of the output value or output of oil and natural gas and can go up to 50%.

In accordance with the *Administrative Regulations on Collection of Mineral Resource Compensation Fee* (《矿产资源补偿费征收管理规定》), in China, the mineral resource compensation fee is calculated by the formula "Resource Compensation Fee = Sales Revenue of Minerals × Rate of Compensation Fee × Coefficient of Recovery (recovery ratio of oil and gas industry)." The rate of compensation fee applicable to oil and gas industry is 1% and since the recovery ratio is usually less than 1, the mineral resource compensation fee collected on oil and gas industry by China is less than 1% of the sales revenue, significantly lower than the overseas level, as well.

In accordance with the definition of special oil gain levy stipulated in the *Administrative Measures for Collecting Special Oil Gain Levy* (《石油特别收益金征收管理办法》) promulgated by the Ministry of Finance on March 25, 2006 that "the special oil gain levy mention in the *Measures* refers to the gains that the state levies on the excess income portion obtained by oil exploitation enterprises because the sale price of domestic oil exceeds a certain level," special oil gain levy has a basic difference from resource tax and resource compensation fee. The threshold of special oil gain levy is US$40 per barrel and special oil gain levy is collected by five tax rate levels based on price, effective as of March 26, 2006. Afterwards, the Ministry of Finance changed that threshold to US$55 per barrel, effective as of November 1, 2011.

Synthesizing the aforesaid discussion and analysis on the resource tax system of oil and natural gas, the absolute rent for oil and natural gas collected in China is on the low side, so it causes the transfer of lots of resource and wealth, while the allocation of such wealth transfer will lead to low production efficiency, weakening incentive mechanism and rent-seeking behavior.

On the other side, since the special oil gain levy in petroleum industry belongs to the differential rent concept, so for that portion, as long as the special oil gain levy exists and related tax rate is proper, no matter whether the price condition suitable for the collection of special oil gain levy or not (after November 1, 2011, depending on whether the crude oil price exceeds US\$55 per barrel; during other periods, depending on whether the price is higher than US\$40 per barrel), there exists no short-paying issue, for differential rent alone. Therefore, when computing the short-paid resource tax in petroleum industry:

a.   Before March 2006, when special oil gain levy was collected, the short-paid resource tax includes two parts. One part is the difference between the payable resource tax calculated at the standard of 10% (the lower limit of general standard abroad) and the resource tax and resource compensation fee actually paid, for the part that the crude oil price does not exceed the threshold. The other part is the payable special oil gain levy, for the part exceeding the threshold (see Table 13).
b.   After March 2006, when special oil gain levy was collected, the short-paid resource tax only includes the difference between the payable resource tax calculated at the standard of 10% and the resource tax and resource compensation fee actually paid, for the part that the oil price does not exceed the threshold (Table 14).

According to the statistics in the Table 14, during the period 2001–2011, the short-paid resource rent of petroleum industry is RMB307.886 billion, and in consideration of the short-paid land rent, the buyer's monopoly during that period causes welfare transfer and loss of RMB474.716 billion.

Table 13.   Calculation of the First Part Short-Paid Resource Rent

Time	2001	2002	2003	2004	2005
Crude oil output (Unit: 100 million tons)	1.64	1.67	1.70	1.76	1.81
Price (US$/barrel)	22.55	21.67	26.63	30.77	45.18
Short-paid absolute rent (Unit: RMB100 million)	—	—	—	—	112
Short-paid absolute rent (Unit: RMB100 million)	194	190	238	285	361
Total short-paid (Unit: RMB100 million)	194	190	238	285	473

Source: The website of Statistics Bureau; annual reports of CNPC and SINOPEC (2001–2011); the exchange rate data come from the monetary policy performance reports of Central Bank (2001–2011).

Table 14.   Calculation of the Second Part Short-Paid Resource Rent

Year	2006	2007	2008	2009	2010	2011
Crude oil output (Unit: 100 million tons)	1.85	1.86	1.90	1.89	2.03	2.04
Price (US$/barrel)	59.95	65.93	86.23	54.05	73.96	102.30
Short-paid absolute rent (Unit: RMB100 million)	308	309	290	311	301	181

Source: The website of Statistics Bureau; annual reports of CNPC and SINOPEC (2001–2011); the exchange rate data come from the monetary policy performance reports of Central Bank (2001–2011).

3. Welfare Loss and Transfer Caused by the Seller's Monopoly and Increase in Marginal Cost

The seller's monopoly mainly refers to the welfare transfer and loss caused by the higher monopoly prices exercised by the monopoly manufacturers and this part is represented by the area of the light grey rectangle part in the figure. In number, it equals to $(P_1 - P_0)Q_1$. When calculating welfare loss, since the welfare transfer and loss caused by the buyer's monopoly has been calculated in the front part of this report, in order to avoid repetition,[4] in the computation concerning the welfare transfer and

---

[4]We assume that domestic oil companies can, at the same cost, realize the same profit margin as overseas oil companies through market competition.

loss caused by the seller's monopoly, we replace the petroleum products price P_0 in a perfectly competitive market with the average price of petroleum products in overseas mature market. P_1 is the average price of domestic petroleum products during the period of computation; Q_1 is the consumption quantity of domestic petroleum products during the period of computation. Since, in March 2006, the domestic pricing mechanism of petroleum products underwent a great change in that the pricing of petroleum products was changed from the previously direct link with the petroleum products markets of Singapore, Rotterdam, and New York (with a price weight of $6:3:1$) to the indirect link with overseas crude oil market (in principle, Petroleum Products Price = The Crude Oil Market Price of the Three Places + Oil Refining Cost + Cost–Profit Ratio), we only calculate the welfare loss and transfer caused by higher monopoly prices in 2006 and afterwards, that is, after the changes in the pricing mechanism of petroleum products.

On the other side, since the quality standard of petroleum products executed in China and that executed in Europe and US are not uniform, the comparability between the petroleum products prices at home and abroad reduces. Therefore, prior to the price comparison between petroleum products at home and abroad, it is essential to make necessary amendments to the quality standard and price of petroleum products at home. Furthermore, among the executive standards for petroleum products at home, Beijing Standard is the highest level at home, so we choose the petroleum products of Beijing as the subject to be compared with those abroad.

(1) *Comparison on the quality of domestic and overseas oil products.* European petroleum products standard is the leading petroleum products standard in the world, so generally, China consults the European standard when formulating domestic petroleum products standard. For instance, National Standard IV (National Standard V is not issued yet), National Standard III, National Standard II, and National Standard I are equivalent to European Standard IV, European Standard III, European Standard II and European Standard I respectively. But the petroleum products quality standard executed in China is lower than the level of the standard executed in Europe during the same period. For instance, excepting Beijing which

executes a standard equivalent to European Standard V and Shanghai, Guangzhou, and Shenzhen which execute National Standard IV, the rest of the places in China execute National Standard III. At present, 5.7% of the domestic car fleet reach National Standard IV; 48.0% reach National Standard III; 19.8% reach National Standard II; 17.0% only reach National Standard I; the rest almost cannot reach National Standard I (Qu Jian, 2013). The comparison between the petroleum products executive standards and times of implementation of Beijing and those of Europe are shown in Tables 15 and 16.

Within the time interval from 2006 to 2011 that we researched, Europe basically executed standards such as European Standard IV, European Standard V, and European Standard V+, while Beijing basically executed standards such as European Standard III, European Standard IV and executive standards of Beijing were one stage lower than those of Europe in the same period.

(2) *Comparison between petroleum products executive standards of Beijing and Europe.* Since within our investigation period, the petroleum products executive standards of Beijing are Beijing Standard A and Beijing Standard B, which are equivalent to European Standard III and European Standard IV, we make a comparison among related standards.

The quality standards of petroleum products can be measured from two indexes, i.e., the combustion performance and environmental protection performance of fuel oil. The octane number of petroleum products represents the combustion performance of petroleum products; and the environmental protection performance of petroleum products can be compared from the aspects of sulfur content, benzene content, and the content of olefin and benzene.

The higher the octane number is, the better the anti-detonating quality will be. Thus, an engine can adopt a higher compression ratio, which can improve the power of an engine and increase the service efficiency of petroleum products. The international grade of petroleum products is divided on the basis of octane number. For example, No. 92 gasoline and No. 95 gasoline in Beijing represent the octane numbers of gasoline.

Table 15.   Petroleum Products Executive Standards of Beijing and Times of Implementation[b]

Year	1998	2004	2005	2008	2012
Executive standard	National Standard I (European Standard I)	Beijing Standard A (European Standard II)	Beijing Standard B (European Standard III)	Beijing Standard C (European Standard IV)	Beijing Standard V (European Standard V)

[b]The European Standards in the brackets show the equivalent quality standard of the petroleum products of Beijing at the time indicated.

Table 16.   Petroleum Products Executive Standards of Europe and Times of Implementation

Year	1993	1996	2000	2005	2009	2011	2014
Executive standard	European Standard I	European Standard II	European Standard III	European Standard IV	European Standard V	European Standard V+	European Standard VI

As for the environmental protection performance of petroleum products, the most important index is sulfur content. In general, in order to control the carbon monoxide (CO), hydrocarbon compound (HC), nitrogen oxides (NO_x), etc., produced in the combustion of petroleum products in an engine, it is essential to add a three-way catalyst in the air exhausting device of engine, and it can eliminate more than 95% of pollutant emission. But if the sulfur content discharged from the combustion of petroleum products is relatively higher, the three-way catalyst can be poisoned, which will seriously influence the role of three-way catalyst in reducing pollutant emission. The international standard dividing the environmental protection performance of petroleum products is on the basis of sulfur content. Fuel oil is generally divided into the following four types: non-clean fuel oil with sulfur content larger than 500 ppm (one-millionth); clean fuel oil with sulfur content larger than 50 ppm but less than or equal to 500 ppm; super clean fuel oil with sulfur content larger than 10 ppm but less than or equal to 50 ppm; and sulfur-free fuel oil with sulfur content less than or equal to 10 ppm (Liao Jian, 2008).

Apart from sulfur content, the content of benzene generated in the combustion process of petroleum products is the main object that all petroleum products standards strictly control as well. The reason is that benzene is carcinogenic and jeopardizes the public health. Olefin content and aromatics content are pollutant emissions under key monitoring, but less attention is paid to them in comparison with benzene content and sulfur content.

From Tables 17 and 18, it can be known that except for octane number, Beijing Standard B and Beijing Standard C have basically the same criteria for the emission of other pollutants as other standards. The formulation of both the petroleum products emission standard of Beijing and the national emission standard usually take the European standard as the reference, so the petroleum products price of Beijing and that overseas have some comparability.

(3) *Unification of benchmarks of petroleum products prices.* Since the petroleum products standards executed in Beijing and in Europe and US during the same period are different (except 2008–2009 when both

Table 17. **Comparison between Beijing Standards and European Standards of Gasoline**

	European Standard III	Beijing Standard B	European Standard IV	Beijing Standard C
Sulfur content (ppm)	<150	<150	<50	<50
Olefin content (v%)	<18	<18	<18	<25
Aromatics content (v%)	<42	<42	<35	—
Olefin + Benzene content (v%)	—	—	—	<60
Benzene content	<1.0	<1.0	<1.0	<1.0
Octane number (RON)	91/95	90/93/95	91/95	90/93/97

Table 18. **Comparison between Beijing Standards and European Standards of Diesel**

	European Standard III	Beijing Standard B	European Standard IV	Beijing Standard C
Sulfur content (ppm)	<350	<350	<50	<50
Total aromatics (v%)	—	—	—	—
Polycyclic aromatic hydrocarbons (v%)	<11	<11	<11	<11
Cetane number	>51	>47/49/51	>51	>47/49/51

	2006	2007	2008	2009	2010	2011	2012
National standard			National Standard II			National Standard III	
Beijing standard		European Standard III			European Standard IV		

Figure 2. Comparison of Beijing Standards and National Standards of Petroleum Products

Note: The national executive standard refers to the standard executed in regions except Beijing, Shanghai, Guangzhou, and Shenzhen.

Beijing and Europe and US exercise standards equivalent to European Standard IV), a direct comparison will lead to underestimating the oil price of Beijing. Therefore, it is necessary to make revisions to the petroleum products price of Beijing to a certain extent before the price comparison. We have first compared the domestic standards and the Beijing standards of petroleum products. See Figure 2.

From Figure 2, it can be seen that Beijing standards are apparently higher than the national ones during the same period and Beijing standards are closer to the executive standards of Europe and US, which is why we choose the petroleum products price of Beijing as the comparison scale with overseas petroleum products price.

The domestic quality standard of petroleum products has been very slow in upgrading and lagged behind emission standards for vehicles for a long time. For example, the National Stage IV Emission Standard for vehicles was issued in 2005, while the corresponding National Stage IV Standard for gasoline was not launched until 2011, with the execution time having a three-year transition period, which means that petroleum products have time until 2014 to upgrade to the National Stage IV Standard. At present, the National Stage IV Standard for diesel has not been formulated yet, neither has the National Stage V Standard for petroleum products (including gasoline and diesel). That causes our current quality standard of petroleum products to lag far behind the current standards of Europe and US, and is the main reason for the air pollution and haze in China.

Since petroleum products executive standards of Beijing are closer to the foreign level, we make a selective analysis on the comparison between Beijing Standards and European Standards. See Figure 3.

From Figure 3, it can be understood that in order to make the prices of petroleum products in Beijing comparable with those in Europe and US, it is needed to translate the prices of petroleum products during the period from 2006 to 2008 into those under European Standard IV; to translate the prices of petroleum products during the period from 2009 to 2011 into those under European Standard V; and to translate the prices of petroleum products during the period from 2011 to 2012 into those under European Standard V+.

What is of note is that in July 2005, in order to compensate for the rise in oil refining cost incurred by the petroleum products in Beijing

	2006	2007	2008	2009	2010	2011	2012
European standard	European Standard IV				European Standard V		European Standard V+
Beijing standard	European Standard III				European Standard IV		

Figure 3. Petroleum Products Executive Standards of Beijing and Europe and Times of Implementation

executing European Standard III, under the background that the retail prices per ton of gasoline and diesel were uniformly raised by RMB250 and RMB150 respectively, throughout the country (except Beijing), the retail prices per ton of gasoline and diesel in Beijing were raised by RMB460 and RMB340 respectively. That is to say, the retail prices of gasoline and diesel in Beijing were respectively raised by RMB210 and RMB190 when the executive standard upgraded from European Standard II to European Standard III. In October 2008, in order to compensate the rise in oil refining cost caused by the implementation of European Standard IV on petroleum products of Beijing, Beijing individually raised the retail prices per ton of gasoline and diesel by RMB200 and RMB290, respectively. After May 2012, when Beijing began to execute Beijing Standard V (equivalent to European Standard V), the prices were not raised consequently (Generally, the retail prices of petroleum products are raised after a new standard has been executed for half a year.).

In order to made prices comparable, we add RMB200 and RMB290 respectively to the retail prices per ton of gasoline and diesel of Beijing during the period from 2006 to 2008, as necessary compensations to the upgrade from European Standard III to European Standard IV during that period. In the same way, according to the average value of price range raised for two oil quality upgrades in Beijing in 2005 and 2008, we add RMB205 and RMB240 to the retail prices per ton of gasoline and diesel respectively, during the period from 2009 to 2011, as necessary compensations to the upgrade from European Standard IV to European Standard V in Beijing during that period. During the period from 2011 to 2012, besides raising the retail prices per ton of gasoline and diesel by RMB205 and RMB240 respectively, as compensation for the upgrade from European Standard IV to European Standard V, we further raise the retail prices per ton of gasoline and diesel by RMB102 and RMB120 respectively, as compensations for the upgrade from European Standard V to European Standard V+.

(4) *Price comparison of petroleum products and the calculation on the welfare loss caused by the seller's monopoly.* According to the aforesaid principles, on the basis that the quality of petroleum products is revised according to the highest retail prices of petroleum products in Beijing,

previously published by NDRC and Beijing Development and Reform Commission, we have revised the pre-tax price according to the taxation regulations concerning domestic petroleum products again, and obtained the pre-tax price comparison between the petroleum products of Beijing and international petroleum products. The consumption tax standard for petroleum products is that gasoline was RMB0.2/liter, while diesel was RMB0.1/liter before 2009. In the *Circular on the State Council Concerning Implementing the Reform of Petroleum products Prices and Taxation Expenses* promulgated by the State Council in December 2008, it is specified that the standard executed for petroleum products consumption tax is changed to that gasoline is RMB1/liter, and diesel is RMB0.8/liter from January 1, 2009. We calculate the value-added tax standard by the value-added tax rate of 8.62% calculated from the value-added tax amount that oil monopoly enterprises actually borne. Based on the aforesaid standards, we obtain the comparison between pre-tax prices of petroleum products at

Table 19.   Comparison between Gasoline Prices (Pre-tax) at Home and Abroad (Unit: US\$/gallon)

	2006	2007	2008	2009	2010	2011
Belgium	2.26	2.50	3.20	2.21	2.72	3.49
France	2.12	2.36	3.02	2.15	2.59	3.38
Germany	2.15	2.38	2.91	2.15	2.58	3.31
Italy	2.42	2.64	3.34	2.46	2.88	3.66
Netherlands	2.49	2.87	3.51	2.31	2.68	3.44
Britain	2.14	2.35	2.95	1.93	2.46	3.21
USA	2.40	2.62	3.15	2.19	2.63	3.36
Weighted average of foreign countries	2.30	2.57	3.06	2.18	2.64	3.38
China	2.07	2.26	2.80	2.72	3.22	3.92

Note: The foreign price is a weighted average with the population size of all countries as the weight. A consumption tax of RMB1/liter is deducted from the domestic price and the actual value-added tax rate deducted, according to the value-added tax data of SINOPEC from 2005 to 2011, plus imported crude oil added-value tax, is about 8.62%. For detailed discussion, see the appendix of Sub-Report I.
Source: US Energy Information Administration; the information of all previous price adjustments of petroleum products released in the website of the National Development and Reform Commission and the website of Beijing Municipal Development and Reform Commission.

Table 20. Comparison between Diesel Prices (Pre-tax) at Home and Abroad (Unit: US$/gallon)

	2006	2007	2008	2009	2010	2011
Belgium	2.39	2.64	3.82	2.30	2.84	3.75
France	2.26	2.48	3.61	2.17	2.64	3.57
Germany	2.27	2.56	3.63	2.26	2.70	3.64
Italy	2.60	2.79	3.96	2.53	2.95	3.92
Netherlands	2.47	2.77	3.94	2.27	2.67	3.70
Britain	2.31	2.50	3.58	2.15	2.58	3.48
USA	2.22	2.43	3.39	2.00	2.54	3.36
Weighted average of foreign countries	2.33	2.54	3.50	2.13	2.64	3.52
China	2.15	2.44	3.03	2.95	3.51	4.25

Source: US Energy Information Administration; the information of all previous price adjustments of petroleum products released in the website of the National Development and Reform Commission and the website of Beijing Municipal Development and Reform Commission. For the estimation of domestic tax rate, see the note for Table 19.

Table 21. Welfare Loss Caused by Price Monopoly (Unit: RMB 100 million)

	2006	2007	2008	2009	2010	2011
Gasoline	−385	−503	−454	971	1,177	1,169
Diesel	−537	−311	−1,395	2,635	3,179	2,849
Total	−922	−813	−1,850	3,607	4,356	4,018

Source: The sales data of gasoline and diesel come from annual reports on domestic sales data of gasoline and diesel of CNPC and SINOPEC over the years (2006–2011); the sales volumes of gasoline and diesel in SINOPEC petroleum products sales are calculated by 1:2.

home and abroad, after revisions on pre-tax prices (see Tables 19 and 20). The foreign price is a weighted average of refined oil prices of all countries according to the population of all countries, as a reference for the domestic refined oil price. Meanwhile, we have estimated the welfare transfer and loss caused by the existence of margin between petroleum products prices at home and abroad (see Table 21).

Table 22. Summary on Welfare Losses of Oil Monopoly Enterprises over the Years (Unit: RMB100 million)

Year	2001	2002	2003	2004	2005	2006	2007	2008	2009	2010	2011	Subtotal
Net welfare loss	1,405	1,405	1,405	1,405	1,405	1,405	1,405	1,405	1,405	1,405	1,405	15,452
Government subsidy	—	—	—	—	98	58	61	672	11	27	81	1,008
Short-paid financing costs	96	96	130	160	197	200	241	268	383	474	634	2,878
Short-paid land rent	136	140	327	343	355	369	419	421	440	484	524	3,958
Short-paid resource rent	194	190	238	285	473	308	309	290	311	301	181	3,079
Loss caused by monopolistic high prices	—	—	—	—	—	−922	−813	−1,850	3,607	4,356	4,018	8,396
Total	1,830	1,830	2,100	2,192	2,528	1,418	1,621	1,206	6,156	7,046	6,843	34,770

Due to the difference between domestic petroleum products and foreign average price, a total welfare loss of RMB839.6 billion was caused during the period from 2006 to 2011.

The international oil price slumped after the outbreak of 2008 financial crisis, but the domestic petroleum products was indirectly linked with the pricing mechanism that the crude oil prices of three places fluctuate within 4% in 22 consecutive days, so China's petroleum products price was not reduced by the similar margin with the fall in the international oil price. Therefore, from Tables 19 and 20, it can be seen that the difference between the domestic petroleum products and the overseas petroleum products price arose and expanded rapidly after 2008, and the pricing mechanism of petroleum products is one of direct reasons for this part of welfare loss.

Based on the analysis above, we have summarized the sum of welfare losses caused by oil monopoly groups during 2001–2011. See Table 22.

Based on the calculation above, during the period 2001–2011, petroleum industry totally caused welfare loss and transfer of RMB3.477 trillion, accounting for 113% of profits of the whole petroleum industry during that period.

III. Summary

The monopoly mechanism of petroleum industry is the root cause for the aforesaid welfare loss. The pricing mechanism of petroleum products directly determines the welfare loss caused by the seller's monopoly and the Harberger welfare loss also comes from the pricing ability of petroleum enterprises surpassing that of the market. The loss caused by the seller's monopoly is equivalent to subsidies granted by the state on the compensations to be paid by the petroleum industry for production factors, while in a market-oriented system, most of these subsidies can be avoided without affecting the production and sales of oil. Within the computation period, the limit of welfare loss and transfer reaches 113% of the net profits of oil industry during that period.

Appendix: Calculation on Value-added Tax Rate of Oil

I. Oil Value-Added Tax

1. Value-Added Tax in the Retail Price of Petroleum Products

The retail price of petroleum products is a price including tax, so the retail price of petroleum products can be divided into pre-tax price and tax in the structure of composition, while the tax part can be divided into tax included in price and tax excluded in price based on the relation between tax and price. Thus, in general, we can express the retail price of petroleum products as follows: The Retail Price of Petroleum Products = Pre-tax Price + Tax Included in Price + Tax Excluded in Price. In the composition of petroleum products price, consumption tax is the tax included in price and value-added tax is the tax excluded in price.

The nature of value-added tax (tax excluded in price) means that the tax base of value-added tax shall be pre-tax price. However, in reality, the tax base of value-added tax includes not only pre-tax price, but also the tax included in price. So taxes are repeated between the value-added tax and consumption tax of petroleum products to some extent. For instance, if calculated by the current consumption tax standard for gasoline, i.e. RMB1/liter, and value-added tax rate of 17%, when buying 1 liter gasoline, it is equivalent to repeating the collection of value-added tax up to RMB0.17.[5] Thus, we can give the equation on the composition of petroleum products price:

$$P = X + aX + (X + aX) \times 17\%.$$

In the above formula, P is the retail price of petroleum products; X is the pre-tax price of petroleum products; a is the tax rate level of consumption tax.[6]

---

[5] Here, the repetition of tax collection is not further discussed.

[6] Suppose that consumption tax exercises ad-valorem collection.

The consumption tax of petroleum products exercised the standard of RMB0.2/liter for gasoline and RMB0.1/liter for diesel before 2009, but exercised the standard of RMB1/liter for gasoline and RMB0.8/liter for diesel after 2009 (*Circular on the State Council Concerning Implementing the Reform of Petroleum Products Prices and Taxation Expenses*, 2008). In accordance with relevant regulations at home, the value-added tax rate applicable to oil is 17% (*Provisional Regulations of the People's Republic of China on Value-added Tax*, 2008). However, in reality, the actual increment standard of value-added tax is not transparent, that is, CNPC and SINOPEC did not pay the tax in strict accordance with the value-added tax rate of 17%. Thus, it is particularly critical to determine the rate of value-added tax of oil. In this section, we put emphasis on the estimation of value-added tax rate of petroleum products.

2. Obtaining the Pre-Tax Oil Price

Since the petroleum products price includes consumption tax as a tax included in price, and value-added tax as a tax excluded in price, to obtain the pre-tax price from the retail price of petroleum products, the procedures below shall be followed:

(1) Calculate the unit value-added tax amount, and minus it from the retail price. From the equation on the composition of petroleum products price, we can learn that: Value-added Tax = Retail Price × (17/117);

(2) Minus the unit consumption tax from the value calculated from the formula above and then the pre-tax price of petroleum products can be obtained.

II. Calculation on Value-Added Tax Rate of Oil

1. Estimation on Value-Added Tax Rate

For lack of data related to the value-added tax of oil and due to the phenomenon that the value-added tax may be reduced in fact and other reasons, the rate of value-added tax actually borne by petroleum enterprises is not the theoretical rate of 17%, and above all, the value-added tax borne by such enterprises is not transparent, so it is necessary to estimate the value-added tax rate.

Based on the data related to value-added tax in previous annual reports of SINOPEC,[7] we determine that the annual rate of the value-added tax borne by SINOPEC during the period 2005–2011 is 3.5%, far lower than the VAT rate of 17% stipulated in the *Provisional Regulations of the People's Republic of China on Value-Added Tax.* Based on the conservatism principle, we assume that the paid value-added tax disclosed in previous annual reports of SINOPEC is the amount deducting the value-added tax of its import crude oil, because as the provisions stipulate, the formula for computing the tax payable is as follows: Tax Payable = Output Tax Payable for the Period–Input Tax for the Period (*Provisional Regulations of the People's Republic of China on Value-Added Tax*, 2008). Thus, the paid value-added tax in the annual reports of SINOPEC shall be the balance between the value-added tax corresponding to the sales of petroleum products (output tax payable for the period) and the value-added tax corresponding to the import of crude oil (period input tax).

On the other hand, when computing the absolute share of value-added tax in the retail price of petroleum products, it is essential that while the value-added tax corresponding to the value-added part of petroleum products needs to be estimated, the value of crude oil shall also be subject to value-added tax. And it is the sum of both parts above that is the absolute value of value-added tax in petroleum products price. Therefore, we add the value-added tax corresponding to its import crude oil on the basis of related value-added tax provided in annual reports of SINOPEC and then estimate the value-added tax rate of oil.

According to the data in Table 1, the average value of oil value-added tax rates during the period 2005–2011 is 8.62%, which is the level of value-added tax that we finally choose in our report.

---

[7] CNPC and CNOOC do not disclose information related to specific value-added tax.

Table 1.   Calculation on Previous Value-Added Tax Rates of SINOPEC (Unit: RMB100 million)

Year	2005	2006	2007	2008	2009	2010	2011
Value-added tax disclosed in annual reports	302	328	438	502	503	680	806
Value-added tax corresponding to imported crude oil	443	563	631	932	603	915	1,215
Total value-added tax borne on oil	745	891	1,069	1,434	1,106	1,595	2,021
Value-added tax rate (in %)	9.32	8.39	8.87	9.93	8.22	8.34	8.06

Note: Since the data regarding the import price of crude oil disclosed by the General Administration of Customs take 2005 as the initial time, we chose the data during the period from 2005 to 2011 in the table above.
Source: Annual reports of SINOPEC over the years (2005–2011).

2. Test on the Method of Estimation

The value-added tax rate is a value estimated by us. Further, we want to run a simple test on the method for estimating the value-added tax rate through the limited data that we obtained. Zhou Mingchun[8] provides rates of value-added tax borne by CNPC during the period 2000–2003 which are 10.1%, 10.1%, 9.3%, and 9.4% respectively (Zhou Mingchun, 2009) in his *Research on Oil Tax System*. Related data are provided in Table 2.

The data of value-added tax in Table 2 are not from good sources, because the value-added tax tends to decline on the whole.[9] Here, we verify the aforesaid method for estimating annually value-added tax mainly by use of the data of value-added tax of CNPC during the period 2000–2003. The main steps are shown as follows:

We suppose that the ratios of value-added taxes borne by CNPC and SINOPEC are close to the ratios of both companies' annual business volume and their annual sales volume of petroleum products.

---

[8] Zhou Mingchun is Chief Financial Officer of CNPC; for related information, see the website of CNPC: http://www.petrochina.com.cn/PetroChina/gsjs/.
[9] Refer to related contents in the next section.

Table 2.   Value-Added Taxes Borne by CNPC

Year	2000	2001	2002	2003
Value-added tax (Unit: RMB100 million)	248	243	228	285
Burden rate of value-added tax (%)	10.1	10.1	9.3	9.45

Source: *Research on Oil Tax System*, Zhou Mingchun, p. 34.

(1) Calculate the ratio of annual sales volume of petroleum products and the ratio of annual business volume of CNPC and SINOPEC, represented as a and b respectively;

(2) Use the value-added tax disclosed in the annual reports of SINOPEC and the total value-added tax borne by oil in the third line of Table 1 to compute the ratio of value-added taxes borne by CNPC and SINOPEC during the period 2000–2003, represented as c and d respectively;

(3) Compare c and d with a (or b) to see which one is closer to a (or b); and the closer one is the more reasonable is the method for estimation of value-added tax. The detailed data are shown in Table 3.

From related ratios computed in Tables 3 and 4, it can be seen that the value estimated with the method for estimating value-added tax rate including import crude oil value-added tax is closer to the related value-added tax data in the *Research on Oil Tax System* of Zhou Mingchun (0.8 is closer to 0.75 or 0.73 compared with 1.34). This verifies our method for estimating the value-added tax rate to a certain extent.

III. Influences of Trend of Oil Value-Added Tax Rate on Welfare Loss

1. Variation Trend of Oil Value-Added Tax Rate

From the estimated data related to value-added tax in Table 1, it can be found that the rate of value-added tax borne by SINOPEC tends to decline and this can be better expressed through Figure 1.

Table 3.   Ratios of Petroleum Products Sales Volumes and Ratios of Business Volumes of CNPC and SINOPEC over the Years

	Petroleum products sales volume of CNPC (Unit: 10,000 tons)	Petroleum products sales volume of SINOPEC (Unit: 10,000 tons)	Ratio of petroleum products sales volume (*a*)	Business volume of CNPC (Unit: RMB100 million)	Business volume of SINOPEC (Unit: RMB100 million)	Ratio of business volume (*b*)
2000	4,389	6,769	0.65	2,420	3,253	0.74
2001	5,449	6,774	0.80	2,413	3,043	0.79
2002	5,405	7,009	0.77	2,444	3,451	0.71
2003	5,834	7,592	0.77	3,038	4,431	0.69
Annual average value	5,269	7,036	**0.75**	2,579	3,545	**0.73**

Note: All the ratios above are obtained after dividing the values of CNPC by the corresponding values of SINOPEC.
Source: Related annual reports of CNPC (H share) and SINOPEC.

Table 4.   Ratio of Value-Added Tax Borne by CNPC and SINOPEC

	CNPC value-added tax	SINOPEC value-added tax (excluding crude oil part)	Ratio (c)	CNPC value-added tax	SINOPEC value-added tax (excluding crude oil part)	Ratio (d)
2000	248	163	1.52	248	280	0.88
2001	243	240	1.01	243	338	0.72
2002	228	164	1.39	228	273	0.84
2003	285	199	1.43	285	366	0.78
Annual average value	251	192	**1.34**	251	314	**0.80**

Note: All the ratios above are obtained after dividing values of CNPC by the corresponding values of SINOPEC; the price of imported crude oil of SINOPEC adopts the realized price of crude oil in the current year.

Source: Related annual reports of CNPC (H share) and SINOPEC; data related to the value-added tax of CNPC, p. 34, *Research on Oil Tax System, Zhou Mingchun.*

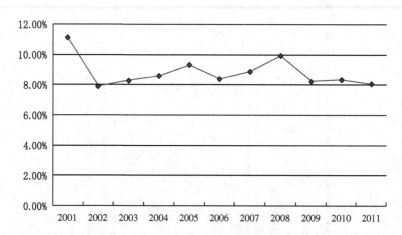

Figure 1.   Variation Trend of Oil Value-Added Tax Rates over the Years
Source: The data of 2005 come from Table 1; the data during the period 2001–2004 are the data estimated by the same method, and prices of import crude oil adopt the realized prices over the year.

Table 5. Influences of Decrease in Value-Added Tax Rate on Welfare Loss (Unit: RMB100 million)

Year	2006	2007	2008	2009	2010	2011
Welfare loss caused when the added-value tax is 7.62%	−827	−708	−1,716	3,763	4,561	4,279
Welfare loss caused when the added-value tax is 8.62%	−922	−813	−1,850	3,607	4,356	4,018
Loss of added value	94	105	134	156	205	262

2. Influences on Welfare Loss

From Figure 1, it can be found that the value-added tax rate tends to decline, and the most direct influence of the decline in value-added tax is the decrease in the value-added taxes paid by CNPC and SINOPEC. If the after-tax retail price remains unchanged, the decrease of value-added tax means the increase in pre-tax price. Measuring the influence of changes in value-added tax rate on welfare from the perspective of the pre-tax price of domestic petroleum products,[10] we have estimated the change in the seller's welfare loss when the value-added tax rate falls by one percentage point (see Table 5).

For the computing method, see related content in Sub-Report I.

From Table 5, it can be found that the fall in value-added tax rate will cause more welfare loss and the amount of welfare loss also increases as the value-added tax rate falls by one percentage point. From the data of 2011, it can be found that if the value-added tax rate falls by one percentage point based on the current level, the whole society will suffer a welfare loss of RMB26.2 billion.

---

[10]Refer to the content related to the seller's welfare loss in Sub-Report I.

Legal Analysis on Administrative Monopoly in Petroleum Industry

I. Law and Policy Foundations of the Current Monopoly System in Petroleum Industry

1. Establishment of Monopoly System in Petroleum Products and Crude Oil Markets and the Related Policy Foundation

The establishment of the current monopoly system in petroleum products and crude oil markets is promoted and facilitated by a series of policies promulgated by various ministries and commissions of the central government on the pretext of developing market economy and reform. On April 5, 1994, the State Council approved and transmitted the *Circular on Suggestions for the Circulation System of Crude Oil and Petroleum Products* (《关于原油、成品油流通体制意见的通知》) (hereinafter referred to as *94 Circular*) of the State Development Planning Commission and the State Economic and Trade Commission, which is the first one of these policies. It was stipulated therein that "the reform on the circulation system of crude oil and petroleum products is an important work for rationalizing oil price and solving the difficulties of crude oil manufacturing enterprises. It is an inevitable requirement for strengthening macro-control, rectifying market order and establishing socialist market economy system, and matters to the overall situation of reform, development, and stability."

Obviously, the primary task of 1994 reform of circulation system is to solve the difficulties of crude oil manufacturing enterprises, among which

100% are actually state-owned enterprises, i.e., the CNPC and SINOPEC at that time. In short, the primary target is to help them "get out of the red." To that end, this policy granted CNPC and SINOPEC a position as quasi-government departments, even a position as the "planning commission" in petroleum industry, so that they could solve problems confronted in development of market economy by means of planned economy. The State Development Planning Commission and the State Economic and Trade Commission gave the State Council suggestions that "China National Petroleum Corporation shall forecast the overall demand and supply of domestic crude oil and put forward proposals on the balance between domestic production of crude oil and import and export crude oil and the program for linking transportation with sale. SINOPEC shall put forward suggestions for the total oil demand of the whole society and the total amount of resources (including crude oil processed domestically, imported crude oil, domestic petroleum products and imported petroleum products). The State Development Planning Commission will, on the basis of gathering and coordinating opinions of all aspects, organize the formulation of the total balance plan, resource allocation plan and import and export plan concerning crude oil and petroleum products. The State Economic and Trade Commission will participate in the formulation of plans and make coordination with departments concerned about issues in the implementation of plans." The State Council approved and transmitted such suggestions.

Moreover, SINOPEC and CNPC also obtained the monopoly on crude oil supply. Because the *94 Circular* explicitly stipulated that "The State Development Planning Commission gives quotas of domestic crude oil and imported crude oil to SINOPEC, while SINOPEC and China National Petroleum Corporation put forward a detailed allocation plan of every oil refinery plant and both are responsible for organization of implementation. China National Petroleum Corporation shall, at the high price specified by the state, provide all its unplanned crude oil, except for oil fields use and reasonable losses, to SINOPEC for processing; the detailed allocation plan of every oil refinery plant shall be negotiated by and between China National Petroleum Corporation and SINOPEC." In addition, the *94 Circular* also stipulated that in order to strengthen the management on crude oil and petroleum products markets, and fully implement the aforesaid reform measures, a crude oil and petroleum products market surveillance group (or office) will be established, and it is in the charge of the State Development Planning Commission and the State Economic and Trade Commission, with departments concerned and CNPC and SINOPEC and other enterprises jointly (for details, see Table 1). For the purpose of maintaining the achievements of the reform on the circulation system in oil industry by the *94 Circular* — a system of monopoly by SINOPEC and CNPC, a series of policies concerning clearing and rectification were introduced in order to further strengthen such a system, on the pretext of maintaining market economy order.

From Table 1, it can be observed that the establishment of China's current petroleum industry monopoly system dates from the 1994 reform of circulation system in petroleum industry and is strengthened on the basis of a succession of policies on clearing and rectification. The main reason why the central government introduced such policies on clearing and rectification is to remove the "mess" caused by the market competition, and help state-owned enterprises caught in business difficulties in the competition. And the means for clearing and rectification is to grant both state-owned enterprises monopoly position by administrative means, replacing competition with monopoly, replacing market supervision with market access approval, so in fact it replaces market economy with planned economy.

2. Legal Foundations of the Monopoly System in Oil Exploitation Sector

Different from the monopoly system of crude oil and petroleum products markets, whose establishment mainly depends on policies, the monopoly on crude oil exploitation sector is guaranteed by laws. Among the various clearing measures listed in the main policy for clearing and rectifying oil industry — Document No. 38, the only one with a higher level law basis is the clearing and rectification pertinent to small oil refineries in exploitation link and the mentioned law is the *Mineral Resources Law of the People's Republic of China*. Paragraph 2 of Article 16 in the *Mineral Resources Law of the People's Republic of China* stipulates that the competent departments authorized by the State Council may conduct

Table 1.   Policies Facilitating the Establishment of Monopoly System in Petroleum Industry

Name of policy	Main content of policy	Reasons
The *Circular on Suggestions for the Circulation System of Crude Oil and Petroleum Products* of SDPC and SETC approved and transmitted by the State Council on April 5, 1994.	(1) The import of crude oil and petroleum products shall be included in the state planning and quota management. The import quotas shall be uniformly examined, approved and issued by SDPC. (2) The SDPC gives quotas of domestic and imported crude oil to SINOPEC, and SINOPEC and CNPC are responsible for related allocation of the quotas. (3) The total resources of domestic petroleum products, import petroleum products and the petroleum products produced by foreign-funded enterprises shall be subject to the state-directed allocation. (4) The factory price and selling price of crude oil and petroleum products shall be subject to planned prices. (5) CNPC and SINOPEC participate in the formulation of related supporting measures and related laws and regulations organized by ministries or commissions concerned.	(1) To rationalize oil price and solve the difficulties of crude oil manufacturing enterprises. (2) To strengthen macro-control, rectify the market order, and establish socialist market economy system.

(Continued)

Table 1. (*Continued*)

Name of policy	Main content of policy	Reasons
The *Suggestions on Clearing and Rectifying Small Refinery Plants and Regulating the Circulation Order of Crude Oil and Petroleum Products* (G.B.F. [1999] No. 38) of SETC and other four departments transmitted by the General Office of the State Council in 1999.	(1) All crude oil produced at home or imported shall be subject to the uniform allocation of the state, and shall not be sold without authorization. (2) All petroleum products shall be handed over to CNPC and SINOPEC for centralized wholesale.	(1) There are too many small oil refineries and their blind development intensifies the contradiction between the overcapacity of refinery industry and the unreasonable layout. (2) They compete with large and medium-sized state-owned oil refining enterprises for crude oil and market and interfere and break the normal production and circulation order of crude oil and petroleum products. (3) Poor efficiency and serious waste of resources. (4) Smuggling. (5) Oil refining with indigenous methods has serious damage. (6) The phenomenon that there are too many wholesale and retail enterprises of petroleum products, and that the redundant construction and poor management of gasoline stations is serious, resulting in disordered circulation channel and market order of petroleum products.

(*Continued*)

Table 1. *(Continued)*

Name of policy	Main content of policy	Reasons
The *Implementation Opinions on Clearing and Rectifying Circulation Enterprises of Petroleum Products and Regulating the Circulation Order of Petroleum Products* promulgated by five ministries or commissions including SETC in 1999 (G.J.M.M.Y. No. 637).	(1) Gasoline, kerosene, and diesel shall be uniformly wholesaled by CNPC and SINOPEC, and no newly-established petroleum products wholesale enterprise will be approved. (2) It strictly controls storage conditions and access examination and approval system of petroleum products. (3) It makes strict conditions and examination and approval system for retail gasoline stations.	To implement the stipulations of Document No. 38.
The *Suggestions on Further Rectifying and Regulating Market Order of Petroleum products* (G.B.F. [2001] Document No. 72) of five ministries or commissions including SETC transmitted by the General Office of the State Council in 2001.	(1) All newly-built gasoline stations in every region shall be constructed by CNPC and SINOPEC as their wholly-owned or holding subsidiaries. (2) Petroleum products shall be subject to the centralized wholesale of CNPC and SINOPEC.	Petroleum products market is disordered because of the blind and redundant construction of gasoline stations and the vicious market competition.

examination of and grant approval to mining of such specified minerals as oil, natural gas, radioactive minerals, and issue mining licenses.

Article 38 of the *Rules for Implementation of the Mineral Resources Law of the People's Republic of China* (《矿产资源法实施细则》) promulgated in 1994, stipulates that "Collectively-owned mining enterprises are permitted to exploit the following mineral resources: (I) Mineral deposits and mineral spots unfit for large or medium-sized mines to be constructed by the state; (II) the designated scattered minerals within the mine areas of the state-owned mining enterprises with the consent from the state-owned mining enterprises and the approval from the competent department in charge at higher level; (III) the remaining ore bodies in the already closed mines which are confirmed by the original department in charge of the mining enterprise that the resumption of mining is safe and will not result in serious environmental consequences; (IV) other mineral resources allowed to be exploited by the collectively-owned mining enterprises pursuant to the state plan." Article 39 of the *Rules* stipulates that "The scope of mineral resources to be exploited by the privately-run mining enterprises shall be decided in reference to the provisions in Article 38." That is to say, privately owned enterprises are treated the same as collectively-owned ones and can only exploit mineral resources which state-owned enterprises are unwilling to exploit.

There have more explicit provisions in the *Regulations of the People's Republic of China on the Exploitation of Onshore Petroleum Resources in Cooperation with Foreign Enterprises* (《中华人民共和国对外合作开采陆上石油资源条例》) and the *Regulations of the People's Republic of China on the Exploitation of Offshore Petroleum Resources in Cooperation with Foreign Enterprises* (《中华人民共和国对外合作开采海洋石油资源条例》). Article 7 in the former and Article 6 in the latter both explicitly stipulate that CNPC and SINOPEC Group (hereinafter referred to as "Chinese Petroleum Companies") shall be responsible for business matters in respect of the exploitation of on-shore petroleum resources in cooperation with foreign enterprises and for negotiating, entering into and implementing contracts for the cooperative exploitation of on-shore petroleum resources with foreign enterprises. China National Petroleum Corporation shall have the exclusive right to engage in petroleum exploration, development, and production in cooperation with foreign enterprises in areas approved by the State Council for exploitation of on-shore petroleum resources in cooperation with foreign enterprises. The China National Offshore Oil Corporation (CNOOC) shall have exclusive and overall responsibility for the work of exploiting offshore petroleum resources in the People's Republic of China in cooperation with foreign enterprises. CNOOC is a state corporation with corporate capacity, it enjoys the exclusive rights of oil exploration, development, production and sales within the foreign cooperation sea area. That is to say, in terms of industry access of oil and mine exploitation, China's related legislations adopt different access standards for enterprises of different ownerships, and the law treatments enjoyed by enterprises discriminate based on the difference in corporate ownership. Such differential treatment give state-owned enterprises a monopoly position in oil exploitation sector.

3. Administrative Licensing System of Market Access Legalized and Strengthened State-Owned Enterprises' Administrative Monopoly in Petroleum Industry

(1) The policies which give CNPC and SINOPEC monopoly position in crude oil and petroleum products markets have no legal basis and obviously violate the *Law of the People's Republic of China for Countering Unfair Competition* (《反不正当竞争法》) promulgated in 1993 (see Table 2). Article 7 of the Law stipulates that "A local government and its subordinate departments shall not abuse their administrative power to force others to buy the goods of the operators designated by them so as to restrict the lawful business activities of other operators ...."

(2) The State Council oversteps the legislative power of the National People's Congress (NPC), legalizes a series of clearing and rectification policies of petroleum industry giving state-owned oil enterprises the monopoly position, and further strengthens the monopoly system.

From the Table 3, it can be observed that the monopoly of state-owned enterprises was legalized by the administrative laws and regulations of the

Table 2.   Legal Basis of Document No. 38

Document No. 38[a]	Legal basis
Ban on oil exploitation sites without mining license.	*Mineral Resources Law of the People's Republic of China*
Ban on oil refining facilities and exploitation sites with indigenous method.	*Decision of the State Council on Some Issues of Environmental Protection* (《国务院关于环境保护若干问题决定》)
Shutdown of small oil refineries.	1. *Circular on the State Council on Exercising Strict Control over Expansion of Oil Refining Capacity* (《国务院关于严格控制扩大炼油能力的通知》) ([1991], No. 54); 2. Not listed in the 1998 national allocation plan of crude oil.
Crude oil (domestic and import) is subject to the unified distribution by SINOPEC and CNPC.	No legal ground or policy basis is mentioned.[b]
Centralized wholesale of petroleum products.	No legal ground or policy basis is mentioned.
Clearing and rectification concerning the retail market of petroleum products.	No legal ground or policy basis is mentioned.
The retail of petroleum products carries out the mode of centralized distribution and chain operation.	

---

[a]The *Suggestions on Clearing and Rectifying Small Refinery Plants and Regulating the Circulation Order of Crude Oil and Refined Oil* (G.B.F. [1999] No. 38) of SETC and other departments transmitted by the General Office of the State Council in 1999.

[b]When explaining the background of the policy, Document No. 38 mentioned six reasons: (1) There are too many small oil refineries and their blind development intensifies the contradiction between the overcapacity of refinery industry and the unreasonable layout. **(2) They compete with large and medium-sized state-owned oil refining enterprises for crude oil and market, and interfere and break the normal production and circulation order of crude oil and petroleum products**. (3) Poor efficiency, and serious waste of resources. (4) Smuggling. (5) Oil refining with indigenous methods has serious damage. (6) The phenomenon that there are too many wholesale and retail enterprises of petroleum products and the redundant construction and poor management of gasoline stations is serious, resulting in disordered circulation channel and market order of petroleum products.

Table 3. Laws, Administrative Laws and Regulations and Administrative Rules Related to Oil Monopoly

	Oil exploitation	Import and export of crude oil and petroleum products	Crude oil market	Petroleum products market
Legalizations of NPC	*Mineral Resources Law* (《矿产资源法》) promulgated in 1996[c]	*Foreign Trade Law of the People's Republic of China* (《对外贸易法》) promulgated in 2004[d]	Section 2, Article 14, *Administrative License Law* (《行政许可法》)	Section 2, Article 14, *Administrative License Law* (《行政许可法》)

(Continued)

[c] Paragraph 2 of Article 16 in the *Mineral Resources Law of the People's Republic of China* stipulates that the competent departments authorized by the State Council may conduct examination of and grant approval to mining of such specified minerals as oil, natural gas, radioactive minerals, and issue mining licenses.

[d] Article 9 of the *Foreign Trade Law* promulgated in 2004 stipulates that "Foreign trade dealers engaged in import and export of goods or technologies shall register with the authority responsible for foreign trade under the State Council or its authorized bodies unless laws, regulations and the authority responsible for foreign trade under the State Council do not so require. The specific measures for registration shall be laid down by the authority responsible for foreign trade under the State Council. Where foreign trade dealers fail to register as required, the Customs authority shall not process the procedures of declaration, examination and release for the imported and exported goods." Article 11 of the *Foreign Trade Law* promulgated in 2004, stipulates that "The State may implement state trading on certain goods. The import and export of the goods subject to state trading shall be operated only by the authorized enterprises unless the state allows the import and export of certain quantities of the goods subject to state trading to be operated by the enterprises without authorization. The lists of the goods subject to state trading and the authorized enterprises shall be determined, adjusted and made public by the authority responsible for foreign trade under the State Council in conjunction with other relevant authorities under the State Council."

Table 3. *(Continued)*

	Oil exploitation	Import and export of crude oil and petroleum products	Crude oil market	Petroleum products market
Administrative Laws and Regulations	*Rules for Implementation of the Mineral Resources Law of the People's Republic of China* (矿产资源法实施细则)[e] in 1994, the *Regulations of the People's Republic of China on the Exploitation of Onshore Petroleum Resources in Cooperation with Foreign Enterprises* (《中华人民共和国对外合作开采陆上石油资源条例》),[f] the *Regulations of the People's Republic of China on the Exploitation of Offshore Petroleum Resources in Cooperation with Foreign Enterprises* (中华人民共和国对外合作开采海洋石油资源条例)[g]	2001, *Regulation on the Administration of the Import and Export of Goods* (《货物进出口管理条例》).[h]	Approval on the operation qualification for the wholesale, storage, and retail of petroleum products, Project 183, No. 412, the State Council.[i]	Approval on the operation qualification for the wholesale, storage, and retail of petroleum products, Project 183, No. 412, the State Council.

(Continued)

[e] Article 38 of the *Rules for Implementation of the Mineral Resources Law of the People's Republic of China* promulgated in 1994 stipulates that collectively-owned mining enterprises are permitted to exploit the following mineral resources: (I) Mineral deposits and mineral spots unfit for large or medium-sized mines to be constructed by the state; (II) the designated scattered minerals within the mine areas of the state-owned mining enterprises with the consent from the state-owned mining enterprises and the approval from the competent department in charge at higher level; (III) the remaining ore bodies in the already closed mines which are confirmed by the original department in charge of the mining

enterprise that the resumption of mining is safe and will not result in serious environmental consequences; (IV) other mineral resources allowed to be exploited by the collectively-owned mining enterprises pursuant to the state plan. Article 39 stipulates that the scope of mineral resources to be exploited by the privately-run mining enterprises shall be decided in reference to the provisions in Article 38.

f Article 7 stipulates that "China National Petroleum Corporation and SINOPEC Group (hereinafter referred to as "Chinese petroleum companies") shall be responsible for business matters in respect of the exploitation of on-shore petroleum resources in cooperation with foreign enterprises, and for negotiating, entering into and implementing contracts for the cooperative exploitation of on-shore petroleum resources with foreign enterprises. China National Petroleum Corporation shall have the exclusive right to engage in petroleum exploration, development, and production in cooperation with foreign enterprises in areas approved by the State Council for exploitation of on-shore petroleum resources in cooperation with foreign enterprises."

g **Article 6 stipulates that** the China National Offshore Oil Corporation (CNOOC) shall have exclusive and overall responsibility for the work of exploiting offshore petroleum resources in the People's Republic of China in cooperation with foreign enterprises. CNOOC is a state corporation with corporate capacity, and it enjoys the exclusive rights of oil exploration, development, production and sales within the foreign cooperation sea area.

h Articles 45–52 of Chapter IV in the *Regulation on the Administration of the Import and Export of Goods* make provisions for state-run trade, and sets a permission for the Ministry of Foreign Trade and Economic Cooperation at that time. In order to prevent special importers from abusing the privilege of state-run trade, Article 52 therein stipulates that "The state-run trade enterprises and the enterprises to engage in designated management shall carry out their business activities under normal commercial conditions, and may not choose providers according to non-commercial considerations, nor may they reject the entrustment of other enterprises or organizations on the basis of non-commercial considerations."

i Five hundred administrative license items retained in the *Decision of the State Council on Establishing Administrative License for the Administrative Examination and Approval Items Really Necessary to be Retained* promulgated on July 1, 2004 according to the provisions of Section 2 of Article 14 in the *Administrative License Law*.

Table 3. *(Continued)*

	Oil exploitation	Import and export of crude oil and petroleum products	Crude oil market	Petroleum products market
Administrative rules		2002, *Interim Methods for Operation and Management on State-Run Trading and Importing of Crude Oils, Petroleum Products and Chemical Fertilizers* (《原油、成品油、化肥国营贸易进出口管理试行办法》)	*Measures for the Administration of the Crude Oil Market* (《原油市场管理办法》)	*Measures for the Administration of the Petroleum Products Market* (《成品油市场管理办法》)

State Council before the *Administrative License Law* was promulgated in 2004, and such administrative laws and regulations shall be cleared after the promulgation of the *Administrative License Law* and the *Legislative Law*. On the contrary, instead of being cleared, they are strengthened through the revisions of laws. For example, the revision of *Foreign Trade Law* (对外贸易法) in 2004 legalized the state-run trade of oil; No. 412 *Decision* of the State Council legalized the licensing system on market access of crude oil and petroleum products without legal basis.[1] Based on the decision of the State Council on retainment of permission, the *Measures for the Administration of the Petroleum Products Market* and the *Measures for the Administration of the Crude Oil Market* promulgated by the Ministry of Commerce in 2006 further strengthened the state-owned monopoly in oil industry (see Table 4).

II. Current Market Access System in Petroleum Industry has no Legality

1. The legal basis for the administrative licensing of Project 183 "approval on the operation qualification for wholesale, storage and retail of petroleum products" in the *Decision of the State Council on Establishing Administrative License for the Administrative Examination and Approval*

---

[1] Project 183 "approval on the operation qualification for wholesale, storage, and retail of petroleum products (the Ministry of Commerce and administrative department in charge of commerce of provincial people's government)" in the *Decision of the State Council on Establishing Administrative License for the Administrative Examination and Approval Items Really Necessary to be Retained* promulgated in 2004. The *Decision* explains that "in accordance with the *Administrative license Law of the People's Republic of China* and the provisions concerning the reforms of administrative approval system, the State Council comprehensively clears items requiring administrative approval of all its subordinate departments. Items requiring administrative approval established by laws and administrative laws and regulations shall continue their effectiveness according to law; for the items requiring administrative approval established by normative documents other than laws and administrative laws and regulations but necessary to be retained and meeting provisions of Article 12 of the *Administrative license Law of the People's Republic of China*, a total of 500 such items are hereby decided to be retained with administrative license established according to provisions of Article 14 of the *Administrative license Law of the People's Republic of China*."

Table 4.   Evolution Relationship between Current Licensing Systems and Document No. 38

	1999, Document No. 637[a]	2001 G.B.F. No. 72[b]	Measures for the Administration of the Petroleum Products Market promulgated in 2006	2008 F.G.J.M. [2008] No. 602[c]
Higher level law and policy basis	1999, Document No. 38	(September 28, 2001 G.B.F. [2001] No. 72) *Decision of the State Council on Rectifying and Regulating the Order of the Market Economy* (《国务院关于整顿和规范市场经济秩序的决定》) of the State Council	*Decision of the State Council on Establishing Administrative License for the Administrative Examination and Approval Items Really Necessary to be Retained* (《国务院对需要保留的行政审批项目设定行政许可的决定》) promulgated in 2004.	No higher level law or policy is mentioned.
Wholesale of petroleum products	1. The wholesale of domestic petroleum products is monopolized by SINOPEC and CNPC; 2. An enterprise engaging in the wholesale of petroleum products must meet the following conditions:	Petroleum products are subject to the centralized wholesale of CNPC and SINOPEC. The layout plan of wholesale enterprises of petroleum products	Entry conditions: 1. It must have secular and stable supply channels of petroleum products; (a) it must have an oil refining enterprise which observes the industrial policies of the state, is capable of processing crude oil of at least 1 million tons at one time,	Speeding up the reorganization of private petroleum products enterprises. 1. CNPC and SINOPEC shall speed up the reorganization work of private wholesale

(Continued)

[a] Circular on Printing the *Implementation Opinions on Clearing and Rectifying Circulation Enterprises of Petroleum Products and Regulating the Circulation Order of Petroleum Products*.

[b] Circular concerning *Suggestions on Further Rectifying and Standardizing the Market Order of Petroleum Products*.

[c] Circular of NDRC and the Ministry of Commerce on Issues Related to Operation of Private Petroleum Products Enterprises.

Table 4. *(Continued)*

1999, Document No. 637	Measures for the Administration of the Petroleum Products Market promulgated in 2006 2001 G.B.F. No. 72	2008 F.G.J.M. [2008] No. 602
(a) it shall be approved by competent department of petroleum products market at the provincial level or above, and shall be registered by law; (b) its registered capital shall not be less than RMB5 million; (c) it shall have wholly-owned or holding petroleum products depots with a capacity not less than 4,000 cubic meters; (d) the construction of oil depots shall be approved by provincial-level people's government or the department designated by provincial-level people's government,	throughout the country is formulated by both groups, and shall be examined and approved by the State Economic and Trade Commission. and whose annual productive capacity of gasoline and diesel oil which observe the product quality standards of the state is at least 500,000 tons; or (b) it must be an import enterprise qualified for petroleum products import; or (c) it has signed a petroleum products supply agreement for at least 1 year in consistence with its business scale with an enterprise qualified for wholesale of petroleum products with at least 200,000 tons of annual business volume of petroleum products; or (d) it has signed a petroleum products supply agreement for at least 1 year in consistence with its business scale with an import enterprise whose annual import volume of petroleum products is at least 100,000 tons;	enterprises by means of acquisition, shareholding and joint operation, in continuous accordance with the enterprise development strategy and market layout of petroleum products. 2. Private wholesale enterprises shall, on the principle of fairness, reciprocity, and negotiation, carry out reorganization and combination, adjust enterprise structure and improve services and the concentration of

(Continued)

Table 4. (*Continued*)

1999, Document No. 637	2001 G.B.F. No. 72	Measures for the Administration of the Petroleum Products Market promulgated in 2006	2008 F.G.J.M. [2008] No. 602
and shall meet the *Code for Design of Oil Depot* (G.B.F. 74–84); (e) it shall have receiving and unloading conditions such as petroleum products pipeline, railway special line or water transport terminal for petroleum products; (f) it shall have sound management systems and must have qualified professionals and technicians with regards to the inspection, metrology, storage and fire safety.		2. The applicant must be a qualified Chinese enterprise legal person with a registered capital of at least RMB30 million; 3. Where the applicant is a branch of a Chinese enterprise person, its legal person must have the qualification for engaging in the wholesale of petroleum products; 4. It must have a petroleum products depot with a capacity of at least 10,000 cubic meters, whose construction shall abide by the local urban and rural planning and oil depot layout planning; and shall be checked accepted by the related departments in charge of state land and resources, planning and construction, safety and supervision, public security and firefighting, environmental protection, meteorology and quality inspection, etc.;	petroleum products operation. 3. CNPC and SINOPEC shall be responsible for supplying oil to private wholesale enterprises which have signed a long-term supply agreement. 4. The petroleum products produced by local oil refineries (except those with wholesale qualification) shall strictly observe the provisions of delivering to CNPC and SINOPEC for centralized wholesale.

(*Continued*)

Table 4. *(Continued)*

	1999, Document No. 637	2001 G.B.F. No. 72	Measures for the Administration of the Petroleum Products Market promulgated in 2006	2008 F.G.J.M. [2008] No. 602
			5. It must be equipped with such facilities to unload petroleum products as conduit pipes, railway special lines, highway transport vehicles or the ports for transporting petroleum products over water whose capacity shall be at least 10,000 tons.	
Import and domestic circulation of petroleum products	It shall be determined by the State Economic and Trade Commission and the Ministry of Foreign Trade and Economic Cooperation separately.			
Storage of petroleum products	1. Entry conditions: (a) it shall be registered by law; (b) the construction of oil depots shall be approved by provincial-level people's government or the department designated by provincial-level	It is essential to strictly control the newly-built and expanded storage facilities of petroleum products; those necessary to be constructed shall be approved by provincial-level economic and trade	Entry conditions: 1. It shall have a petroleum products depot with a capacity of at least 10,000 cubic meters, whose construction shall abide by the local urban and rural planning and oil depot layout planning and shall be checked and accepted by the related departments in charge of state land and	

(Continued)

Table 4. *(Continued)*

1999, Document No. 637	2001 G.B.F. No. 72	Measures for the Administration of the Petroleum Products Market promulgated in 2006	2008 F.G.J.M. [2008] No. 602
people's government, and shall meet the *Code for Design of Oil Depot* (G.B.J. 74-84); (c) the storage tank and unloading conditions shall meet the current national standards and the regulation of metrological verification, and shall meet the requirements of safety and environmental protection; (d) it shall have sound management systems and must have qualified professionals and technicians with regards to the inspection, metrology, storage and fire safety.	commission on the principles of being helpful to orderly competition and rational distribution, and shall be submitted to the State Economic and Trade Commission for record	resources, planning and construction, safety and supervision, public security and firefighting, environmental protection, meteorology and quality inspection, etc.; 2. The applicant must be a qualified Chinese enterprise legal person with a registered capital of at least RMB10 million; 3. It must be equipped with such facilities to unload petroleum products as conduit pipe, railway special line, highway transport vehicles or ports for transporting petroleum products over water whose capacity shall be at least 10,000 tons; 4. Where the applicant is a branch of a Chinese enterprise legal person, its legal person must be qualified to engage in the storage of petroleum products.	

(Continued)

Table 4. (*Continued*)

	1999, Document No. 637	2001 G.B.F. No. 72	Measures for the Administration of the Petroleum Products Market promulgated in 2006	2008 F.G.J.M. [2008] No. 602
	2. Strictly control the newly-built and expansion projects.			Reasonably supply oil to private petroleum products enterprises:
Gasoline station	1. Entry conditions: (a) it shall be approved by prefecture-level economic and trade commission, and shall be registered by law; (b) it shall have stable channels to supply petroleum products, and have signed an oil supply agreement with enterprises qualified for wholesale of petroleum products; (c) gasoline stations shall meet the national standard *Code for Design of Small Oil*	Newly-built gasoline stations in every area shall be subject to the uniform wholly-owned or holding construction of CNPC and SINOPEC.	1. It must abide by the local development planning for the gasoline station industry and the technical specifications and requirements; 2. It must have secular and stable channels to supply petroleum products, and have signed a petroleum products supply agreement for at least 3 years in line with its business scale with an enterprise qualified to engage in the wholesale business of petroleum products; 3. The design and construction of the gasoline station must abide by the related standards of the state and have been checked by the related	(1) CNPC and SINOPEC shall be responsible for supplying oil to private retail enterprises signing a long-term supply agreement with them. The supply and demand parties shall strictly perform articles of the agreement.

(*Continued*)

Table 4. *(Continued)*

1999, Document No. 637	2001 G.B.F. No. 72	Measures for the Administration of the Petroleum Products Market promulgated in 2006	2008 F.G.J.M. [2008] No. 602
Storage Depots and Service Stations (GB50156-92) and requirements of related technical specifications; (d) it shall meet the requirements of the over-all planning of the local government, and the operation facilities shall meet the regulations of the current national standards and the regulation of metrological verification, and meet the regulations of firefighting and environmental protec-tion, with complete approval procedures;		departments responsible for state land and resources, planning and construction, safety and supervision, public security and firefighting, envi-ronmental protection, meteorology and quality inspection, etc.; 4. It must have professional and technical personnel with regards to the inspection, metrology, storage and firefighting and safe production of petroleum products; 5. The marine gasoline stations (vessels) and land-based gasoline stations (sites) for the supply of petroleum products used for vessels must observe, in addition to the above-mentioned provisions, the related provisions on ports, water transportation safety and prevention and control of water pollution, etc.;	(2) CNPC and SINOPEC may correspondingly reduce the quantity of supply to private wholesale enter-prises that sell oil to buyers other than their subordinate gasoline stations and the retail gaso-line stations that have signed contract with them; (3) It shall have strict control over the construction of retail gasoline stations.

(Continued)

Table 4. *(Continued)*

1999, Document No. 637	2001 G.B.F. No. 72	Measures for the Administration of the Petroleum Products Market promulgated in 2006	2008 F.G.J.M. [2008] No. 602
(e) it shall have professionals and technicians with regards to fire safety and petroleum products; (f) it shall have sound financial systems and other management systems; (g) it shall meet the conditions for installation of tax-control devices or the use of tax-control fuel dispensers.		6. As for the gasoline stations built in rural areas and only sell diesel, the administrative departments of commerce of the provincial people's government shall institute specific conditions for their establishment under this measures.	Departments in charge of commerce in every province, municipality, and autonomous region shall strictly approve newly-built gasoline stations according to the development planning of the gasoline stations in every region and provisions of related technical specifications.

Note: From 1999, Document No. 38, the 2001 Document No. 72, the *Measures for the Administration of the Crude Oil Market* and the *Measures for the Administration of the Petroleum Products Market* promulgated by the Ministry of Commerce in 2006, to 2008 Document No. 602 promulgated by NDRC and other departments, no matter whether policy documents or administrative rules, they all exactly followed the provisions and spirit of Document No. 38, and continued to strengthen the oil monopoly system.

Items Really Necessary to be Retained (《国务院对确需保留的行政审批项目设定行政许可的决定》) promulgated in 2004 is no longer in existence.

(1) The premise for the administrative licenses retained is that they must meet the terms and scope for setting administrative license stipulated in the Article 12 of *Administrative License Law*, while Decision No. 412 did not give any explanation on the necessity of retainment.

(2) The administrative licenses retained in accordance with Article 14 of the *Administrative License Law* (《行政许可法》) are temporary. Temporary administrative licenses can become regular through legislation of NPC or be cancelled in the event of no use. Such administrative licenses have so far been retained for more than 8 years, but the State Council has neither submitted to NPC for legislation, nor made any explicit explanation on retaining them or not, so they are very likely to become permanent.

2. Terms Regarding the Establishment of Administrative License on Market Access of Petroleum Industry is Discriminatory and Illegal.

(1) The *Rules for Implementation of the Mineral Resources Law* (《矿产资源法实施细则》) makes differential treatment toward enterprises of different ownerships, so it is discriminatory and illegal. It violates the basic principle of fair competition of market economy, so it is illegal.

(2) The state-run trade in the context of import and export is not equal to the monopoly trade of state-owned enterprises concerning the import and export of crude oil and petroleum products. According to Article 17 of GATT I994, State Trading Enterprises (STEs) refers to "enterprises that engage in the trade involving import and export with the exclusive or special authority, in form or in fact, granted by the government." Some scholars construed it as a kind of governmental, or quasi-governmental, enterprises that are guaranteed to enjoy special protection and/or privilege by their home government. Article 4 of the *Interim Methods for Operation and Management on State-Run Trading and Importing of Crude Oils, Petroleum Products and*

Chemical Fertilizers (《原油、成品油、化肥国营贸易进出口管理试行办法》) promulgated by the Ministry of Commerce in 2002, also explicitly stipulates that "state trading enterprises are the enterprises or institutions which obtain the import operation right of some state trade and management, as chartered by the state." Therefore, **state trade is not equal to monopoly trade of state-owned enterprises. The monopoly position on the import of crude oil and petroleum products granted to state-owned enterprises is based on government's policy documents, but these documents have no legal grounds.**

3. The current access terms on the wholesale, storage and retail of crude oil and petroleum products markets follow the policies of the former State Economic and Trade Commission, and such terms are tailor-made for the state-owned enterprises that have already obtained monopoly position and are impossible to meet for potential entrants of the market. Therefore, such access licensing systems are purely discriminatory and unfair. They not only obviously violate the 36 suggestions on developing non-public economy issued by the central government, including the new 36 suggestions, but also violate the policy of the ruling party to make unswerving efforts to encourage, support and guide the development of the non-public sector of the economy while unswervingly consolidating and developing the public sector of the economy and to allow fair competition between the two sectors, so they are illegal.

III. Solutions

1. According to Article 20 of the *Administrative License Law*, the Adminstrative Licenses Losing Legality Can Be Cleared and Cancelled.

Article 20 of the Administrative License Law stipulates that "The establishment organ of the administrative license shall periodically evaluate the administrative license it sets; if it considers that an already established administrative license can be solved by any of the methods listed in Article 13 of this Law, it shall modify the requirements for the establishment of the administrative license or abolish it in time. The executive organ of an administrative license shall evaluate the information of the implementation of the administrative license and necessity of its existence and shall report the relevant opinions to the establishing organ of the administrative license. The citizens, legal person or other institutions may put forward opinions and suggestions to the establishment organ and executive organ about the establishment and implementation of the administrative license."

On the occasion that the new administration announces to carry out further clean-up on unreasonable administrative licenses, China Chamber of Commerce for Petroleum Industry (CCCPI) as a non-governmental organization representing private petroleum enterprises may apply to the State Council for including the administrative licenses (market access limitations) that violate related policies including the 36 suggestions on developing non-public economy in the scope of administrative license to be cleared up by the new administration.

2. The Establishment of Such License Policy Documents Completely Contradicted the 36 Suggestions on Developing Non-Public Economy of the State Council, So It Is Possible to Submit to the State Council to Formulate Implementation Rules of the 36 Suggestions, and Clear Such Policy Documents and Propose New Legislations to NPC to Reform-Related Administrative Licenses.

In the *Several Suggestions of the State Council on Encouraging and Guiding the Development of Individual and Private Economy and Other Non-Public Sectors of the Economy* (《国务院关于鼓励与引导个体私营等非公有制经济发展的若干意见》) promulgated in 2005, it is stated "to relax the market control over non-public sectors of economy" and the specific policy measures, include "to implement the principle of equal access and fair treatment." It is required that "related national departments and local people's departments shall complete the clearing and amend laws, regulations, and policies on restricting the market access of non-public sectors of the economy as soon as possible." And it is explicitly stipulated that "non-public capital is allowed to enter the monopolized industries and fields." "We will accelerate the reform of monopolized industries and further introduce market and competitive mechanisms to such industries and fields as power, telecommunications, railway, civil aviation, and oil."

It is stipulated in the *Several Suggestions of the State Council on Encouraging and Guiding the Healthy Development of Private Investment* (《国务院关于鼓励和引导民间投资健康发展的若干意见》)   (G.F. [2010] No. 13) promulgated in 2010 that "to be standard in setting the investment access standard threshold, to create an equal competition and access market environment. The market access standard and the preferential and supportive policies shall be open and transparent; various types of investment entity shall be equally treated, and no additional conditions shall be individually set for private capitals." And it is explicitly stipulated that private capitals are encouraged to participate in the construction of oil and natural gas. And private capitals are encouraged to enter the field of oil and natural gas exploration and development, and to carry out cooperation with state-owned petroleum enterprises in oil and natural gas exploration and development. Therefore, it is required that "Regulations, policies and provisions against the development of private investment shall be cleared and amended, so as to effectively protect the legal rights of private investment, cultivate, and maintain the investment environment of equal competition. When formulating the laws, regulations and policies concerning private investment, it is essential to listen to the opinions and suggestions of related chambers of commerce and private enterprises, so as to fully reflect the reasonable requirements of private enterprises."

Although policies have been promulgated for many years, related departments are still negative toward the relaxation of petroleum industry market access and take no action in that aspect. Thus, it is essential to submit to the State Council an appeal to clear the related policy documents.

3. To Ask Anti-monopoly Law Enforcement Agencies to Carry Out Anti-monopoly Investigation on the State-owned Monopoly in Petroleum Industry, and to Make It Clear That State-Owned Monopoly in Petroleum Industry Does Not Enjoy the Exemption Stipulated in Article 7 of the *Anti-Monopoly Law.*

Article 7 of the *Anti-Monopoly Law* stipulates that "The state shall protect the lawful business activities of those Operators from industries of vital economic or national security importance which hold positions of control in the state-owned economy or industries which are specialized providers of particular products or services, regulating the business activities of such. Operators as well as the prices of their products and services pursuant to law and safeguarding the interests of consumers while at the same time promoting technological advance." The State Council and all ministries and commissions have always granted state-owned enterprises monopoly position at the excuse that petroleum industry concerns national economy and the people's livelihood or national security. But facts prove that such assumptions are not established. Therefore, state-owned enterprises in petroleum industry cannot enjoy the exemption stipulated in Article 7 of the *Anti-Monopoly Law*.

4. To Promote Private Enterprises and Consumers to File Judicial Litigations against State-owned Monopoly Enterprises' Abuse of Their Monopoly Position in Petroleum Industry, to Disclose the Inefficiency and Unfairness Caused by State-Owned Monopoly in Petroleum Industry and Promote the Market Reform in Petroleum Industry.

To say the least, even if state-owned monopoly enterprises in oil industry can invoke Section 1 of Article 7 in the *Anti-Monopoly Law* for pleading, Section 2 thereof, also stipulates that the operators referred to in the preceding paragraph shall conduct business operations lawfully and in good faith, imposing strict self-regulation and accepting the supervision of the general public. They shall not use their positions of control or their status as exclusive provider to harm consumers' interests.

Therefore, it is feasible to submit the research results of this project to public law groups and rights protection lawyers engaging in protection of consumers' legal rights, promote and support them to file anti-monopoly civil actions against state-owned oil monopoly enterprises on behalf of consumers, educate the general public, and promote the anti-monopoly reform in petroleum industry.

References

Ade Crooks: "Analysis: Politics, science and technology rebuild the oil gas outlook in America," *Financial Times*, May 21, 2013, source: http://www.ftchinese.com/story/001050516#s=o.

Ajay Makan (2013). "Prediction about IEA raising petroleum production dramatically in North America," *Financial Times*, May 5, 2013, source: http://www.ftchinese.com/story/001050432.

Blog of East Money: "Brief introduction of world petroleum pricing system," April 27, 2009, source: http://blog.eastmoney.com/fzqhgxq/blog_120143053.html.

BP (2012). *BP Statistical Yearbook of World Energy in 2012*.

BP (2013). *BP World Energy Outlook in 2030*.

BP (June 2012). *BP World Energy Yearbook*.

BP (June 2012). *Statistical Yearbook of World Energy*, bp.com/statistical review.

Business Counselor's Office of Chinese Embassy in Russia (2011d): "Russian Anti-monopoly Bureau suggests lower the excise tax on gasoline as well as the other petroleum products," April 22, 2011, source: http://ru.mofcom.gov.cn/aarticle/jmxw/201104/20110407512516.html.

Caijing (2012). "Invisible barrier: The hardship behind monopoly reform in petroleum industry in China,"

CCTV.com (August 19, 2003). "North of Shaanxi Oil Field: Private investment withdrew in embarrassment," source: http://www.cctv.com/financial/20030820/100297.shtml.

Chemlogo Net (May 25, 2011). "American CFTC accused three companies of manipulating crude oil price," source: http://www.hxchem.net/index.php/D/newsdetail55427.html.

Chen, Desheng and Lei Jiasu: "Comparison of strategic petroleum reserve system among France, Germany, America and Japan and reference for China," *Pacific Journal*, the 2nd issue in 2006.

Chen, Li: "Research on Regulation Reform of Oil and Gas Industry in China," thesis for master's degree of Fudan University, April 20, 2007.

Chi, Qingjia: "China issued *Antimonopoly Act* and made European and American transnational enterprises worried," *Elite Reference*, August 6, 2008, source: http://news.ifeng.com/opinion/detail_2008_08/06/1318464_0.shtml.

工商联石油业商会上书商务部：建议成立石油交易平台. China Chamber of Commerce for Petroleum Industry Appeals to the Ministry of Commerce (November 30, 2011): Proposal on Establishing a Trading Platform for Oil, source: http://www.022net.com/2010/11-30/423653403281271.html.

2013 年 2 月中国石油化工行业月度分析报告，中商情报网. Monthly Analysis of China's Oil and Chemical Industry (February, 2013), China Competition Information Center (March 05, 2013), source: http://www.askci.com/news/201303/05/152127179863772.shtml.

China News Network: "Russian Anti-monopoly Bureau punished Rosneft by 5.3 billion roubles," October 28, 2009, source: http://news.qq.com/a/2009 1028/001281.htm.

China Think Tank for Strategy: "America started to import petroleum from surrounding countries again," *China Business News*, July 11, 2011.

China-consulting.cn: "Development status of major Russian oil gas companies," source: http://www.china-consulting.cn/article/html/2011/0124/675408.php.

Chnvc.com (October 11, 2010). "History of crude oil price," source: http://210.177.73.246/news-189.html.

CNPC News Center (August 14, 2009). "America will severely punish oil market manipulating behaviors," source: http://news.cnpc.com.cn/system/2009/08/14/001252073.shtml.

CNPC News Center (August 20, 2012). "American government is considering releasing petroleum reserve to stabilize oil prices," source: http://news.cnpc.com.cn/system/2012/08/20/001388728.shtml.

CNPC News Center (May 22, 2007): "Foreign petroleum reserve systems," source: http://center.cnpc.com.cn/bk/system/2007/05/22/001094768.shtml.

Commercial Department in Chinese Embassy in Singapore (January 11, 2012): "Analysis of key industries in China invested by Singapore during the 12th Five-Year Plan," source: http://sg.mofcom.gov.cn/article/yuyan/201201/20120107923070.shtml.

Cui, Shoujun: "Shale gas revolution drives the adjustment of world energy structure," *Oriental Morning Post*, the 010 edition on March 19, 2013.

Daniel, Yergin: *Petroleum, Power and Money*, Xinhua Publishing House, 1992.

Daniel, Yergin: *Seek: Energy, Safety and Rebuild Modern World*, Penguin Press, 2011.

Daqing Daily (multimedia digital edition) (July 28, 2012). "The rankings of the largest 25 global petroleum companies are released," *Daqing Daily* (multimedia digital edition).

Dictated by Yue Changtai and sorted out by Wang tao and Feng jie: "How does environmental protection movement change from resistance to negotiation? Trilateral Committee: The "window" beyond the law," *Southern Weekend*, November 29, 2012, source: http://www.infzm.com/content/83318.

Dong, Shizhuang: "Petroleum Economy in Singapore," *Petroleum Enterprise Management*, the 10th issue in 1995.

Douglass C. North, *Structure and Transition in Economic History*, Shanghai Sanlian Bookstore, Shanghai Peoples Publishing House, in 1994.

Du, Dongya: "Comparative study on Chinese and foreign legal system," *China Petroleum and Chemical Industry*, the 4th issue in 2005.

Economic and Commercial Counselor's Office of Chinese Embassy in Russia (2011a): "More than ten areas in Russia are suffering oil shortages," April 28, 2011, source: http://ru.mofcom.gov.cn/aarticle/jmxw/201104/20110407523184.html.

Economic and Commercial Counselor's Office in Chinese Embassy in Russia (2011b): "Russian Department of Energy will propose the suggestion about oil exploitation permission to the government within two months," July 14, 2011, source: http://ru.mofcom.gov.cn/aarticle/jmxw/201107/20110707646551.html.

Economic and Commercial Counselor's Office of Chinese Embassy in Russia (2011c): "Russian government will offer VAT exemption to the oil export to customs union states," November 2, 2011, source: http://ru.mofcom.gov.cn/aarticle/jmxw/201111/20111107811135.html.

Economic and Commercial Counselor's Office of Chinese Embassy in Russia (2011e): "Russian government will cancel the oil export preferential duty on some oil-producing regions since May 1," May 6, 2011, source: http://ru.mofcom.gov.cn/aarticle/jmxw/201105/20110507535191.html.

Economic and Commercial Counselor's Office of Chinese Embassy in Russia (2012a): "Russian government will restrict state-owned companies from buying new assets," November 7, 2012, source: http://ru.mofcom.gov.cn/aarticle/jmxw/201211/20121108421781.html.

Economic and Commercial Counselor's Office of Chinese Embassy in Russia (2012b): "Russian government will restart petroleum reserve fund next year," March 28, 2012, source: http://ru.mofcom.gov.cn/aarticle/jmxw/201203/20120308040582.html.

Economic and Commercial Counselor's Office of Chinese Embassy in Russia (2012c): "It is hopeful for Russian government to permit private enterprises exploiting offshore oilfields in 2013," October 19, 2012, source: http://ru.mofcom.gov.cn/aarticle/jmxw/201210/20121008391907.html.

Economic and Commercial Counselor's Office of Chinese Embassy in Russia (2012e): "Russian government extended the grace period of oil and mineral resources royalty tax in Siberia," September 25, 2012, source: http://ru.mofcom.gov.cn/aarticle/jmxw/201209/20120908358550.html.

Economic and Commercial Counselor's Office of Chinese Embassy in Russia (2012d): "Russian government will lower petroleum export tax since January 1," January 5, 2012, source: http://ru.mofcom.gov.cn/aarticle/jmxw/201201/20120107915354.html.

Economic and Commercial Counselor's Office of Chinese Embassy in Singapore (April 20, 2007): "Brief introduction of import and export and transship cargo in Singapore," source: http://sg.mofcom.gov.cn/article/maoyi/laogong/200704/20070404594042.shtml.

Economic and Commercial Counselor's Office of Chinese Embassy in Singapore (February 18, 2009): "Provisions about tax administration on import commodities in Singapore," source: http://sg.mofcom.gov.cn/article/maoyi/laogong/200902/20090206050376.shtml.

Economic and Commercial Counselor's Office of Chinese Embassy in Singapore (May 19, 2010). "Information on Singapore's efforts in developing into an international trade center," source: http://sg.mofcom.gov.cn/article/yuyan/201005/20100506922140.shtml.

EIA (2012a). "Petroleum & Other Liquids — Number and Capacity of Petroleum Refineries," source: http://www.eia.gov/dnav/pet/pet_pnp_cap1_dcu_nus_a.htm.

EIA (2012b): "Japan—Background," June 4, 2012, source: http://www.eia.gov/countries/cab.cfm?fips=JA.

EIA (2013). "Markets & Finance — FRS Respondent Companies," source: http://www.eia.gov/emeu/finance/page1b.html.

EIA (2013a). "India—Overview," March 18, 2013, source: http://www.eia.gov/countries/cab.cfm?fips=IN.

EIA (2013b). "Singapore—Country Analysis Brief Overview," February 12, 2013, source: http://www.eia.gov/countries/country-data.cfm?fips=SN.

EIA (2013c). "Singapore—Overview," March 12, 2013, source: http://www.eia.gov/countries/cab.cfm?fips=SN.

Exxon Mobil (2011). *Energy Outlook in 2040.*

Fan, Qing and Zhuang Qingda: "Study on Taiwan fishery oil subsidy policy and policy implication of Vietnamese fishery department," *Paper Announcement Campaign of Taiwan Aquaculture Society in 2010*, 2010.

Feng, Lianyong, *International Petroleum Economics*, Petroleum Industry Press, 2009.

Feng, Lianyong and Chen Daen: *International Petroleum Economics*, Petroleum Industry Press, 2009.

Feng, Shi: "[Overseas Petroleum Enterprises] Road of tax reform of petroleum products in India," *Gas Station Service Network*, September 2, 2009, source: http://www.jyz.com.cn/zz/ShowArticle.asp?ArticleID=123788.

Finance channel of PhoenixNet: "Details of Rosneft," source: http://finance.ifeng.com/company/data/detail/2735.shtml.

France *Figaro Newspaper*, "A new scramble for world petroleum reserve is under way," reprinted in *Reference News*, April 12, 2005.

Global B2B Website (March 25, 2005). "The energy demand of Taiwan basically depends on imported petroleum," source: http://china.53trade.com/news/detail_20466.htm.

广州日报- 2009 年 8 月 3 日- A5: 国内版-陈同海日均挥霍 4 万元. *Guangzhou Daily* (August 03, 2009): Chen Tonghai Spends RMB40,000 on a Daily Basis, A5, source: http://gzdaily.dayoo.com/html/2009-08/03/content_655018.htm.

Gu, Dejin: "Indian environmental basic law and judicial activism in implementation," *Journal of China University of Geosciences (Social Sciences Edition)*, the 3rd issue in 2009.

Gu, Haibing, Liu, Guopeng and Zhang, Yue: "Analysis of Japanese economic security legal system," Fujian Forum — *Humanistic and Social Science Edition*, the 7th issue in 2009.

Guo, Chen: *Crude Oil in Current Gasoline Shortages in China and Solutions*, oil and natural gas storage and transportation, the 9th issue in 2011.

Han, Jie and Luo Sha: "China started Golden Sun Demonstration Program officially," *Xinhua Net*, July 21, 2009, source: http://news.xinhuanet.com/society/2009-07/21/content_11747614.htm.

He, Miao: "Discussion on Indian energy law transition and its inspiration to China," *Seeking*, the 3rd issue in 2012.

He, Wei, *Discussion on Characteristics of Monopolized Industries in China*, Economist, the 6th issue in 2003.

Hou, Yan, "Study on Indian Competition Law," thesis for master's degree of Central South University, May 1, 2009.

Hu, Hongting, Economic Analysis of "Gasoline Shortages" Phenomenon in China at High Oil Prices, thesis for master's degree of HUST, May 24, 2009.

Hu, Zheng and Li Hui: "Study on fuel oil market in Singapore," *World Petroleum Economy*, 2002.

Huaxia Net: "Oil subsidies are not adjusted inside the island fisheries and fishermen are very angry to the unfair situation," July 30, 2007, source: http://www.huaxia.com/xw/tw/2007/00658352.html.

IEA (2012a). "*World Energy Outlook in 2012*," 2012.

IEA (2012b). *Iraq Energy Outlook*, 2012.

IMF: *World Economy Outlook*, 2012.

International Finance News (November 22, 2010). "What exactly happened in gasoline shortages?"

International Petroleum Net: "Gasoline Shortages in the great energy country Russia," 2011a, June 10, 2011, source: http://oil.in-en.com/html/oil-11201120171040768.html.

International Petroleum Net: "Japanese government plans to offer more subsidies to energy programs," 2011b, December 21, 2011, source: http://oil.in-en.com/html/oil-13461346821233593.html.

International Petroleum Net: "Japanese petroleum reserve system," May 18, 2007, source: http://www.in-en.com/finance/html/energy_2007200705189 1691.html.

International Petroleum Net: "US Senate vetoed the proposal of cancelling tax preference acts upon petroleum enterprises," May 4, 2012, source: http://www.cippe.net/news/html/201205/72500.html.

Jiang, Chunhai, *Study on Resource Exhaustion Cities and Social Stability Issues*, national social science fund program, October 1, 2008.

Jiang, Chunliang: "Petroleum: Lifeblood of Taiwan," *China Petroleum*, July 2000.

Jiang, Lei, "Central enterprises of oil trade gathered together again and SINOPEC strongly proposed to maintain the old system," *Economic Observer Newspaper*, May 14, 2010.

Jiang, Rong, *Survey on "Taking back the Power" of Private Petroleum Enterprises in the North of Shaanxi*, China Business Journal, August 9, 2004a.

Jiang, Ya: "Authorization clarification in Japanese mineral resources legislation," *Land and Resources Information*, 2010b, July 23, 2010, source: http://www.mlr.gov.cn/zljc/201007/t20100723_155680.htm.

Jiang, Ya: "Operation mode of Japanese oil, gas and metal mineral resource organization and its inspiration to China," *Land and Resources Information*, 2010a, May 21, 2010, source: http://www.mlr.gov.cn/zljc/201005/t20100521_149881.htm.

Jin, Guozhong, *Educational Circles Question "Oil Field Nationalization in the North of Shaanxi*," Economic Information Daily, August 25, 2004.

Jing, Chunmei: "Opinions on Chinese energy development strategy," *China Energy News*, the 005 edition on February 4, 2013.

Judith Rees (June 14, 1990). *Natural Resources: Allocation, Economics and Policy*, Routledge, 2nd Edition.

Judith, Rees (2002). *Natural Resources: Allocation, Economics and Policies*, Commercial Press.

Ke, Ao and Wang Qiang, "Historical events during the three decades since reform and opening up in electric industry in China," *Lead*, the 12th issue in 2008.

Keith Cowling and Dennis C. Muller (1978). The Social Cost of Monopoly Power. *The Economic Journal*, Vol. 88 (December), pp. 727–748.

Kong, Xiangyun: "Openness of petroleum products market in Taiwan and prospect for cross-straits cooperation," *International Petroleum Economics*, November 2002.

Lan, Bihua: "Inspiration of economic development strategy in Singapore to economic development in Longgang District, Shenzhen," *Reform and Strategy*, the 03rd issue in 2007.

费加罗报：油价狂飙 为何没冲垮全球经济，中国网. Le Figaro (May 30, 2006). "Oil Price Rocketing Up without Crashing Global Economy", china.com.cn, source: http://www.china.com.cn/chinese/HIAW/1224067.htm.

Li, Chunlian, "CNPC and SINOPEC were accused of intentionally causing gasoline shortages to recover high oil price," *Securities Daily*, October 20, 2011.

Li, Dongchao: "Debate about advantages and disadvantages on American natural gas export," *China Business News*, May 28, 2012, source: http://www.yicai.com/news/2012/05/1761425.html.

Li, Huiyi: "Nationalization restricted petroleum growth in Russia," April 22, 2008, source: http://www.ftchinese.com/story/001018826?full=y.

Li, Lu and Qiu Yuanbin, "Brazilian Petroleum: A new star in the field of energy," *Imp-Exp Executive*, the 9th issue in 2012.

Li, Shu: "Problems and solutions of petroleum price regulation in China," *Journal of Northeast University of Finance*, the 5th issue in 2008.

Li, Shufang and PAN Mao: "Japanese petroleum policy after World War II and its inspiration to China," *Asian-Pacific Economy*, the 2nd issue in 2004.

Li, Wei: "Oil prices in Japan: regulation and marketization," *Sanlian Lifeweek*, April 1, 2012, source: http://www.china5e.com/news/news-217274-1.html.

Li, Xiaodi: "Oil consumption policy and the implementation effect after the oil crisis in the 1970s," *International Petroleum Economics*, the 11th issue in 2006.

Li, Xingmeng, *Case Analysis of Public Crisis Management of "PX Program" — Perspective of Governmental Responsibility and Information Communication*, Legal System and Society, the 2nd issue in 2011.

Li, Yuping: "CPC in Taiwan," *Oil Forum*, the 3rd issue in 1998.

Liao, Jian, *Beijing Oil Products is Upgraded and Uses EU Standard*, China Petrochemical News, March 13, 2008.

Liao, Weijing, "Natural gas output created a new height in Russia," *Economic Daily*, January 13, 2012.

Lin, Liqin: "Development and inspiration of petrochemical industry cluster in Jurong, Singapore," *Journal of Shijiazhuang University of Economics*, the 3rd issue of the 34 volume in June 2011.

Lin, Na, "Inspiration of Brazil petroleum system reform to Chinese petroleum industry," *International Business and Finance*, the 1st issue in 2011.

Liu, Endong: "American energy emergency mechanism and reference," *International Seminar of Emergency Management in 2010*, 2010.

Liu, Xiaoxuan and Zhou Xiaoyan, "Inspection of configuration relationship between financial resources and real economy — and discussion on reasons for imbalance of economic structure," *Finance Research*, the 2nd issue in 2011.

Liu, Yanan: "India announced to integrate gasoline price with market," *Xinhua Net*, June 25, 2010, source: http://news.xinhuanet.com/fortune/2010-06/25/c_12264986.htm.

Liu, Ying: "Regulation of American government on petroleum price in the 1970s," *Inquiry into Economic Issues*, the 4th issue in 2012.

Long, Shu (February 12, 2012): Is There Interest Involved in CNPC's "Tuangou Fang" (Group Purchased Houses)?, Opinion China, source: http://opinion.china.com.cn/opinion_97_34997.html.

Lu, Ao: "Artificially manipulating market is unfair — is it a disaster for Singapore petroleum industry in 2007?" *Financial Report of the 21st Century*, June 30, 2003.

Lu, Li: "Price regulation mode of Singaporean government and its inspiration to China," *Price Theory and Practice*, the 7th issue in 2008.

Luo, Chengxian: "Abolishment of Japanese Specific Oil Products Import Act and its effect," *International Petroleum Economy*, the 2nd issue in 1996.

Ministry of Foreign Affairs (2012a). "Profile of Russia," in December 2012, source: http://www.fmprc.gov.cn/mfa_chn/gjhdq_603914/gj_603916/oz_606480/1206_606820/.

Ministry of Foreign Affairs (2012b). "Profile of Japan," in December 2012, source: http://www.fmprc.gov.cn/mfa_chn/gjhdq_603914/gj_603916/yz_603918/1206_604546/.

Ministry of Foreign Affairs (2012c). "Profile of India," in November 2012, source: http://www.fmprc.gov.cn/mfa_chn/gjhdq_603914/gj_603916/yz_603918/1206_604930/.

Ministry of Foreign Affairs (2012d). "Profile of Singapore," in August 2012, source: http://www.fmprc.gov.cn/mfa_chn/gjhdq_603914/gj_603916/yz_603918/1206_604786/.

Ministry of Land and Resources: *Investigation Evaluation of National Shale Gas Resources Potential and Favorable Area Optimization in China*, 2012.

Mu, Shuang: "Change from monopoly to open competition," *Petroleum Enterprise Management*, the 10th issue in 2001.

Mu, Xuejiang, "What shall we learn from Brazilian petroleum," *China Petroleum Enterprises*, the 10th issue in 2010.

National Development and Reform Commission: "Analysis report on foreign petroleum legislation situation," November 3, 2005, source: http://biz.163.com/05/1103/05/21K40I1O00020QFA.html.

News Center of China Shale Gas Network (February 5, 2013a). "Can America escape from the "Shale Gas Curse?" China Shale Gas Network.

News Center of China Shale Gas Network (February 5, 2013b). "News from China Shale Gas Network: American experience was discussed heatedly on Munich Security Conference," *Xinmin Evening News*.

Official Website of Formosa Petrochemical Co. Ltd.: http://hanweb.fpg.com.tw/han3/2/1/1/0/0/0/0/www.fpcc.com.tw/about_us/company.asp.

Oilchina.com (November 4, 2013). "Indian government loosened restriction on petroleum import and private enterprises are allowed to be middlemen," source: http://news.sina.com.cn/w/2003-11-04/10381054958s.shtml.

Oilchina.com: "Japan National Oil Corporation — JNOC," source: http://www.oilchina.com/syswsc/gwdsygsgk/zhsygs/rbgjsygs.htm.

Organization of the Petroleum Exporting Countries: *World Oil Outlook 2012*, in 2012.

Ou, Lingxiang: "Legal system guarantees Japanese energy security," *China Petrochemical News*, the 8th issue on January 15 in 2010, source: http://enews.SINOPECnews.com.cn/shb/html/2010-01/15/content_96493.htm.

Pan, Hongqi, "The reform of petroleum products pricing mechanism is imperative," *China Youth News*, September 9, 2011.

Pan, Jia and Thompson Paine: "Comparison between Chinese and American petroleum industry management in the post-crisis era," *Baoding University Journal*, in July 2011, the 4th issue in the 24th volume.

Pan, Xuezheng and Ran Xiaorui: "Why does the petroleum products price rise in Chinese Mainland, while it drops in Taiwan? The price regulating mechanism aroused attention," Longzhong Petrochemical Net, March 23, 2013, source: http://finance.huanqiu.com/china/2013-03/3760774.html.

Partner Net: "Russian government plans to loosen the restriction on oil exploitation by foreign enterprises," July 19, 2010, source: http://www.hlj.gov.cn/zerx/system/2010/07/19/010084351.shtml.

People Network • Tianjin Window: "The oil price is high in the great petroleum country and the Russian people feel unhappy," April 29, 2011, source: http://www.022net.com/2011/4-29/486850392521689.html.

People Network: "American government terminated offering subsidies for ethanol fuel taxes," January 11, 2012, source: http://www.cpcia.org.cn/html/19/20121/97515716.html.

Perman, R., Y. Ma, J. McGilvray and M. Common (2003). *Natural Resource and Environmental Economics*, 3rd edition, Pearson Education, Harlow.

Petroleum & Petrochemical Today (2012). "The rankings of the largest 25 global refining companies in 2011," *Petroleum & Petrochemical Today*, the third issue in 2012.

Profile of the 6th-light plan from the Official Website of Formosa Petrochemical Co. Ltd.: http://hanweb.fpg.com.tw/han3/2/1/1/0/0/0/0/www.fpcc.com.tw/six/six_1_dtl.asp.

Proposal of the National Federation of Industry and Commerce: "Proposals about seriously implementing the No. 3 document of the State Council to create a fair playing field for private petroleum enterprises," 2006.

Qu, Jian, *Unsynchronized Standard and Reality in the Automobile Age*, February 2, 2013.

Ren, Jianjin: "Analysis of the Cluster of Singapore Petrochemical Industry and Influence Factors," thesis for master's degree of Jilin University, in April 2009.

Reported by US Research Group on National Energy Policy and translated by Information Center of Ministry of Land and Resources: *American National Energy Policy*, China Land Press, in December 2001.

Research Group of Unirule Institute of Economics (2009). *Impact of Economic Marketization on Energy Supply and Demand and Carbon Emission*.

Research Group of Unirule Institute of Economics (August 2, 2012). *Causes, Behaviors and Eradication of Administrative Monopoly in China*.

Research Group of Unirule Institute of Economics (July 12, 2011). *Property, Performance and Reform of State-owned Enterprises*.

Roger, Ultraman *et al.*, *Natural Resources and Environmental Economics*, China Economics Publishing House, in 2002.

Roger, Ultraman: "The discovery of oil and natural gas will change the global politics," *Financial Times*, May 24, 2012, source: http://www.ftchinese.com/story/001044696.

Russian News Network: "Russia acquired TNK-BP and BP Anti-monopoly Bureau might ask to reduce the number of gas stations," October 26, 2012, source: http://rusnews.cn/eguoxinwen/eluosi_caijing/20121026/43603590-print.html.

Russian News Network: "Russian government expects the highest ever annual total petroleum output," July 10, 2008, source: http://rusnews.cn/eguoxinwen/eluosi_caijing/20080710/42199304-print.html.

Seth, Kleinman: "Global petroleum demand will drop," *Financial Times*, April 7, 2013, source: http://www.ftchinese.com/story/001049776?full=y.

Shang, Baosan: "The land area is vast and the Yellow River is unique in the whole world," May 2, 1990, source: http://www.dongying.gov.cn/html/2009-2/200922520564939263.html.

Shanghai Evening Post (March 22, 2011). "CNPC appeals to decrease the special oil gain levy again."

Shao, Yunpeng, Primary Investigation on Benefit Sharing System Reform of Onshore Crude Oil Resource in China, Journal of Shanxi Economic Management Cadre College, the 1st issue in 2011.

Sheng, Hong, "Foreign exchange quota transaction: A case of plan-right transaction," Social Sciences Quarterly in China, totally 13 issues (November 1995), 1995.

Sheng, Hong, "Research on the transient process of market-oriented reform in China," *Economic Research*, the 1st issue in 1996.

Sheng Hong (1992, January): Division of Labor and Transaction, Shanghai: The Joint Publishing Company.

Sheng, Hong, *Economics of Transition in China*, Shanghai Sanlian Bookstore, 1994.

Shi, Huaxin (1994). "Practice of the national governments around the world holding petroleum resource and controlling the import, price and circulating of crude oil and petroleum products," *Petrochemical Industry Trends*, No. 9.

Shi, Zhiliang *et al.* (July 15, 2012). "An invisible barrier in petroleum industry," *Caijing*.

Shi, Zhongtian (2008). *Gasoline Shortages Forced Price Rising*, Window of Northeast, No. 1.

Singapore Maintains Advantages of Petrochemical Engineering Center, originally published in *Singapore United Morning Post* on January 26, 2002.

SINOPEC News Net (April 19, 2010). "Indian government plans to establish the first strategic petroleum reserve facility next year," source: http://finance.stockstar.com/JL2010041900001922.shtml.

Sun, Yana and Bian Shu (2005). "Natural resources and economic development in Russia," *Markets of Russia, Central Asia and Eastern Europe*, No. 3.

The State Council, "Circular on the State Council about Implementing Petroleum Products Price and Tax Reform," December 18, 2008.

The State Council, "Interim Regulations on Added-value Tax in the People's Republic of China," November 10, 2008.

Tian, Li (January 27, 2012). "The import volume of crude oil dropped by 3.5% year-on-year in December in India," *Caixun Net*, source: http://finance.sina.com.cn/money/future/20120127/155911262250.shtml.

Tian, Xiaoxian (September 2012). *Study of Problems and Countermeasures of Excise Tax on Petroleum Products in China*, China Management Information, Vol. 15, No. 17.

Translated and compiled by Huang Feng: "Summarization of oil and gas industry in Singapore," *Economic Analysis of Petroleum and Chemical Engineering in China*, the 17th issue in 2006.

US Energy Information Administration, Natural Gas, Consumption, http://www.eia.gov/dnav/ng/ng_cons_sum_dcu_nus_a.htm.

Wang Muheng (Translated) (1979). "Petroleum refining industry in Singapore," *Southeast Asian Studies*, No. 2.

Wang, Bo (2000). "Development history and features of petroleum industry in Taiwan before 1949," *Journal of Fujian Provincial Party School of the Communist Party of China*, No. 12.

Wang, Cailiang (2007). "Government regulation to petroleum production in American petroleum history," *SINOPEC*, No. 5.

Wang, Jian (2012). "Antimonopoly affairs in the petroleum products market in China," *Science of Law*, No. 2.

Wang, Jiashan and Li Shaoping (December 2005). "Reflecting on uniformly levying mining royalty on oil and gas resources," In Oil–Gas Field Surface Engineering, Vol. 24, No. 12.

Wang, Lu (November 7, 2011). "CNPC and SINOPEC monopoly caused gasoline shortages in private petroleum enterprises," *Economic Information Daily*.

Wang, Lu (November 07, 2011a): "The Two Bucket of Oil Caused Conundrum of 'No Oil for Refining' for Private-Owned Oil Companies", Economic Information.

Wang, Lu and Zhou Nan (December 14, 2011). "Gasoline Shortages happened again and intensify the shortage of diesel in many areas in South China," *Economic Information Daily*.

Wang, Lu and Zhou, Nan (December 14, 2011b): "Oil Shortage: Getting Worse in South China", Economic Information.

Wang, Muheng (1994). "Petrochemical industry in Singapore," *Southeast Asian Affairs*, No. 3.

Wang, Muheng (1994). "Petroleum refining industry in Singapore," *Southeast Asian Affairs*, No. 2.

Wang, Naiyang (1988). "Development road of petrochemical industry in Taiwan," *Science & Technology Review*, No. 4.

Wang, Songhan (August 14, 2006). "Inspiration from the development of petrochemical industry in Taiwan," *China Chemical Industry News*, the 005 edition.

Wang, Wen, Lao Mu, Zong He, Hao Hong and Chang Zhipeng (December 26, 2003). *We Are Not Afraid of Gasoline Shortages*, Jiangsu Economic News.

Wang, Xiaosu (2012). "OPEC released *World Petroleum Outlook in 2012*," *China Petroleum and Chemical Engineering Standard and Quality in November* (half bottom), No. 14.

Wang, Xiaosu (March 26, 2012). "Indian government raised petroleum tax substantially," *China Energy News*, the 7th edition, source: http://www.mofcom. gov.cn/aarticle/i/dxfw/jlyd/200808/20080805747574.html.

Wang, Xiaozong and Wu Peng (January 21, 2011). "Decoding Chinese strategic petroleum reserve," *China Economic Weekly*.

Wang, Yang (August 6, 2008). "Comments of foreign countries on China's Antimonopoly Act," *Business Counselor in Chinese Mission to EU*, source: http://www.mofcom.gov.cn/aarticle/i/dxfw/jlyd/200808/20080805747574. html.

Wang, Yonghong (August 17, 2009). "30-year course of paid land use system reform in China," *Chinese Territory Resource News*.

Website of America EIA: http://www.eia.gov/.

Website of Ministry of Land and Resources of the People's Republic of China: http://www.mlr.gov.cn/.

Website of National Bureau of Statistics of the People's Republic of China: http:// www.stats.gov.cn/.

Website of National Development and Reform Commission of the People's Republic of China: http://www.sdpc.gov.cn/.

Wei, Jie (September 28, 2007). "Simple analysis of the impact of Antimonopoly Act on tobacco industry," *Tobacco Online*, source: http://www.tobaccochina. com/news/analysis/wu/20079/2007927952_272706.shtml.

Wikipedia: "Oil Industry Safety Directorate," November 2, 2012, source: http:// en.wikipedia.org/wiki/Oil_Industry_Safety_Directorate.

World Economic Forum and HIS Cambridge Energy Research Institute (2012). *Promote Growth by Energy — Latest Energy Outlook Report in 2012.*

Written by Clyde Russell I and translated and compiled by Wang Yang: *"Russell Special Column*: China may change the mechanism of petroleum products pricing to improve transparency," *Thomson Reuters*, July 3, 2012, source: http://cn.reuters.com/article/columnistNews/idCNCNE86206420120703.

Written by Yang, Jingmin *et al.*: *Modern Petroleum Market — Theory, Practice, Research and Innovation*, Petroleum Industry Press, in 2003, pp. 155–167.

WTRG Economics, "Oil Price History and Analysis," http://www.wtrg.com/prices.htm.

Wu, Gaozhi and Ou Qingxian (2010). "Comparative study on fishing moratorium management system in Taiwan and Chinese Mainland," *Paper Announcement Campaign of Taiwan Aquaculture Society in 2010.*

Wu, Jiandong (2007). "Innovation strategy of reform of China submarine natural gas," Ocean World, 2007b, No. 2.

Wu, Jiandong (Feburary 19, 2009). "Pricing power of international crude oil changes substantially," *Southern Weekly*, C19 Edition.

Wu, Jiandong (January 24, 2007). "Gas energy promotes the leapfrog transformation of China energy structure," *Sina Finance*, 2007a, source: http://finance.sina.com.cn/review/zlhd/20070124/10393277349.shtml.

Wu, Jiandong (November 1, 2012). "It is hopeful for China's clean energy to realize "independence," *Shanghai Securities News*.

Wu, Shunhuang (June 4, 2012). "The Real India: Indian oil price drops again after it is raised," *Sina Finance*, source: http://finance.sina.com.cn/world/yzjj/20120604/080212214351.shtml.

Wu, Weizheng, Pan Junqiang and Wang Jinhai (September 15, 2011). *How Huge Is the Risk of PX Program, People's Daily.*

Wu, Zhong (1995): "Current situation and development trend of petrochemical industry in Taiwan," *Petrochemical Industry Trends*, No. 5.

Xia, Guangqi (April 29, 2011). "Even President Obama ordered to investigate crude oil speculation strictly, it is still hard to rock the oil price," *Financial Management Weekly*.

Xie, Xiaoyan: "Source of research on the legal environment of oil and natural gas investment in Russia," *Central Asia and Eastern Europe Market of Russia*, the 11th issue in 2010.

Xu, Keqiang (November 13, 2001). "Russian government will reduce petroleum exploitation quantity temporarily," source: http://www.stockstar.com/info/darticle.aspx?id=SS,20011113,00330560&columnid=401,7,59,58.

Yang, Jisheng (2002). *It is a Mess in the Petroleum Industry Which is Hard to be Regulated*, China Investment, No. 9.

Yang, Lei (February 27, 2008). "There has been no state-owned petroleum monopoly enterprise in Brazil for ten years," *Southern Weekend.*

Yang, Rong (2004). "International reference of governmental regulation reform in petroleum industry," *Productivity Research*, No. 10.

Yang, Xueyan, Luo Hong, Li Peiling and Jia Wenrui (2004). *Discussion on International Business Environment and Strategy of Chinese Petroleum Industry*, Petroleum Industry Press.

Yang Zhongxu and He Jiajin (July 16, 2012). Glass Door in the Oil Industry: Obstacles for Private Oil Enterprises in the "Upstream, Middle Stream, and Downstream", *Caijing.*

Yu, Chun (March 29, 2013). "BP: China will replace America to be the largest petroleum importing country in the world in 2017," *NBD*, source: http://www.nbd.com.cn/articles/2013-03-29/727467.html.

Yu, Chunling (2011): "Discussion on petroleum economy in Russia," *World History*, No. 5.

Yu, Huan (August 31, 2009). "Aspects of petroleum products in America, Japan and European countries," *China Energy News*, 12th edition.

Yu, Li and Meng Tao (2004). *Problems and Standards of Buy-off Offer in State-Owned Enterprises — Take the Resource-Exhaustion State-Owned Enterprises in Northeast Old Industrial Base for Example*, Social Science Front, No. 6.

Yue, Jianguo (December 20, 2007). "Is Chinese petroleum system integrated with that of America," *China Youth News.*

Yue, Xiaowen (2012). "Overview of petroleum gas industry in Russia in 2011," *International Petroleum Economics*, No. 4.

Zhai, Ruimin (March 5, 2012). "Private enterprises failed to participate in petroleum reserve once again due to expiration of bidding contract," *Finance Channel of Netease.*

Zhang, hong and Wang Huiliang (July 2011). "Market-oriented reform of petroleum products in typical surrounding countries and regions and its inspiration," *International Petroleum Economics.*

Zhang, Hongmin (2005). "Indian petroleum industry and the industrial policy change," *International Petroleum Economics*, No. 13.

Zhang, Qi'an (March 10, 2011). "Chamber of Petroleum Commerce in Federation of Industry and Commerce appealed to loosen the restriction on private oil enterprises about importing crude oil," *Financial Network.*

Zhao, Haofeng (2008). *Discussion on the Realization of Citizen Environmental Rights by Taking Xiamen PX Program Event for Example*, Modern Business Trade Industry, No. 11.

Zhao, Nong and Liu Xiaolu (January 2007). *Barrier for Entering and Exiting: Theory and Its Application*, China Market Price, No. 1.

Zhao, Qingsi (2009). "Mandatory petroleum import quota plan in America and its influence," *Hubei Social Sciences*, No. 10.

Zhao, Xinshe (November 03, 2008): Private-Owned Oil Companies: From Winner to Loser, SinaNews, source: http://news.sina.com.cn/c/2008-11-03/154416579276.shtml.

Zhong, Jingjing (September 8, 2009). "CNPC indirectly held 100% stock rights of Singapore petroleum," *Beijing News*.

Zhou, Mingchun as chief editor, *Research on Petroleum Tax System*, China Market Price, January 2009.

Zhou, Ruohong (April 2001). "Reflections on petroleum pricing mechanism," *Petroleum & Petrochemical Today*.

Zhou, Wenshui (2005). *Strong Administrative Power behind Oil Field Incident in the North of Shaanxi*, Trend of Our Time, No. 13.

Zhou, Zhiwei (2011). "Road of the internationalization of Brazilian petroleum," *Shanghai State-owned Assets*, No. 7.

Zhu, Chengzhang (1995). "Petroleum enterprises will change from privately-operated to state-owned in Taiwan," *Technology and Industry Across the Straits*, the 4th issue.

Zhu, Qian (2008). *Environmental Information in a Fight Shall be Released Timely — Discussion on the Urban Master Planning Environmental Impact Assessment of Xiamen PX Program*, Science of Law, the 1st issue.

Zhu, Yunzu (2001). "Opening-door policy of Brazilian petroleum industry," *International Petroleum Economics*, Vol. 9, No. 3.

Index